THREE FLAGS AT THE STRAITS

ere Marquette

Peche du
Poisson blanc

I.^t de
Missilimakinac

age des
ouats
Hurons
Iesuits
nakinak

uvages

Lac

des Hurons

I.^t du
bois Blanc

Surprenant portant tantost icy tantost la

A

Alexander Henry

Books by Walter Havighurst

★

PIER 17   1935
THE QUIET SHORE   1937
THE UPPER MISSISSIPPI (*Rivers of America*)   1938
THE WINDS OF SPRING   1940
NO HOMEWARD COURSE   1941
THE LONG SHIPS PASSING   1942
LAND OF PROMISE   1946
SIGNATURE OF TIME   1949
GEORGE RODGERS CLARK: SOLDIER IN THE WEST   1952
ANNIE OAKLEY OF THE WILD WEST   1954
WILDERNESS FOR SALE   1956
VEIN OF IRON   1959
THE MIAMI YEARS   1959
LAND OF THE LONG HORIZONS   1960
THE HEARTLAND   1962
PROUD PRISONER   1963
VOICES ON THE RIVER   1964
THE GREAT LAKES READER   1966

With Marion Boyd Havighurst

HIGH PRAIRIE   1944
SONG OF THE PINES   1949
CLIMB A LOFTY LADDER   1952

THREE

PRENTICE-HALL, Inc., Englewood Cliffs, N.J.

FLAGS AT THE STRAITS

The Forts of Mackinac

By Walter Havighurst

977.48
H

Three Flags at the Straits: The Forts of Mackinac
by Walter Havighurst

© 1966 by Walter Havighurst

Library of Congress Catalog Card Number: 66-22081

Printed in the United States of America

T 92025

PRENTICE-HALL INTERNATIONAL, INC., *London*
PRENTICE-HALL OF AUSTRALIA, PTY. LTD., *Sydney*
PRENTICE-HALL OF CANADA, LTD., *Toronto*
PRENTICE-HALL OF INDIA PRIVATE LTD., *New Delhi*
PRENTICE-HALL OF JAPAN, INC., *Tokyo*

ACKNOWLEDGMENTS

For kind assistance in the preparation of this book I am indebted to various persons. Dr. Eugene T. Peterson, Director of Historic Projects for the Mackinac Island State Park Commission helped me to grasp both the excitement and the problems of restoration of the past in the Straits area. Mr. W. S. Woodfill of Mackinac Island gave me the benefit of his library and of his extensive knowledge of Mackinac history. From Robert V. Doud of Mackinac Island I learned some vivid details of local memory and tradition. Dr. George S. May, Research Archivist of the Michigan Historical Commission, kindly directed me to sources I might otherwise have missed; my debt to his own writing is suggested in my bibliography. To the late Stewart H. Holbrook, who planned the *American Forts Series* with his unfailing zest and perception, I am indebted for many stimulating exchanges of knowledge and opinion.

For other assistance I offer thanks to Mr. Herman D. Ellis of the Mackinac Bridge Authority; to Miss Geneva Kebler, Reference Archivist of the Michigan Historical Commission; to the late Mrs. Carroll Paul and to Mr. Ernest H. Rankin of the Marquette County Historical Society, and to members of the staffs of the Newberry Library, the William L. Clements Library, the Burton Collection of the Detroit Public Library, the Buffalo and Erie County Historical Society, and the State Historical Society of Wisconsin.

Walter Havighurst
Oxford, Ohio

Prologue

ECHOES ON AN ISLAND

When Detroit was a lifeless waterway and Chicago was only a name for wild garlic, Michilimackinac was a center of dominion and power. A wilderness capital, known only to a few thousand half-clothed savages, it became part of the history of France, England and the United States.

"Michilimackinac"—later shortened to "Mackinac"—was a name of many meanings. To the Indians it signified the strait between Lake Huron and Lake Michigan, and the turtle-shaped island near the narrows as well.

The Ojibwa syllables also were applied to the French mission and military post at St. Ignace, and later to the fort and mission across the straits near the present Mackinaw City.

At the height of its early history, Michilimackinac's mission touched Indian tribes a thousand miles away. Its councils drew tribesmen from vast territories. Its fur trade spanned half a continent. Now it is remote and tranquil, a place of beauty and repose. The wilderness capital has become a wilderness retreat.

From Old Fort Point on the southern shore of the straits, the four-mile narrows widen into Lake Huron and Lake Michigan, and the northern mainland fades into the west. It is a spacious scene: vast sky, wide water, a shoreline dark with forest. Those long horizons dwarf the settlements; the straits towns of Mackinaw City and St. Ignace are almost lost between the deep woods and the big sea water.

Mackinac was first known to white men in the 1630s. Before the founding of Philadelphia and New York it had become a busy station in the wilderness. In three and a half centuries its history has been concentrated on a sequence of three sites. The first French and Indian settlement huddled on the north point of the straits, the site of the present St. Ignace, where a bark chapel and a timbered fort stood amid brush huts of the Hurons and the Ottawas. It was abandoned about the year 1700. Eighteenth-century Michilimackinac occupied the south point, directly opposite the former post, near the present Mackinaw City. The palisaded fort, built by the French and taken from them by the English, guarded the straits until the eve of the American Revolution. In 1780 the flags, the cannon, the military post and the trading houses were moved to Mackinac Island, which became a center of Indian commerce and diplomacy. The island remained a British post until Jay's Treaty brought it under American control in 1796. Recaptured by the British in 1812, it was returned permanently to America in 1815.

Time brought little change to the green shores and the restless blue water until the great bridge arched the straits in the 1950s. Linking Mackinaw City and St. Ignace, the bridge poured life into the mainland settlements. But Mackinac Island, ringed in deep waters, keeps its airy beauty and repose. Blue water reaches to the sky, and the lake wind murmurs in the Mackinac spruce and tamarack as it did before history began.

"Michilimackinac"—Frenchmen first heard this singsong name in the talk of Ojibwa tribesmen. Voyageurs and priests repeated it many times before it was first written on their rude maps and in the reports of their journeys. Saying the word was simpler than spelling it. Pronunciations varied, though it was always given six syllables, with twin stresses on the first and fourth of them. Some Indians called it "Mich-in-i-mack-in-ong." Father Marquette wrote "Michilimakinong;" Hennepin made it "Missilimackinack;" explorer Joutel's version was "Micilimaquenay." The scholarly Jesuits used thirteen different spellings in the many volumes of their *Relations*. The diarist Robert Navarre spelled by ear with various results, and merchant John Lee wrote by whim—"Michilimakenaz," "Michamakenil" and "Michaelmackinac." A recent historian gathered a solid paragraph of various spellings; in records between 1681 and 1855 he found 68 different versions, ranging from "Mitchinimackenucks," "Mishinimakinang," "Eshelemackinac," "Micilimaquinay" and "Mochenemockenugong" to the modern, abbreviated, phonetic "Mackinaw."

An old, dark, savage name, harshly musical, it would inevitably be shortened—not by the Indians, who loved the many syllables, nor by the French, who respected the native folkways, but by the English and Americans. When he lowered the British ensign on the southern point and raised it on the legend-haunted island, Captain Patrick Sinclair stated that the place should be "Mackinac." The final syllable was illogical; the word was pronounced "Mackinaw." Present-day spellings are contradictory—Mackinaw City but Mackinac Island; Mackinac County but mackinaw coat, boat, trout and blanket. The visitor who carefully gives two "ack" syllables to the island name is wrong; however spelled, the word has but one pronunciation—"Mack-in-aw."

In its meaning "Michilimackinac" also had variations. The name begins with the familiar "Michi" of "Michigan" and "Mississippi" (originally "Michisipi")—meaning "great." It was commonly thought that the whole name meant "Great Turtle," and so the island appeared—oval, dark, steep-sided, rising out of the water like a giant tortoise. The turtle was held in reverence by the tribes, and Mackinac Island was a place of wonder. But, after long study of Algonquin language and mythology, Henry Rowe Schoolcraft concluded that the original name of the island was "Mishi-min-auk-in-ong," which meant a place of dancing spirits. The term has also been translated as a local form of "Turtle Spirits."

In the *Algic Researches*, Schoolcraft recounted the Ojibwa legend of Osseo, the Son of the Evening Star. Marvelous things befell Osseo, who at last descended from the sky and so came upon our mortal earth. In *The Song of Hiawatha* Longfellow versified the tale:

> And the youth, the fearless bowman,
> Suddenly felt himself descending,
> Held by unseen hands but sinking
> Downward through the empty spaces,
> Downward through the clouds and vapors,
> Till he rested on an island,
> On an island green and grassy,
> Yonder in the Big-Sea-Water.

Osseo's sky people, transformed into birds, alighted with him
on the island. There they resumed their original shapes, though
diminished in stature.

> They remained as Little People . . .
> And in pleasant nights of summer
> When the evening star was shining
> Hand in hand they danced together
> On the island's craggy headlands,
> On the sand-beach, low and level.

So the spirits—Mishiminaukinong—gave a name to the magic
island, and the Indians felt their presence.

> Still their glittering lodge is seen there
> On the tranquil summer evenings,
> And upon the shore the fisher
> Sometimes hears their happy voices,
> Sees them dancing in the starlight!

Still another legend tells how Michoban, chief of the spirits,
dwelt upon the island. There he first instructed men to weave
nets for the taking of fish. When he departed he left spirits called
"Imakinaks," and from those airy inhabitants the island took
its name. It is true that, when the Indians feasted on mackinaw
trout and whitefish, they thanked the spirits of the island.

Whatever its ancient origin, "Michilimackinac" was a name
of wonder. With its cliffs, crags, caverns, mysterious glens and
grottoes, the island was a haunt for many manitous.

No Indian people lived on Mackinac Island, though many sojourned there. Its beauty and tranquillity, its safety from attack
and the rich fishing in its waters gave it a special place in savage
life and lore. There the tribesmen brought their dead for burial;
human bones accumulated in its limestone caves.

This haunted island was a home of Michoban, the great spirit
of the lakes. Coming with sunrise over the eastern waters he
would alight on "Manitou's Landing Place," the white, shelving
shore at the foot of a hollowed cliff. Through that magic gateway
he would climb the hill to his lofty limestone wigwam; the cave
on its west side was his doorway. For the mundane white men

Michoban's Gateway was merely "Arch Rock," and his Great
Wigwam became "Sugar Loaf."

The Indians carried tales of the magic island, and the white
men made it known beyond the range of tribal commerce. Geologists know that it was once submerged—as the savage legends
told—and that the slowly receding water washed away the limestone, leaving pinnacles and hollows. Now it rises in six terraces
(the carriage horses know each new lift of land) from the harbor
beach to the height of Fort Holmes, which surveys it all. Its
landmarks have been pictured in textbooks of geology.

Arch Rock hangs in the air 140 feet above the water, a precipitous cliff whose calcareous stone bank eroded, leaving a natural bridge. It looks airy and fragile framing the blue of Lake
Huron, though tradition says that a lady once rode horseback
across the span. When Captain Marryatt visited the island in
1837, Schoolcraft took the seaman-novelist to see this wonder.
Always a show-off, Marryatt insisted on crossing the arch, and
halfway across he stumbled. "My heart was in my throat," wrote
Schoolcraft, "but like a true sailor he crouched down, as if on
a yard-arm, and again rose and completed his perilous walk."
Ten years earlier Thomas McKenney, in his *Tour of the Lakes*,
had predicted its collapse. "The arch is crumbling, and a few
years will deprive the island of Michilimackinac of a curiosity
which it is worth visiting to see." That was a century and a
half ago, and the arch still frames the restless blue water.

Other landmarks are nearly as notable. Sugar Loaf, 284 feet
above the water, rises out of the forest in a great cone of limestone. Halfway up is a niche to which climbers ascend. In 1843
Margaret Fuller reported a ladder leading to the rocky shelf.
On the western heights of the island, midway on the leafy Stone
Cliff Trail is the Crack in the Island—a shallow fissure that some
geologists ascribe to an ancient earthquake. Near the eastern
cliffs, on the ghostly old Murray Road, the Great Gardens are
outlined in crumbling stone walls amid second-growth spruce
and hemlock. The gardens were already overgrown in Schoolcraft's time, 130 years ago. He said that no one knew their origin.
They must have been cleared for farming, though the island

soil is thin and snow has been recorded in every month of the year.

When the American flag first hung over the fort on the hill, a motley life thronged the half-moon harbor below. After the long, locked winter came the boisterous life of spring. When ice went out of the straits the first canoes came over the flashing water. Mackinac was magic to the voyageurs, as it had been to the ancient tribesmen. After the winter solitude, at the end of a journey through dark woods and lonely waters, there was the white-walled island with welcoming voices and the smoke of many fires. There were hot food and brandy, the beat of Indian drums and the lilt of fiddle music. To this place red men and white men had brought their songs and their firelight. Campfires twinkled along the canoe-strewn shore, and in the harbor sloops and schooners swayed against the sky. Indians and woodsmen brought the winter harvest of furs to be cleaned, graded, bundled and stamped for transport to the East and the great fur markets abroad. At the same time trade goods came ashore from the schooners—knives and skillets, traps and axes, coppered brass kettles, twist and carrot tobacco, striped shirts and blankets, beads, bells and buckles and kegs of whiskey and rum. Midsummer brought a full tide of trade and revelry—as in the modern tourist traffic. With the colored leaves of autumn the voyageurs and tribesmen scattered, and winter silence settled on the island.

At Mackinac the voyageurs roistered, gambled, feasted. With feathers in their red wool caps and fringed sashes trailing, they swaggered around the trading houses and through the Indian camp on the shore. By the leaping light of a beach fire they bragged of their capacity to "carry, paddle, drink or sing" with any man. At night when the trading posts were dark and campfires sank along the harbor, they slept beneath upturned canoes. On land or water that craft was home.

Mackinac is a remote small island, sundered from the mainland by miles of deep water and sealed from transportation by months of ice and snow. But to and through it flowed the currents of

life on the northwestern frontier. What other place in America
has seen such a procession of savage and civilized leaders—Jean
Nicolet, Claude Allouez, Jacques Marquette, Robert de La Salle,
Henry de Tonty, Louis Hennepin, Antoine de Cadillac, Charles
de Langlade, Matchekewis, Alexander Henry, Wawatam, Minavavana, Robert Rogers, Jonathan Carver, Lewis Cass, Gurdon
Hubbard, William Beaumont, Henry Rowe Schoolcraft?

In the mid-nineteenth century its fur trade dwindled, and its
military importance ceased. It might well have become only a
site of memory, like La Pointe on Lake Superior or L'Arbre
Croche on Lake Michigan. But its wild beauty and its bracing
air have become known to the world, and these qualities, along
with its historical associations, have given it tourist fame. Before
the Civil War, people made the long journey to the tranquil
island. Since then travel has grown easier—by steamer, train,
highway and air—and the visitors have multiplied. They found
the old island paths and made new ones, paths through spruce,
larch and laurel; through glades bright with wild roses, daisies,
blue gentians, Indian pipes; through shadowed glens carpeted
with moss and fringed with fern, to sudden outlooks over wide
blue water.

One of the oldest of American resorts, Mackinac Island became
a national park in 1875; for a generation it and Wyoming's Yel-
lowstone comprised the national-park system. In 1895 the island
was transferred to the State of Michigan and became Michigan's
first state park. Under Michigan law, motor vehicles were kept
from the island roads. Without machinery and motor traffic, away
from the twentieth century's hurrying change, Mackinac has retained a tranquil charm. Carriage drives were cleared through
the woods in the 1870s. Steam-ferry service to the island began
in 1881. The Grand Hotel was built in 1887. By 1900 Mackinac
Island was a meeting place for travelers from many lands.

But the eventful past was not forgotten. On an island, where
every road returns one to the same place, the past accumulates.
It cannot get away. It builds up, legend upon legend, tradition
upon tradition. The island's people have memories that began,
like an inheritance, before they were born.

CONTENTS

PART ONE: THE FRENCH

*Missilimackinac is an Island of note in these regions. . . . It is
situated exactly in the strait connecting the Lake of the Hurons
and that of the Illinois, and forms the key and the door, so to
speak, for all the peoples of the South, as does the Sault for
those of the North.*

FATHER DABLON

THE GALLANT NORMAN

Near Arch Rock on the eastern cliff of Mackinac Island, overlooking miles of blue water, stands a bronze memorial tablet designating the place as "Nicolet Watch Tower." It is not known that Jean Nicolet ever peered from this lookout, but he paddled past in 1634, the first white man to enter the strait that widened into Lake Michigan.

Nicolet was a Norman. The old Normandy ports of Rouen, Honfleur, Cherbourg and Le Havre furnished the crews that sailed ships to New France, and young men from those harbors looked westward toward the New World wilderness. From Cherbourg three brothers went to Canada. One was a sailor who climbed the Quebec hills with a rolling step; another strode those streets in the swishing cassock of a priest. The third was the "gallant Norman" who extended the maps of New France to present-day Wisconsin.

Samuel de Champlain, the founder of Quebec, felt the lure of the western woods and waters. To extend French trade and exploration, he sent young men to live with the Indians, to learn their languages and customs and their canoe routes through the interior. This was a new profession, and it required an arduous training. The camps of the savages were a language school. The rivers and portages were a testing ground; the exile, hardship and danger either broke a man or nourished him. (Etienne Brulé, the first white man to see Georgian Bay, became a depraved and brutal savage; two years before Nicolet's great voyage he was killed in a brawl over a Huron woman.) To this stern training school Champlain sent young men who would become his agents, interpreters and ambassadors in the wilderness.

In 1618, while his ship was loading at Cherbourg, Champlain became acquainted with a sturdy, clear-eyed, high-minded youth to whom he offered a career in Canada. The governor chose better than he knew; he could not then have seen the self-discipline, the religious faith, the quick mind and stubborn memory and the boldness that would carry Jean Nicolet deeper into America than any European had gone.

Arrived at Quebec, young Nicolet found himself in a small outpost of France. Old World and New World met on the river-front, where birch canoes bobbed against the hulls of French merchantmen. On the quay a circle of Indians squatted around a fire, boiling a mixture of fish and pounded corn. From the heights one could look westward over the broad St. Lawrence and the fading hills.

After a season in Quebec, Nicolet went to live with the Hurons on Allumette Island, two hundred miles up the Ottawa River. There he was in primitive country, far from shops and cafés, from the clangor of church bells and the boom of signal cannon. For two years Jean Nicolet heard no syllable of French and saw no white man. He endured privation, hunger, hardship, swarms of mosquitoes, smoke-filled lodges, flies, fleas, dogs and dirt. He went on winter hunts and summer trading journeys, paddling through white water, carrying loads over steep and muddy portages. He froze with the Indians in bitter weather, feasted with them on fish and beaver, ate acorns and boiled lichen in times of famine. Once he went for seven weeks with no more nourishment than pounded fish bones and the bark of trees.

When he returned to the St. Lawrence, Nicolet was more Indian than European. He spoke the guttural Huron tongue, his body was hardened and his face was dark with weather. He knew the streaming northern lights, the cold winter daybreak, the Indian lore of woods and sky. But he still wore the crucifix about his neck.

Soon he was back in the wilds, deeper in the west this time. Adopted by a tribe on Lake Nipissing, Nicolet lived in a cabin a little apart from the Indians' brush-walled village. He did his own fishing, hunting and trading, but he had a place at the tribal fire, and he spoke in the councils. He was at home in the wilderness, yet he sorely missed the holy sacraments. Missionaries were sojourning in the Huron towns around Lake Simcoe and in southern Georgian Bay, but no priest had come to remote Lake Nipissing.

Nine winters darkened the northern land and besieged the tribal camps. Nine times the rivers raced with spring water. Nicolet listened to tales of dread and wonder, and he told about French cities across the great sea. He taught the use of needle and thread, of awl and gimlet. The tribesmen gave him a Huron name—"Achirra" and Nicolet called them his "brothers." Yet this devout man felt his soul imperiled. "It is easier," wrote one of the Jesuit missionaries, "to make an Indian out of a Frenchman than a Frenchman out of an Indian." Nicolet must have felt the pull of savagery. When at last he returned to Quebec, he went first to the chapel where votive candles flickered on the altar and saints looked down from the walls.

It was 1633 when Nicolet came back to the St. Lawrence. For a season he enjoyed half-forgotten comforts—crisp French bread, a bed with clean linen, French speech and songs and fiddle music. Then came a new mission.

More than any other governor of New France, Champlain was an explorer. He knew the lure of the woods and the toil of the water routes. He had gone as far as the shore of Georgian Bay, where he had tasted the inland ocean. On his map Lake Huron was "Mer Douce"—the Sea of Sweet Water. From the Hurons he heard of a people in the west who lived on the edge of a farther sea and who traded with a still more distant people who had neither beards nor scalp locks. To Champlain this suggested the Chinese; in his mind leapt up the old dream of a short route to Asia. This stubborn myth was an inheritance from the sixteenth century map-makers, who showed an arm of the North Sea reaching in toward the sources of the Ottawa River. Nicolet himself had heard Nipissing tales of a "sea-water people," whom he pictured in Chinese robes.

To search for the fabled passage to India, Champlain needed a daring and resourceful man, and the man was ready.

On the 1st of July, 1634, Jean Nicolet left Quebec in a party of two canoe brigades. One fleet went only as far as Three Rivers, halfway to Montreal; there Nicolet helped to drive stakes for a fort on the north bank of the St. Lawrence. Soon he was on the way again, with a canoe caravan in charge of the brawny Jesuit Jean de Brébeuf.

Working at the paddles and portages like any boatman, wading in numbing water, hauling the craft through swirling rapids, Nicolet reached his old abode on Allumette Island. There Father Brébeuf remained, while Nicolet journeyed on to his savage friends on Lake Nipissing. From that familiar place he descended the French River to the shore of Georgian Bay. Beyond lay the unknown realm that he was to explore.

With seven Huron paddlers in a bark canoe he set out for the mysterious west. Following the intricate northern coastline he came to an Indian town beside the St. Mary's rapids. Nicolet rested there, a few miles from vast Lake Superior, which he never saw. Instead he turned southward, journeying down the St. Mary's to Point Détour. Then he steered toward the setting sun.

At the end of summer the slanting light does strange things to the northern waters. Islands float on the horizon; they hang suspended in the sky and melt into sunlight. Fog moves in silver banks, and double rainbows beckon and vanish. Sun dogs hang on the evening horizon as two moons rise in the east. At midnight ghostly banners stream up in the northern sky. Jean Nicolet was on the edge of an unknown world.

Two days from Point Détour he saw ahead a humped island, like a giant turtle. As the canoe neared, limestone cliffs showed white beneath the dense green forest cover. With a singsong muttering, the Indians broke off twists of tobacco and dropped them in the water; praise and appeasement took them past the sacred island with its many manitous. The paddles quickened as they neared the narrows. The first white man was entering the Straits of Mackinac.

Beyond the narrows a new sea (Nicolet had no better name than "the second lake of the Hurons") widened into unguessed distance. A week's journey brought them to Green Bay, which ended in a reedy river mouth. From the woods rose the smokes of a large village.

For this moment Nicolet had brought a ceremonial robe. He donned it, a silk and brocade dress covered with birds of paradise. In that garb, fit to meet the merchants of Cathay, Nicolet stepped ashore with two pistols in his hands.

At this famous moment in New World history some half-clothed Winnebagos came out of the forest. When the visitor loosed the thunder in his upraised hands, they scattered in the woods. But they soon were back, welcoming the magic white man. "In former times," wrote Nicolas Perrot half a century later, "the Puants [Winnebago tribesmen] were the masters of this bay, and of a great extent of adjoining country. This nation was a populous one, very redoubtable . . . . If any stranger came among them he was cooked in their kettles." But Nicolet had arrived at a place (the Red Banks a few miles above the present city of Green Bay) sacred in the tribal lore. His dress, his bearing and his firearms made him godlike to their wondering eyes.

At news of the great man's arrival, the scattered warriors assembled. Each chief gave a banquet. After a ceremonial feast of 120 beavers, Nicolet spoke of peace, friendship and commerce. He urged an alliance of the Winnebagos with the Huron and Ottawa nations and told of French warehouses on the St. Lawrence filled with Indian trade goods.

At Green Bay Nicolet heard of other tribes in the interior and of westward flowing rivers. This was not China but a new realm of American wilderness. To see it for himself, he paddled southward, up the Fox River, portaging around swift chutes and rapids. After fifty miles the river led to Lake Winnebago. The horizon-reaching water looked like an ocean, but soon the shores closed in again to the river leading southward.

A few days' paddling against the stream brought him to the home of the Mascoutins, a people of Algonquian stock, whose language he could understand. They told him of a broad river (the Wisconsin) a short portage from the dwindling Fox and of a "great water" which that river entered. Their reference was to the Mississippi, but Nicolet took it for the western ocean—on his return to the St. Lawrence he reported having been but three days' journey from the sea.

Instead of seeking that ocean, Nicolet turned southward—leaving an epic discovery for Marquette and Jolliet. He must have seen the northern Illinois prairies, the great grassland with its winding, wooded water courses.

Returning northward, he visited the Potawatomi; he sat with them in the slow smoke of their oak and hickory fires while snow swirled through the bare Wisconsin woods. No doubt he played on Indian superstition, using compass, mirror and magnet to impress them with his manitous.

Spring unlocked the bays and rivers. The woods turned green, and again the lake was restless. While flocks of waterfowl winged northward, Nicolet and his seven paddlers pushed their canoe into flashing water. They retraced their long journey, through the Straits of Mackinac, along the broken southern shore of Manitoulin Island, up the French River, over Lake Nipissing and so to the seaward-flowing Ottawa. There Nicolet joined a Huron brigade on its summer trading voyage to the French settlements on the St. Lawrence. No one feted him there, and Nicolet never wrote an account of his exploration. But at Quebec old Governor Champlain must have listened with quickened heartbeat while he told his story, and Father Vimont wrote a brief record of it for the *Jesuit Relations*. This was the last fulfillment for Champlain, who died on Christmas day of that year, 1635.

After the great adventure that crowned his sixteen years in the wilderness, Nicolet became a household man. At Quebec in 1637, he married Margaret Couillard, daughter of a St. Lawrence farmer and goddaughter of Champlain. As interpreter and trading clerk, Nicolet lived at Three Rivers, where every year fleets of Indian canoes came down from the wilderness. Sometimes his thoughts must have followed them when their shouts faded and their craft disappeared around the river bend. On a windy night in November 1642, on an errand to Quebec, he was drowned in a storm that lashed the St. Lawrence. In all his years as boatman he had never learned to swim.

Jean Nicolet was mourned by Indians and Frenchmen alike. Three years later his wife's sister bore a son, Louis Jolliet, who would also pass the Straits of Mackinac on an epic journey.

Governor Champlain had provided the impulse for exploration, and with his death the horizons of New France contracted. For a generation no agents of the French King counciled with distant tribes. Only the Jesuit missionaries, anxious for the souls of the savages, went to the western wilderness. For more than thirty years no other Frenchman passed the Straits of Mackinac. Nicolet himself was forgotten, and it remained for nineteenth-century historians, searching the voluminous Jesuit records, to rediscover "the gallant Norman."

Jean Nicolet left no descendant of his own name in Canada. But his daughter Marguerite married Jean-Baptiste Le Gardeur, whose son, Jacques le Gardeur, commonly known as "St. Pierre," had a long career in the northwest. As a trader at Chequamegon on Lake Superior, this grandson of Nicolet knew the savage languages, it was said, better than did the savages. He became a distinguished officer of New France, commanding posts on the upper Mississippi and at the Straits of Mackinac. He dealt firmly and fairly with the tribes. In 1747 Le Gardeur de Saint-Pierre followed Nicolet's route of discovery from Michilimackinac to Green Bay. He carried no robe of Chinese damask but a cargo of presents for the Indians—flour, peas, suet, salt beef, beads, traps, knives and kettles. Returning, he led thirty canoes heaped with peltry from Lake Michigan to Montreal. In the uneasy year 1748, when the Indians were restive, he was made commander at the Straits. He allayed an uprising and made peace in the upper country. St. Pierre was "much esteemed among all the nations."

In the twentieth century, Nicolet's monument was raised on Mackinac Island. By then a great commerce passed through the straits where a Frenchman and seven Huron boatmen had paddled into history.

. 2 .

THE CROSS ON THE SHORE

Beneath the white fort on Mackinac Island, Marquette Park slopes down to the half-moon harbor. Over that terrace once rambled the gardens and stables of a United States Army garrison, with paths shaded by the old French lilac trees. The lilacs are still there, a century older now, blowing white, lavender and purple in the long June sunlight. They now shade stone benches on a green lawn where seagulls gather leftovers from picnic lunches. The gulls have a convenient perch in the midst of the picnic parties; they watch from the bronze head and shoulders of Jacques Marquette. From a stone pedestal banked with shrubs and flowers, the prince of the Jesuits looks toward the harbor.

A hundred steps from the Marquette monument is a rounded dark shelter, bark-covered, with a low dim entry. It might be an old Chippewa dwelling or a fur trader's hut—except for the cedar cross, taller than the rounded roof, beside it. Gulls whiten the weathered crossbar. Inside the dark doorway a concealed light shows five life-sized figures—a surpliced priest blessing two kneeling Indians while a pair of voyageurs look on.

An upraised cross and a bark chapel were the first French structures at Michilimackinac, and the illustrious Marquette was the first and most beloved of the French missionaries. His name is honored in many places in the upper country, and his memory is cherished at the Straits of Mackinac.

In the 1660s, while young Louis XIV was making France the great power of Europe, Jacques Marquette was living in a cloister and dreaming of a mission in some distant land. At seventeen he entered the Jesuit college at Nancy. As a novice he followed

10

Loyola's *Spiritual Exercises*, meditating in solitude and darkness, performing menial tasks, studying history, languages, science and philosophy. So he learned repose, endurance and self-discipline. Admitted to the order, he became a teacher in Jesuit schools in Reims, Charleville and Langres. But he had read the annual volumes of the *Jesuit Relations* recounting the toil of missionaries among the Indians of Canada. In his cloister he prayed for an assignment in the New World wilderness.

At last, when he was 29, a mature scholar and a resourceful man, his orders came. In 1666 he sailed for America. For many days he paced the deck in his long black cassock and flat black hat, a crucifix swinging from his waist, picturing the wild land beyond the sea rim. In the Jesuit college at Quebec he met a young Canadian named Louis Jolliet. They quickly became friends, but when Marquette was sent to the interior no one thought that they would ever meet again.

The missionary enterprise looked forlorn in 1666. It had never recovered from the defeats and disasters of 1649, when peaceful Huronia was swept by the ruthless Iroquois. As Marquette looked westward, the Jesuit empire consisted of a few toilworn priests with altars strapped to their backs, wandering with hungry savages, building and abandoning bark chapels in desolate places. As missionary to the Ottawas, veteran Father Ménard had raised the cross at Sault Ste. Marie and on distant Keweenaw Bay—before he died in the northern forests. Father Allouez had followed him to Lake Superior and had gone on to plant a mission at Chequamegon Bay, on the edge of nowhere. Now came word that Allouez wanted more missionaries. Jacques Marquette would answer that call.

Marquette's hands were hardened by canoe paddles, and his shoulders were scarred with portage loads when he arrived at the Indian settlement beside the wide white rapids that the French called "Sault Ste. Marie." With Indian helpers he built a cabin and erected his altar at the foot of the falls—it was near the site of the later Schoolcraft house in the American town. The next spring Father Dablon joined him there. They built a mission church within a log stockade. On its altar Marquette

placed gold and silver ornaments, and he hung pictures of the
saints on its rough walls. These sacred objects he had guarded
throughout the hazardous journey from the St. Lawrence.

Sault Ste. Marie, where the water from Lake Superior fell
twenty feet in two miles, tumbling over reefs and rocks and
teeming with whitefish, was one of the most populous places
in North America. There lived two thousand Algonquian tribesmen and a few French traders. The Indians listened to
Marquette's teaching. Some came to the chapel, along with the
swaggering French voyageurs, for confession and prayer. Marquette patiently instructed the savages, trying to overcome their
heathen fears and sorcery. To Indian children he told stories
of the saints. He made a garden and taught the Indian women
agriculture along with the forgiveness of sins. He won the Indians to himself, if not to Christian doctrine, by kindness and
affection.

In the summer of 1669 Father Allouez, serving the remote
station of La Pointe on Chequamegon Bay near the western end
of Lake Superior, was ordered to found a new mission at Green
Bay on Lake Michigan. Marquette was to replace him at La
Pointe.

In Marquette's time the Jesuits were not sedentary priests and
apostles; they were pathfinders, explorers, map-makers, scouts
in the wilderness. Along with reports of baptisms and conver-
sions, they told of newly found Indian peoples, of tribal myths,
migrations and wars. They reported copper mines, lake and river
currents, portage routes, the locations of capes, bays and islands.
In their *Relations* a zeal for the souls of the savages is mingled
with a zest for exploration and discovery.

It was Jacques Marquette's destiny to be a forerunner of fore-
runners. After eighteen months of pioneer priesthood at Sault
Ste. Marie, he went on to an outpost three hundred miles deeper
in the wilderness. With Indian canoemen he coasted mysterious
Lake Superior, past dune, forest and cliff, through fog, squall
and an early September snowstorm, with no prospect but hardship and difficulty at the journey's end. At La Pointe du St.
Esprit (the Point of the Holy Spirit), Allouez had accomplished

little, as Marquette must have known. But he went with eagerness to this far station.

Near the western tip of Lake Superior, Chequamegon Bay makes a spacious harbor sheltered by the wooded Apostle Islands and a long sandy promontory (La Pointe). Various Indians had settled there, and others came in season for the fishing in the bay and the wild rice in the river marshes. Indian women were harvesting rice and husking corn in withered fields when Marquette arrived.

Immediately he visited the Huron village, where he was welcomed. But the other camps were surly. There the priest was rebuffed and ridiculed; only the old and the sick listened to his prayers. Among the Ottawas he found lewdness, brutality and cruel superstition.

Marquette shared the winter cold and hunger of these Indians. In huts reeking with smoke and smell, with shivering dogs against his back, he tried to sleep. Around him were the mutter and drone of savage voices; outside were wind and snow and the crash of ice in the bay. There, between the frozen swamps and the ice-clogged harbor, the priest carried on his own private devotions and his patient ministry, rejoicing over the piety of a sick man or a submissive woman, thanking God for the privilege of baptizing Indian infants before they died, gladly accepting the "little crosses" of his daily life.

One sick Ottawa, grateful for Marquette's healing, gave him a slave, a captive Illinois tribesman. Patiently the priest studied the captive's language, repeating his words and phrases until the meanings came. He learned that the Illinois country was a month's journey distant from Lake Superior. The tribe had large towns, he learned, in the midst of fertile fields and vast grass-covered hunting grounds. While the captive talked, Marquette's eyes grew distant. Through the Illinois country ran a great river, the "Misipi." In his next report to his superior in Quebec, Marquette spoke of new lands to explore and new nations to redeem from darkness. He hoped to carry the cross to the Illinois people and to follow the great river, which, he believed, would lead to California.

At La Pointe, Marquette heard of another nation, the Sioux, who lived in the forests beyond Lake Superior. On hunting trips the La Pointe Indians had clashed with Sioux hunters; Marquette sent the Sioux presents of glass beads and religious pictures. In primitive formality, the Sioux returned the presents and threatened war upon the settlement at La Pointe. The abject Indians prepared for flight—the Ottawas to their earlier home on Manitoulin Island in Lake Huron and the Hurons to Great Turtle Island in the Straits of Mackinac. The maple woods were gold and scarlet when they reached the Sault.

To Marquette this trip was a kind of homecoming. There he could speak French again, and, while the fugitives fished and feasted, he performed his offices in the mission church. There were long talks with Father Druilettes, who must have told him of the great Indian gathering, just a few months earlier, when the French proclaimed possession of all the Great Lakes country.

After a rest at the Sault, Marquette and his exiles voyaged down the winding St. Mary's River. At the head of Lake Huron the tribesmen separated. One fleet of canoes carried the Ottawas eastward to their old home on Manitoulin Island. The Hurons paddled toward the sunset. Two days' travel brought them to the island of Michilimackinac.

After flight and homelessness, the cliff-walled island was a secure place, and the Hurons made their settlement around the pebbly harbor. There, in a rude bark chapel built by Father Dablon a year before, Marquette spread a clean cloth on the alter and lit a votive candle beside his silver crucifix. For the Hurons there was safety in the winter isolation, but when summer came they grew restless. Winds and currents, fog and storm cut them off from the mainland. The island had little open land for gardens. Perhaps, too, they had an uneasy sense of Michilimackinac's jealous spirits.

Before a year had passed they moved to the north shores of the straits, settling at the site of the present St. Ignace. There, within a pole stockade, they built their long huts with sleeping platforms framing a central fire. Nearby a few French traders raised cabins with stone chimneys. A hundred feet from the sheltered harbor, Father Marquette built the mission church, of alder poles covered with basswood bark, which he named for Saint Ignatius Loyola. The Indian name for their settlement was "Min-is-ing"—"Place of the Big Island"—but the mission name became the lasting designation of St. Ignace.

In the rude chapel, with colored pictures of the saints on the walls and silver vessels on the altar, Marquette taught his converts the Pater Noster in Huron rhymes. He instructed Indian children, their thin voices repeating after him the Ave Maria and the Credo; at the end of the lesson he gave them a few beads or raisins. He made missionary journeys to inland camps and to villages on coastal islands. Today the largest of the Cheneaux Islands is named for Marquette; in its pine woods part of a stone chimney is left from the mission chapel of three hundred years ago. "Citadels of religion," the Jesuits called their forest chapels. They would outlast French trade and empire.

In all his teaching Marquette appealed to the Indians' native sense of wonder. He showed them a magnetic compass, explaining its secret knowledge: No matter where it was consulted, on land or water, in darkness or daylight, it always knew the way to the North Star. This knowledge led to God, who made all things, the moon and stars, the earth and the waters. He told them of his own country, France, of its many towns and its great cities and of its churches with jeweled windows and altars of gold.

In his own mind, while he walked the forest trails and along the shore, Marquette wondered about the terrestrial wilderness around him. Two great fresh-water seas met in the straits, their winds and currents always shifting. From his churchyard he sometimes watched a wall of fog move through the narrows. Winds eddied and changed, and mysterious patterns moved on the water. Perhaps, he reflected, there was a subterranean stream from Lake Superior that came up in the restless straits—like the legendary underground river that flowed from the Holy Land and came to the surface near the shores of Sicily.

For Marquette, lonely St. Ignace was the place he called "home." Yet his thoughts went often to the undiscovered country of the Illinois and the people who had not seen the Christian cross. Daily at his altar he entreated the Virgin Mary "to obtain of God the favor of being able to visit the nations on the Mississippi River." His prayer was especially fervent on the morning of December 8, 1672, the day of the feast of the Immaculate Conception of the Blessed Virgin. And, by a happy chance, the answer to his petition was at that moment on the gray horizon. Over the winter water came a small canoe. It drew near, a canoe with a single paddler; it crossed the little harbor and landed on the sandy beach. Out of it stepped Louis Jolliet, and two friends from years past met in the St. Ignace churchyard.

Jolliet had come alone, after parting from companions in Georgian Bay, with orders for Marquette from Quebec. He was to prepare for a voyage with Jolliet to the undiscovered Mississippi River. "I was all the more delighted with the good news," wrote the joyous Father, "because I saw all my plans about to be accomplished, and found myself in the happy necessity of exposing my life for the salvation of all those tribes."

. 3 .

TO THE GREAT RIVER

Jacques Marquette spent seven winters in the wilderness—one at the Sault, one on Lake Superior, three at the Straits of Mackinac, one at De Pere at the head of Green Bay and one on the lifeless Chicago River. All winters are long in the north, but for him the longest came in 1673, while snows piled up at St. Ignace and his mind went ahead to the great exploration. Louis Jolliet had gone to Sault Ste. Marie before ice locked the St. Mary's. While winter moaned through the pines and blizzards dimmed the straits, the Indians huddled around their fires. In intervals of bright weather they went on hunting trips, men, women and children dragging sleds through the snow. Each night they unrolled their mats of bark and rushes and built shelters in a trampled clearing. Each morning the children, knee-deep in the snow, called "Come porcupine, come beaver, come elk and deer." When hunting was good, the sleds were heaped with smoked venison and bear meat. Sometimes the hunters went home hungry.

That winter, traveling on snowshoes and tramping into scattered camps, Marquette gathered scraps of information about the western country. From wandering hunters, he put together a map of western Lake Michigan, of Green Bay and its southward leading river and of other rivers flowing westward toward the Mississippi. In St. Ignace he rejoiced with the Indians after a successful hunt and fasted when the sleds came back empty. But he daily gave thanks at his altar.

In February the days began to lengthen, and a blinding sunlight came to the icy straits. In the woods the sap was running.

17

The Indians tapped maple trees and kept fires blazing under their sugar kettles. Then the March skies darkened, and new snow erased the forest paths. But at last the winds softened; the sun beamed down. From the straits came a thunder of heaving ice. Undercurrents caught the floes, and the white straits showed gleamings of blue water.

After days of watching, Marquette saw two canoes in the northern channel. They paddled into the bay, and a final thrust beached them on the sand. Out stepped Louis Jolliet and five voyageurs. That winter Jolliet, living in Sault Ste. Marie with his brother Zacharie, had talked to traders and canoemen about the mysterious Mississippi River. The Indians had muttered of evil spirits and destroying monsters in that hostile country, but Jolliet had enlisted five veteran voyageurs to make the journey.

A few days later a canoe brought scholarly Father Philippe Pierson in his tattered Jesuit robe. He moved into the priest's small quarters beside the mission church. His first blessing was given to Marquette and Jolliet and their canoemen, kneeling in the dim chapel while sunlight danced on the water, gulls wheeled over the bay and partridges drummed from the woods. With the restless spring outside, Marquette made a quiet dedication: He placed the whole hazardous voyage under protection of the Blessed Virgin Immaculate, promising that if by her grace they should discover the great river he would establish a mission of the Immaculate Conception among its savage people.

It was a brief task to load the canoes. Some Indian corn and dried meat were the only provisions; the country would supply their needs. Jolliet had a compass and map-making instruments; Marquette had his portable altar, his breviary, some religious pictures and a flask of communion wine. They carried presents for the Indians—beads and buckles, needles, knives and colored garters. After loading these few bundles, the paddlers stepped in—Jacques Tibergé, Pierre Largilier, Pierre Moreau, Jean Plattier, Pierre Porteret. Simple, hardy, unwashed men, they could not know that they were making history.

In the long morning sunlight on May 17th, the two canoes pushed off. They soon vanished around the wooded point.

It was spring, the radiant spring of the north country. Water flashed and gleamed to the horizon, and little waves shattered around the two canoes. White clouds drifted overhead, their shadows changing on the water. A soft wind came from the luring, unknown country.

In a bark canoe, thrusting his paddle in rhythm with three incurious boatmen, Marquette was at the crest of his life. A man of piety and purpose, experienced, disciplined, devoted, he now knew the fulfillment of his deepest yearnings. Ahead of him lay risk, hazard, danger and the promise of discovery, the winning of new lands for France and the salvation of unknown nations. As his paddle reached forward, his eyes went to the horizon, and his heart throbbed under his sober black cassock. "Our joy at being chosen for this expedition roused our courage, and sweetened the labor of rowing . . . we made our paddles play merrily over a part of Lake Huron and that of the Illinois." With that blithe summary he accounted for the long days' toil, night camps on rocky shores, the pursuit of the horizon.

One of their stops was at a huddle of brush huts beside a river stained with tanbark, a village of the Menomini nation. "Wild Oats People" Marquette called them; they gathered grain in the wide rice marshes along the river mouth. The visitors were well received there, but when Marquette spoke of his destination the tribesmen tried to turn him back. They told of warring nations in the western country and of monsters and winged demons on the great river. If one should get past those perils, the headlong current would sweep him into a land of steaming heat and searing sun.

Thanking the Menominis for this advice the Frenchmen traveled on. Ahead of them the shores of Green Bay closed in to the broad mouth of the Fox River. After a brief rest at the De Pere mission, the travelers were on their way, wading icy waters at the rapids, hauling the canoes over reefs and ledges. They paddled up the diminishing river to a palisaded village of the Mascoutins, arriving there on June 7th. Wrote Marquette, "This is the limit of the discoveries made by the French, for they have not yet passed beyond it." That the French had been there, both traders and priests, was evident from a cedar cross upraised in the midst of the rush cabins. Marquette found the cross hung with offerings—white skins, strings of beads, red belts, bows and arrows.

For three days the Frenchmen remained in the Mascoutin village. When they moved on, two Indian guides led them to the carrying place between the dwindling Fox River and the westward-flowing Wisconsin.

The upper Fox was a maze of rice swamps and reed thickets, with no discernible channel. But the guides found a landing place where a muddy path led into the forest. There was the site of the future town of Portage, Wisconsin, the home of Juliette Kinzie, Frederick Jackson Turner and Zona Gale. It was wilderness when Marquette counted 2,700 paces with his altar strapped to his back. That mile-and-a-half portage ended at a sandy shore where a clear brown current hurried westward. On the undiscernible height of land, the Frenchmen had crossed a divide. Wrote Marquette, "We now leave the waters which flow to Quebec, a distance of 4 or 500 leagues, to follow those which will henceforth lead us into strange lands."

For nearly a week the Meskonsing (Wisconsin) carried them southwest, through smiling country, past countless vine-clad islands and wooded bends. Deer and elk watched them from the forest; wild swans flew over, and fish leaped in the stream. At evening the sun sank over a land with all its history yet to come. At last, on June 17th, a month out of St. Ignace, Marquette saw, beyond a low green island, a great current sweeping past in silence and grandeur. A thrust of paddles pushed them into the new stream. With a joy beyond expressing, Marquette entered the Mississippi.

That night they made camp in a willow thicket, and the first fire of civilized men gleamed in the darkening water. Marquette must have gone apart from the others, crossing himself and offering a prayer of thanksgiving for this discovery. Names from French piety have warmed the maps of the upper country ever since the first Jesuits entered the wilderness. Sault Ste. Marie,

Lac de Flambeau, St. Croix and De Pere were more lasting than
were the mission stations. But the name Marquette had promised
to the Virgin—"River of Immaculate Conception"—did not sur-
vive. There were other French names for the Mississippi. Traders
seeking political favor called it "Rivière Colbert" for the French
minister and "Rivière Buade" or "Rivière Frontenac" for the
Governor of New France. In honor of the French monarch it
was named "Rivière St. Louis" and "Rivière Louisiana." But
neither Christian nor political names could supplant the savage "Mee-Zee-see-bee" of the Algonquians; perhaps no Old
World term could fix itself to this timeless feature of the new
continent.

For the first Frenchmen the river had majesty and grandeur.
The dread tales of the savages vanished like morning mist as
the current carried them around countless bends and islands,
past shores of abrupt bluffs, dense woods and sunlit prairies.
It was a deep channel; ten fathoms they measured with a stone-
weighted fishing line. From its depths came huge turtles and
fish as big as floating pine trunks. Once they glimpsed "a mon-
ster with the head of a tiger, a pointed snout like a wildcat's,
a beard and ears erect, a grayish head and neck all black." But
this chimera vanished as quickly as it had appeared. Wrote Marquette, "We saw no more of them."

What they saw was a wild and beautiful country without a
sign of human habitation. From the river they netted sturgeon
and catfish. Ashore they hunted turkey and "wild cattle"—the
first buffalo hunt on record. Months later, when he wrote his
account of the exploration, Marquette remembered standing over
that first slain bison.

> The head is very large, the forehead flat and a foot and a half
> broad between the horns, which are exactly like those of our
> cattle, except that they are black and much larger. . . . When
> you fire at them from a distance with gun or bow, you must
> throw yourself on the ground as soon as you fire, and hide
> in the grass; for if they perceive the one who fired they rush
> on him and attack him. . . . They are scattered over the prairie
> like herds of cattle. I have seen a band of four hundred.

As they went deeper into mystery ("We did not know where we were going," Marquette wrote simply), the strangeness, beauty and solitude of the country hung over them like a spell. A combination of wonder and wariness kept them searching the shores. They felt the silence, as though the wilderness watched them night and day. In the evening they kindled the smallest fire, and when supper was eaten they moved their canoes away from that thin smoke, anchoring in some backwater between dense islands. They slept now in the canoes with a sentry awake to the summer darkness and the high white stars. Marquette must have enjoyed the midnight watch, while Scorpio blazed in the south and Cassiopeia circled around the Pole Star. Over the wilderness river hung the stars he had learned in his youth from the hilltop of Laon.

On the eighth day of the southward journey, they found the first signs of men. Footprints on the west bank of the river led them to a path through a screen of woods and across a little prairie. Leaving the boatmen to guard the canoes, Marquette and Jolliet went visiting. After an hour of watchful walking, they came to an Indian settlement—one village on the bank of a river and two other clusters of dwellings on a ridge above the valley. (This was the Des Moines Valley, on the eastern edge of present-day Iowa.) As they waited, four old men carrying feather-tufted calumets came toward them, lifting the pipes to the sun. They stopped and studied the Frenchmen. Perhaps it was Marquette's Jesuit dress that reassured the savages; word of the "black robes," their medicines and their great manitou often went ahead of the missionaries. When Marquette spoke in the Illinois tongue, they presented the pipes of peace.

A friendly visit followed, the two Frenchmen puffing the ceremonial pipes and the Indians staring at these men from another world. With the entire village following, they were led through woods and prairie to another town. In endless curiosity the Indians ran ahead, waited for the visitors to pass and then ran ahead to watch again. In the house of a sachem, Marquette ceremoniously presented gifts and told of his desire to bring Christian teaching to the Illinois nation. The French, he said, had overcome the warring Iroquois, and there would now be peace in the Illinois country from which these people had been driven. He asked how far it was to the sea where the great river flowed.

In reply, the sachem expressed joy at this meeting with men from distant places. He could not tell where the river ran, but he asked Marquette to bring his religious teaching to the Illinois people. Then he gave gifts—a colored calumet and a young Indian slave. Next day the explorers were escorted to the Mississippi by six hundred Indians, who watched the Frenchmen paddle away. In Marquette's canoe was the Indian slave, a bright and curious youth who seemed happy with his new existence. Within a few weeks he was speaking French and repeating the catechism.

Journeying down the smooth, clear, tranquil Mississippi, the travelers came suddenly upon the monsters they had been warned about. On a sheer rock cliff above the river were two grotesque paintings. The Indian boy turned his head away while Marquette carefully traced the figures and wrote a description of "horns on the head like a deer . . . bearded like a tiger . . . the body covered with scales and the tail so long that it twice makes the turn of the body, passing over the head and down between the legs, and ending at last in a fish's tail." At great pains and peril, some Indian sorcerer had painted in red, green and black, high on the cliff, these grim dragons. Marquette was still wondering about them when he saw something more threatening: a mass of floating timber came rushing out of the huge yellow flood, which white men would call the "Missouri." Indians had told them of this river, the Pekitanoni, which flowed from an endless prairie, but the Frenchmen had not expected a current that would muddy the Mississippi all the way to the sea.

As they paddled southward, the land was lush and mysterious, with unseen buffalo bellowing in the bottomlands and vine-clad islands. At the mouth of the St. Francis River, in what would become the State of Arkansas, a swarm of tribesman came out, some in log dugouts, others swimming and flailing clubs in the water. Either as guests or captives, Marquette and Jolliet were taken to their camp. This tribe had guns, knives and axes, obtained from Spanish traders on the Gulf of Mexico. Some Arkansas warriors wanted to kill the strangers and seize their canoes, but a chief interceded.

That night the two explorers considered their situation. It was the 17th of July; they had traveled for a month on the Mississippi. They were in the realm of New Spain, where they would meet hostility. They had traced the Mississippi, they thought, nearly to the sea (actually they were yet seven hundred miles from the Gulf of Mexico). It was time, they agreed, to return northward.

The return journey was toilsome and slow, as they paddled against the current without the excitement of discovery. They rounded endless bars and islands. They looked for side channels of slack water. They toiled from dawn till dark and slept with smudge fires against the mosquitoes. At last they passed the Ohio, then the Missouri. The Illinois tribesmen had told of another river, scratching the ground to show it leading northeastward toward Lake Michigan.

Halfway up the Illinois they came to a town of 74 cabins. It was home country now, or so it seemed to grateful Jacques Marquette. The tribe welcomed the travelers, and at their departure one of the young men escorted them up the diminishing river. He showed them the prairie portage to the Chicago River, which carried the canoes smoothly into "the Illinois Lake," not yet named "Lake Michigan." At last they had blue water, windy blue skies and the French stations ahead. Their goal was the mission of St. Francis Xavier at the head of Green Bay.

When the canoes were beached there at the mouth of the Fox River, the exploring journey was completed. They had traveled 2,767 miles through wild and unknown country among native nations of whom the French had never heard. They had extended the maps of New France deep into the interior of America and had traced the great river for 1,100 miles. Jolliet's record must have emphasized these accomplishments. All his papers were lost, however, in sight of Montreal, when his homecoming canoe capsized in the rapids. His good fortune, so long continued, failed him in the last quarter-hour. Marquette's record has survived. Carried with some voyageur's baggage and baled peltry through a hundred rapids and over a score of portage trails, it arrived at the Jesuit College of Sainte-Marie in the old waterfront town of Montreal. There, in a long room with leaded windows closed against the noise of Bleury Street, among reports of toil and martyrdom, is the joyous story of discovery.

With all its ardor, Marquette's journal shows a man concerned for the spreading of the word of God rather than for the power of France. Marquette was tired and ill when he wrote the final pages of his narrative—so tired that he telescoped the whole return journey, from the Arkansas to Green Bay, in four paragraphs. He had no thought then of the expanding of French empire, but he still felt a selfless rejoicing over the salvation of souls. His report of an epic exploration ends with gratitude for the opportunity to baptize a dying child at the edge of the Illinois River.

Looking westward from the heights of Quebec two and a half centuries later, Willa Cather wrote in *Shadows on the Rock*:

> When an adventurer carries his gods with him into a remote and savage country, the colony he founds will, from the beginning, have graces, traditions, riches of the mind and spirit. Its history will shine with bright incidents, slight, perhaps, but precious, as in life itself, where the great matters are often as worthless as astronomical distances, and the trifles dear as the heart's blood.

. 4 .

THE END OF THE JOURNEY

In the forty miles between Lake Winnebago and Green Bay, the Fox River falls 170 feet. At the first rapids, just five miles from Green Bay, stood the De Pere settlement clustered around the mission of St. Francis Xavier. There the travel-worn Marquette and Jolliet found rest and refuge. After prayers in the chapel and a meeting with Indian chiefs in the council hut, it must have seemed strange not to be pushing on to new places. Instead they traced maps of their journey and recorded the lands and peoples they had seen. When the days shortened and the winds grew cold, Jolliet left for Sault Ste. Marie, where he would spend the winter. With him went the Indian boy who had been given them by the tribe on the Des Moines River.

When spring unlocked the channels, Jolliet set out with two boatmen and his Indian lad for Quebec. They toiled up the swirling French River and swept down the Ottawa to the broad St. Lawrence. Soon that river narrowed, and they were in the turbulent La Chine rapids. Jolliet may have wondered at that derisive name. There lived the aristocratic Sieur de La Salle, whose estate was named "China" because he dreamed of a canoe route to the Orient. The map in Jolliet's battered chest showed the waterways to distant places, with China still beyond. But he had little time to ponder. The rapids grew loud and white. In bow and stern the paddlers chopped at swirling water, and between them the Indian boy from the prairies watched white-eyed with excitement. They were almost past the cauldron when the canoe smashed on a rock.

26

Somehow Jolliet floundered through the raging water. All else was gone—his men, the Indian youth, his peltry, the chest with his maps and records.

In Quebec, travel-worn and empty-handed, he went to see Father Dablon, to tell of the success he had shared with Jacques Marquette. He had one satisfaction—copies of his maps and his journal had been left in the mission house at Sault Ste. Marie. But that comfort failed when Father Dablon told of news that had just arrived with canoemen from the upper country: Fire had destroyed the mission at the Sault. Everything, he repeated to the stunned Jolliet, had been destroyed; nothing was left but ashes. So vanished the wilderness chapel that the ardent Father Le Clercq had described as "a magnificent church furnished with the richest vestments."

All that was left of Jolliet's exploration was his memories. He recalled, as carefully as he could, the epic journey, while Father Dablon pictured the great river and its varied shores. Despite all that Jolliet had seen of the American interior, the dream of a route to the Orient still beckoned. He described the portage between the Chicago and Des Plaines Rivers, adding that a short canal across the prairie marshes would facilitate travel from Lake Michigan to the Illinois and "to China and Japan."

Father Dablon wrote it all down. Later he would combine this report with Marquette's record for publication in the *Jesuit Relations* for 1678. Of Jolliet's misfortunes he stated, "Having passed through dangers of a thousand kinds, he was wrecked in the very harbor . . . and only escaped by a kind of miracle with his life."

Meanwhile Marquette was at De Pere, patiently and hopefully awaiting the opportunity to return to the Illinois country and establish a mission there. The spirit was willing, but the flesh was weak. All winter he had suffered from a stubborn dysentery, an illness left over from his exhausting travel. But as the summer passed his strength increased. With the bracing airs of autumn he felt himself ready. When the Wisconsin forests were scarlet and gold, he set out to spend the winter among the Illinois.

With two boatmen, he set out on October 25, 1674, paddling into Green Bay and along the coast of the widening estuary. On the shore of Lake Michigan they joined a party of Indians in nine canoes. The tribesmen, Potawatomi and Illinois, had come north with peltry and were returning to their town of Kaskaskia on the Illinois River—the town Marquette had visited fifteen months before.

Winter came early that year. Day after day a cold wind whipped the men in their tossing craft. When nausea overcame him, Marquette would walk the windswept beach within hailing distance of his canoe. His strength was ebbing. The group camped at night in reed shelters thrown up on the sand and pushed off in pitching canoes at daybreak.

After six long weeks they reached the Chicago River, its sheltered water frozen hard. They followed the south branch, carrying canoes and baggage over the snowy prairie. A few miles inland, between the Chicago River and the headwaters of the Illinois, they built a flimsy cabin, where Marquette tried to warm himself beside a fitful fire. While the boatmen hunted on the prairie and fished through the ice, he read his breviary and said his Aves. Twice a week he heard confession from his boatmen and encouraged them in their faith.

Late in March, with the prairie streams alive and brimming, they pushed on. It was blustery weather, high winds, flickers of sunlight, sudden curtains of rain and snow. On the 8th of April, Marquette was welcomed in a tribal town "of five or six hundred fires."

There he went from cabin to cabin, ringing his little chapel bell, with prayer book and religious pictures. Three days before Easter he called the Indians to a council. For him the men had built a tabernacle of saplings, its floor covered with rush mats and bear and buffalo robes. In the center Marquette erected an altar, which he adorned with four large pictures of the Holy Virgin, one picture facing in each direction. Five hundred chiefs and elders took seats around the altar, and another five hundred young men stood around the circle. Rising above his weakness, Marquette gave them the wampum belt of prayer and told the story of crucifixion and resurrection. After eleven days with the Illinois, Marquette began his return journey. An escort of tribesmen accompanied him to the headwaters, where they bade him farewell. With his two boatmen Marquette crossed the Des Plaines prairie to the south branch of the Chicago River and paddled into Lake Michigan. The priest hoped to reach "home" at the Straits of Mackinac before death overtook him.

To use a northward current, the canoes followed the east shore of the lake. Slowly they voyaged past the great dunes and green forests. Marquette was growing weaker. At night the men lifted him from his craft and made him a bed under a canvas lean-to on the shore. They camped at the river mouths—the St. Joseph, the Kalamazoo, the Grand, the Muskegon.

They were halfway up the long coast when Marquette directed his men to land where a small stream flowed past a headland into the lake. It had two extended Indian names—"Notispescago" and "Aniniondibeganining"—but it would become the Marquette River. A wind came up while Marquette's men carried him across the beach to a shelter of poles and bark.

That night, May 16, 1675, "with a countenance beaming and all aglow," Jacques Marquette ended his journey. Perhaps he remembered what he had written during that desolate winter at La Pointe: "No one must hope to escape crosses in our missions, and the best means to live happy is not to fear them, but in the enjoyment of little crosses, hope for another still greater." He thanked his voyageurs for their loyalty and devotion, begged their pardon for all the trouble he had been and with a trembling hand gave them final penance. From his robe he drew a paper listing his own faults since his last confession, asking the men to deliver it to his superior. Then he told his companions to take some rest.

Ernest Hemingway, who later also knew the solitude of the north country, said that the best thing is to die well. Marquette had lived well, perhaps the greater thing, and it was natural for him to die with grace. He was buried at the mouth of the river that years later would bear his name. The boatmen carried his body to a trench in the sand, rang the altar bell, covered the body and set up a cross above it. Then they pushed northward.

For more than a century, voyageurs coasting Lake Michigan and camping at the river mouth knelt at a weathered cross on the empty shore. Seagulls perched on it, the rains darkened it, the sun warmed it and the west wind scoured it with sand. In 1818 Gurdon Hubbard, fur trader from Mackinac, saw at the river mouth the remains of a red-cedar cross—"it was about three feet above the ground and in a falling condition." He reset the cross, planting it firmly upright. The winds of the next winter drifted the dunes, and no one ever saw the cross again.

But the grave had gone from that lonely beach long before. In the spring of 1675, Marquette's two companions completed their voyage to St. Ignace, where they told of the burial of the priest. The next winter some Indians of St. Ignace went south on a hunting trip. On their return, early in the spring of 1676, they camped at the river mouth where Marquette was buried. Crossing themselves as the Father had taught them, they dug into the sand. They found the body intact; even the skin was unbroken. According to tribal custom they dissected it, washed the bones in lake water and dried them in the fresh spring wind. When the bones were packed in a birchbark box, the Indians— thirty canoes, according to Dablon's account—paddled home to the Straits. At sight of Mackinac Island, they threw a kinnikin- nick to its manitous. They had been attached to the man in the black robe, though they grasped little of his doctrine.

At St. Ignace they were met by Father Pierson and a second missionary, Father Nouvel. The Indian population had increased at the Straits; there was a priest in charge of the Huron mission and another ministering to the Ottawas four miles up the shore. Indians had gathered around the bay when the canoes paddled in. The two priests rowed out to greet them. Word went across the water that the hunting party had brought home Father Mar- quette's remains.

On that bright day, June 8, 1677, the priests carried the birch box, with Indians following, over the forest path to the chapel. With funeral rites it was lowered into a small vault under the chapel floor. There it was to remain "as the guardian angel" of the mission.

Indians came often, wrote Dablon, to pray at this tomb. An Ottawa maiden, whom Marquette had baptized and instructed before his great journey, fell ill, and neither Indian nor French medicines could help her. At last Father Pierson told her to go to the chapel for three successive days, each time saying an Ave and three Pater Nosters at the grave of Father Marquette. By the third day she was cured of her malady.

A few years later a French garrison came to St. Ignace and erected Fort de Buade. Its commander in the years 1694–1701 was Antoine de la Mothe Cadillac. When it was decided that Detroit should become the French capital in the west, Cadillac removed the soldiers and trading houses to Detroit. Gradually the Indians drifted away from St. Ignace, and the last Jesuit priest departed in 1706. To prevent sacrilege by wandering savages, he took the altar ornaments and burned the chapel. Wind soughed through the pines, water washed the shore and forest grew over the chapel clearing. Marquette's mission and his grave seemed erased from memory.

A century later some Canadian fishermen built cabins there. A Jesuit priest arrived, and a new church was built in 1834. Slowly St. Ignace grew, a lonely little town between dark woods and the restless water.

One spring morning in 1877, while gulls veered over Moran Bay and the little steamer *Truscott* was loading for Mackinac Island, a half-breed named Peter Grondin was clearing brush at the edge of Patrick Murray's garden. Amid forest trees and undergrowth he found a stone foundation; it measured 36 × 40 feet. He also found bits of iron, copper and looking glass and what appeared to be the outlines of a small well and a cellar.

Patrick Murray went to his priest, Father Edward Jacker, who had read all the Jesuit histories. The priest was excited—it sounded like the site of Marquette's chapel—but he persuaded Murray to postpone excavation until he could send for Bishop Mrak. The bishop arrived September 3rd. In long black vestments, with a rosary swinging from his waist, he dug the first spadeful of earth. Then he gave the spade to Murray, and the digging went on. When nothing was found but roots and some bits of limestone, the bishop walked off. Patrick Murray kept digging. A piece of birchbark, white in the black earth, came up on his shovel. Other bark fragments appeared; they had an orange coloring as if scorched by fire. Then the shovel found a solid sheet of birchbark, such as might have formed the bottom of an Indian macock. Murray was working slowly now, cutting carefully into the damp ground. Up came two fragments of bone. When he finished, 36 pale pieces of bone had come out of the excavation.

The bone fragments were examined by a Cheboygan physician, who declared them human. Father Jacker pronounced them the remains of the missionary-explorer, recovered two centuries after his burial. A few of the relics were sent to Marquette University in Milwaukee. The rest were returned to the grave, on which was erected a marble monument surmounted by a cross. It stands today in Marquette Park on the St. Ignace highway, where the Indians once wore a path to the mission chapel.

THE LOST GRIFFIN

On a late summer day in 1679—the ledgers in the trading houses were marked "August 27"—excitement spread through the settlement of St. Ignace. Indians and Frenchmen trooped down to the shore, staring across the channel below Mackinac Island. There, with four square sails catching the breeze, with flags rippling from two tall masts and an ensign billowing behind, came a canoe bigger than a council house. A puff of smoke went up from its deck, and thunder rumbled over the water. At this first boom of a cannon in the northern straits, the Indians yelped and ran. Some Hurons got muskets and fired in all directions. But the Frenchmen stood waving on the beach, and the savages crept back. Now the fort-in-the-water drew near. The sails came down; men lowered a small boat and rowed ashore. Out of the boat stepped a Frenchman wearing a plumed hat and scarlet cape embroidered with gold, a priest in the peaked hood and gray robe of the Recollet order and a swarthy man with the mooring line wrapped around an iron hand. Three men of history—Sieur de La Salle, Father Louis Hennepin, and Henry de Tonty—had arrived at the Straits. In St. Ignace harbor rode the first commercial ship on the upper lakes, with a silhouetted griffin at her prow and the Fleur-de-Lis fluttering above her raised quarterdeck. Already canoes were circling like seagulls around her.

La Salle was the son of a rich merchant of Rouen. As a youth in that ancient, many-spired city, he had studied for the priesthood in the Jesuit college, but he had never taken orders. He was too willful to submit himself to the Church, and his ambition involved more worldly goals than the saving of souls. Even as a youth he seems to have been austere and solitary; he had no love of pleasure and little taste for society. In him burned a deep and lonely ambition, a hunger for hardship and achievement, a need to defy difficulties. If ever a man was destined for the enterprises of New France, it was Robert Cavelier, Sieur de La Salle.

In 1667, at the age of 23, La Salle came to Canada. Ten years of exploration, which carried him into the Ohio Valley and through the Straits of Mackinac to the southern shores of Lake Michigan, gave him a dream of a chain of trading stations in the Mississippi Valley. At that fortuitous time there came to Quebec a new governor, a bold, ambitious man who saw in La Salle's dream the extension of the power and prosperity of New France. He was Louis de Buade, Comte de Palluau et de Frontenac. Together the Governor and the explorer projected a commercial empire in the West.

The first step was to build Fort Frontenac at the outlet of Lake Ontario; La Salle was placed in command. From there he launched two trading sloops, which did a brisk business on Lake Ontario, diverting the Iroquois trade that had gone to Montreal merchants and to the English at Albany. It was a profitable business, which might have satisfied another man. But La Salle had larger goals.

In 1677 he went to Paris, seeking authority to build forts in the interior and to trade with western tribes not yet reached by French enterprise. His petition was granted by the King's minister, and his relatives in France subscribed 500,000 livres to support his undertaking. In Paris he met a restless Italian army officer, Henry de Tonty, who had lost a hand in the Sicilian wars. When La Salle offered him a share in his enterprise, he did not know that Tonty's iron hand would become famous from Michilimackinac to the Gulf of Mexico. The next summer they sailed for Canada. In Quebec they met a long-striding Recollet friar named Louis Hennepin, who was less interested in evangelism than in adventure and discovery. He would soon join in La Salle's undertakings and would become notorious as his vainglorious "historian."

To begin his inland empire, La Salle planned to build a cargo ship that would carry commerce between the Niagara River and the far northwest. Such a vessel could land the cargo of many hundreds of canoes and could transport materials for construction of other vessels for use on the western rivers. In the fall of 1768 he sent a force of workmen to the Niagara River to build a stockade and a shipyard; at the same time he sent a brigade of voyageurs to the Lake Michigan country to gather furs from the Indians, furs that would become the first return cargo of his trading vessel.

Five miles above Niagara Falls, at the mouth of Cayuga Creek at what is now La Salle, New York, a clatter broke out in the winter woods. French carpenters and shipwrights hewed timbers for the hull of a vessel five times larger than any craft that had ever sailed on the Great Lakes. Some hired Indians threw up bark barracks for the workmen. Hennepin constructed a rude chapel. As winter waned and the spring days lengthened, the framework of a ship took shape on the riverbank.

In bright spring weather the last deck planks were laid, the masts were braced and the *Griffin* was ready for launching. Named for Frontenac's coat of arms, it carried a carved griffin on its prow and a spread-winged eagle at its stern. Its masts and bowsprit stood up like leafless trees. With the men assembled, French and Indians together, Hennepin invoked a blessing on the vessel (ahead of her was nothing but disaster), and the builders joined in a singsong Te Deum. From the deck a swivel cannon boomed. The hawsers were cut, and the ship slid into the water. While the Indians whooped over an extra ration of brandy, the Frenchmen anchored their vessel in the stream.

The *Griffin* was now a house in the water. She was of 45-tons' burden, with two masts, a raised forecastle and a square, high quarterdeck. From port and starboard portholes five cannon pointed over the water. Hauling at lines from the shore, the men towed her upriver to Black Rock, where they made her fast to trees near the riverhead. There they worked on the rigging and waited for La Salle to come from the St. Lawrence. He arrived in midsummer with a file of sweating men who had

lugged an iron anchor over the steep Niagara escarpment. After
loading arms, stores and merchandise, they worked the ship to
the Lake Erie entrance. Meanwhile Tonty, in a canoe with five
men, had been sent ahead to the Detroit River to meet any of
La Salle's traders who might then be returning from the northwest; he would join the *Griffin* when she came along.

A strong east wind was required to carry the *Griffin* through
the rapids at the lake entrance. While they waited, the men
sewed canvas and calked decks; on Sundays Hennepin preached
from the ship's raised quarterdeck to the Frenchmen and Indians
assembled on the shore. At last, on August 7th, there came a
fresh northeast wind. Sails were spread; the towropes tightened.
With wind and manpower, the *Griffin* breasted the current and
sailed into Lake Erie. From the shore, the Indians watched the
ship diminish and disappear. It was beyond their comprehension,
and once over the horizon it must have seemed a dream. But
there were the rope-scarred trees and the trampled ground where
the winged vessel had been moored.

The first ship ever to sail Lake Erie had a good passage in
fine summer weather. In three days she steered into the Detroit
River. At sight of three smoking fires on the shore, the vessel
was slacked off. Out came a canoe with Tonty and his men.
With all aboard, they went on up the Detroit River, admiring
the country of dense forest and grassy plain. Near the present
city of Detroit, they dropped anchor so that a hunting party
could go ashore. When the hunters returned, the ship's rigging
was hung with venison, bear meat and plucked wild fowl, and
in the galley the cook was pressing grapes and promising the
men a taste of wine. Hennepin liked the place so much that
he wanted to found a settlement there, and La Salle had to re-
mind him that their voyage had only just begun.

In one of the "homeland" references that the French liked
to make, Hennepin found the Detroit River current "as strong
as the tide is before Rouen." Slowly they sailed up the river
into a serene lake that had, on a stormy day, been named Lac
de la Chaudière. It was anything but a caldron now, and, because

he arrived there on August 12th, the saint's feast day, La Salle renamed it Lac Sainte Claire for the girl who had begged for the poor in the streets of Assisi. Between the low banks of the St. Clair River they were carried by a favorable breeze. But the wind changed at the entrance to Lake Huron, and the *Griffin* met a current "as strong as the bore before Caudebec." There La Salle sent twelve men ashore to haul on towropes. In the slanting light of the August day, they passed the Port Huron entrance, where now the Blue Water Bridge arches over an endless commerce, and sailed into the open lake.

For a day the *Griffin* had wind in her sails and a scroll of white water at her bow. Then the wind died, and she lay becalmed off Saginaw Bay. Clouds massed in the north, long ripples ran across the water and then the storm struck. Through the darkness the ship ran with shortened sails. The men were afraid of being driven aground, but daylight showed only a waste of broken water. The gale rose, and the *Griffin* pitched like a bark canoe. "We brought down our mainyard and topmast," wrote Hennepin, "and let the ship drive at the mercy of the wind, knowing no place to run into to shelter ourselves. Monsieur de La Salle notwithstanding he was a courageous man began to fear, and told us we were undone; and therefore everybody fell on his knees to say his prayers and prepare himself for death except our pilot whom we could never oblige to pray; and he did nothing all that while but curse and swear against Monsieur de La Salle who, as he said, had brought him thither to make him perish in a nasty lake and lose the glory he had acquired by long and happy navigation on the ocean."

Prayers were made to the sailors' patron, Saint Anthony of Padua, and, in a rare religious mood, La Salle promised to build a chapel in the saint's honor in the western country. The wind subsided "by a kind of miracle," and the ship rolled in lessening seas, while the men crossed themselves in gratitude. The next day brought a light southeast breeze, which carried them past the shores of Bois Blanc Island and into the Straits of Mackinac. So the *Griffin* came to anchor in the sheltered bay of St. Ignace.

While Indian canoes swarmed around the vessel, La Salle and his company paraded to the Ottawa chapel. Kneeling together, La Salle in his scarlet and gold cape, voyageurs in red-sashed blue capotes and Indians in fringed buckskin, they heard a mass and joined in prayers of thanksgiving.

It was peaceful in the chapel but hostile outside. La Salle was out of bounds there: He had no right to trade in the upper country. A year before he had sent fifteen voyageurs to gather peltry. They had been vaguely instructed to trade among the Potawatomis at the southern end of Lake Michigan, but instructions meant little in the wilderness. Since then, some of the men had embezzled their trade goods and gone adventuring for themselves. La Salle surprised four of these deserters at St. Ignace, though it is not clear how he dealt with them. Other deserters were said to be at Sault Ste. Marie; he sent Tonty to recover any goods they might have left. The rest were scattered among wandering tribes, where he might never find them.

After a week at St. Ignace, the *Griffin* raised sail and voyaged westward to the Green Bay peninsula. Things seemed better there, though the ship arrived in stormy weather. The chief of a Potawatomi village, wrote Hennepin, "came to join us in a canoe at the risk of his life, and in spite of the swelling waves we hoisted him with his canoe into our vessel. He told us in a martial tone that he was ready and willing to perish with the children of Onontio (Great Mountain) the governor of the French."

After this welcome, La Salle found on Washington Island several of his traders who had been faithful to their trust. They had gathered a cargo of peltry, worth 12,000 livres. This good turn of events led La Salle to alter his plans—he could not know how disastrously. Instead of taking the *Griffin* to the southern end of Lake Michigan, he decided to send her back to Niagara, in hopes that the furs could be shipped to France before the end of navigation for the season.

Quickly the peltry was loaded. The godless pilot was assigned five good sailors. The rest of the company, in charge of La Salle, would coast down Lake Michigan in four canoes. But it took two more days to finish his paper work—letters, maps, accounts, requisitions for his creditors in Montreal and his backers in Paris. Those two days were good sailing weather, and if the *Griffin* had not waited she could have made a safe journey. La Salle said farewell in good spirits, expecting the ship to return to Lake Michigan with materials and merchandise the next season.

On September 18th, with a parting salute from her cannon, the *Griffin* sailed away from Washington Island, bound for Niagara. La Salle then began his canoe journey to the Illinois country.

That night a storm swept northern Lake Michigan. The forest rocked in a gale, and water crashed and pounded on the shore. The angry lake swallowed up the *Griffin*, though La Salle would not know it until the next season when, with sinking hopes, he waited for her arrival at the southern end of Lake Michigan.

As with many later shipwrecks in the Straits, the fate of the *Griffin* is a lasting mystery. Perhaps the laboring ship never got beyond Death's Door, at the entrance to Green Bay, and was wrecked off Washington Island. Perhaps she broke up on St. Helena Shoal or on Pointe La Barbe, where the north shore bends into the Straits. Legends surround the vanished vessel, and many bits of shipwreck have been called remains of the *Griffin*. It was said in early times that Indians from St. Ignace boarded the ship and set her afire. Another story says that her mutinous men abandoned the vessel to the storm. Perhaps she floundered through the Straits, obscured by mist and cloud, and came to grief on the sharp shores of Manitoulin Island.

Whatever her end, the ill-starred *Griffin* left a lasting memory. For nearly three centuries men have wondered how she came to rest and what cold waters closed over her six seamen. Generations of Lake sailors, peering through mist or moonlight in the northern straits, have glimpsed a ghostly vessel with a silhouetted griffin springing from her prow. The first ship to the upper country haunts those waters still.

. 6 .

THE LAWLESS POST

In the office of the Corps of Engineers, United States Army, at Detroit are the master charts of the United States Lake Survey. They mark the reefs and shoals, the broken shores and chains of islands, the fog horns and flashing beacons, the currents and magnetic variations. They show the paths of modern commerce, the up- and downbound lanes of shipping that converge at Detour Passage. They measure the Straits of Mackinac and the depth of the island channels and the shelving shores.

In Montreal, Quebec and Paris are older maps. They show vague shores, unfixed islands and unmeasured waters. ("No bottom can be found well out in these lakes," wrote La Mothe Cadillac. "Near the land there is 20, 25, 30, 40 or 50 fathoms of water almost everywhere.") They outline a half-known country where the great trade route followed portage paths around the falls of wilderness rivers. The Great Lakes make a vast tilted "U" between Montreal and the Straits of Mackinac. Because of the Niagara cataract and the British-allied Iroquois, French traders cut across the top of the "U." By passing the lower lakes, they came out, after hundreds of miles of wilderness travel, at the North Channel of Lake Huron.

On the left bank of the Seine in Paris, above a gray stone courtyard in the quiet rue de l'Université, stands the old Ministry of the Marine, with the Depôt des Cartes occupying a balconied room on the second floor. There, in a tall cabinet crammed with folio maps of New France, is the great *Carte de l'Amérique Septentrionale*, drawn by Jean-Baptiste-Louis Franquelin, mapmaker for the King, in the 1680s. The ivory parchment, big as a tablecloth, has red and blue border decorations, a flowered scroll and a colored vignette of Quebec City as seen from the east. It shows an inviting waterway—a strong green line on this map of many colors—leading straight west to "Missilimackinac." Behind that broad, straight line lay endless bends and turns, a hundred menacing rapids and 36 rugged portages, but for a century it was the French highway to the heart of North America. Over it passed explorers and priests, Indians and traders, soldiers and surveyors, French officials and lawless *coureurs de bois*. Whatever their destinations they all came to Michilimackinac. "Stand long enough at Charing Cross," wrote Charles Lamb with the murmur of London outside his window, "and you will meet everybody in the world." Every traveler in the upper country sometime came to remote St. Ignace.

The little station that Father Marquette had established with his fugitive band of Hurons in 1671 grew to a restless outpost. "Fishtown" it might have been called. Over the settlement hung an aroma of drying, smoking and roasting fish. "The whitefish of the straits," wrote Lahontan "is a daily manna which never fails. Moreover better fish cannot be eaten." In the center of St. Ignace, enclosed in a log stockade, stood the Jesuit chapel and the adjoining house of Father Pierson. To one side was the Huron village, its bark dwellings also surrounded by a fence of spruce and poplar poles. On the other side were scattered the square cabins of forty or fifty French traders, men who came and went in the wilds while their Indian women kept the home fires burning. On a low, wooded hill overlooking the bay, were the wigwams of the Ottawas. There stood another chapel, with Father Nouvel's hut beside it. Already St. Ignace had become a two-church town. It also had a dozen shops and trading houses with dry goods on the shelves and brandy under the counter. Each spring and fall the beach was black with canoes, and the town swarmed with trappers, traders and Indians from outlying places. During the summer months, hundreds of transient Indians camped on the St. Ignace shore.

It was less than a lifetime since Nicolet had awed the Winnebagos with fire and thunder from his upraised pistols and had fascinated them with cloth blankets and iron kettles. But already the Indians had turned from their ancient arts to abject dependence on the white man's wares. No contest of cultures, it was an unresisting surrender of the primitive integrity. (A century and a half too late came Tecumseh's resistance, the rejection of the white man and all his ways—his cloth, his iron, his gunpowder and his whiskey.) With the first canoe cargoes of blankets, knives, shirts, mirrors and muskets, the savage self-sufficiency gave way. Clothing, weapons, implements, even the Indians' finery came in the canoe and were sold in the trading house. French beads and earrings replaced the native shells and colored porcupine quills. The warriors dressed in blankets and shirts instead of the skins of animals. In the fields, the women cultivated corn with iron hoes and sickles. Iron arrowheads, consigned from Montreal at 2 sols each, soon replaced the chipped flints that had been precious possessions, and as quickly as they could deliver a pack of beaver skins the hunters discarded their spears and arrows for French firearms. The treasured wampum of the tribes gave place to a new currency in beads of French glass and porcelain. And one taste was enough to start an endless appetite for that intoxicating "milk," French brandy.

Like moths to a fire the Indians came to the white man's posts. They left their scattered villages and clustered around the French settlements. Old camp sites were left lifeless while the tribes gathered at the new stations—La Pointe on Lake Superior, La Baye on Green Bay, St. Joseph at the southern end of Lake Michigan, Fort St. Louis on the Illinois River and St. Ignace at the Straits.

At the beginning of French commerce in America, it was thought that the Indian trade could be regulated and controlled by French officials. In a quaintly unrealistic system, the King's ministers issued licenses to merchants on the St. Lawrence. Each spring brigades of canoes came down from the interior, bringing their winter furs to the warehouses at Montreal and Three Rivers. But the trade could not be confined to the St. Lawrence ports. French woods rangers, anxious for profit and drawn by the freedom of the wilderness, went to the tribal camps on rivers and bays. They opened their packs of knives, blankets, hatchets, bells, beads, mirrors and brandy—all the wares of use and fancy—and exchanged them for the Indians' catch of furs. Then, with feathers stuck in their caps, keeping time to the paddles with old songs from Normandy, they went on loaded with peltry worth five times the cost of their trade goods.

These hardy, cheerful, lawless men took like foxes to the wilderness. They were tireless on the portages, indolent in camp, carousing at the trading posts. Short men generally, they had broad shoulders, stocky legs and leathery skin little bothered by black flies and mosquitoes. Their trade goods were put up in packs of a hundred pounds each. At the portages it was common to carry two of these, steadied by a strap over the forehead or across the chest, singing and joking on the way. Some men could carry four, five or even six pieces at a dog trot on a half-mile portage. Around campfires at St. Ignace they bragged of the rapids they had waded, the loads they had carried, the distances they had come since sunrise. When fiddle music sounded, they jumped up to dance with the dark-eyed Indian girls.

Seeing that the trade could not be confined to the St. Lawrence, the Montreal merchants tried a license system. For a fee a man could send out two canoes—the number was soon increased—loaded with trade goods. A voyageur was hired by written agreement for a stated term—one, two or three years. The standard contract gave him his equipment and subsistence plus wages of 350 livres—about $70—a year; the payment was made in beaver skins to be added to the contract cargo. For this the voyageur took a canoe loaded with trade goods to Lake Superior, Wisconsin or Illinois. At the western posts, he would make himself useful as a trader and hunter, and he would return to the St. Lawrence in a canoe loaded with 25 packets of peltry, amounting to some 1,400 pounds. On the return journey he could legally trade his gun, capote and blanket at Michilimackinac for his own interest.

Despite the system, lawless traffic increased. Though officials sealed bales of merchandise and inspected arriving peltry, there were more violators than licensed traders. Traders sent out more than their allotted cargoes, and, once in the woods, many a voyageur broke open his patron's goods and began trading for himself. To regulate a wilderness trade was contrary to nature. All the extremes of the north country—the iron winter and the radiant summer, the dark woods and the luminous water, the alternate feast and famine, the toil of the trail and the indulgence at its end—all its excesses worked against the organization of men.

Wrote the aristocratic Lahontan, who read Homer, Anacreon and Lucian in the wilderness, "The manners of the savages are perfectly agreeable to my palate." The peasant *coureurs de bois* took on savage ways much more readily. They wore eagle feathers in their hair and sometimes daubed themselves with colored clay and charcoal. On greasy hunting frocks they hung fringes of wildcat skin or wolf paws. After solitude and toil a voyageur would come home to a littered Indian camp, where he would lounge on a bearskin, while an uncomplaining squaw boiled his venison and brought fire to light his pipe. As readily as the savages adopted Christian symbols, the voyageur carried snake rattles in his bullet pouch, offered tobacco to the northern lights and whistled through the wing bones of an eagle to appease a thunderstorm. After a beaver feast, he would drive the camp dogs away, convinced that beavers would depart the country if dogs should gnaw the bones of their dead.

In 1687 Baron de Lahontan, in the French military service, went west with orders to command a fort, built by the Sieur Duluth the year before at the foot of Lake Huron. His double mission was to control the vagrant *coureurs de bois* and to counter the growing British trade in that country. Life was dull there, where the Blue Water Bridge now spans the St. Clair channel, and business was slow for his traders; lower Michigan had long been avoided by the western tribes, who feared the far-ranging Iroquois. When his supplies ran short, Lahontan canoed north to the Mackinac Straits to buy some Indian corn. At St. Ignace he found Indian women hoeing beans, corn, peas, squash and melons; red and white men feasting on whitefish in rough cabins, and a fiddler sitting cross-legged on a plank table while woods rangers sang songs of a sweetheart's Sunday ribbons and roses

in May. He found two priests laboring there but was skeptical
of their accomplishments.

> These good Fathers lavish away all their Divinity and Patience
> to no purpose, in converting such ignorant infidels. For all they
> can bring 'em to is that oftentimes they'll desire baptism for
> their dying children, and some few superannuated persons con-
> tent to receive the sacrament of baptism when they find them-
> selves at the point of death.

In a letter to an official in Paris, Lahontan described himself
as being "at the fagg end of the world." Yet he thought Michilimackinac a place of great importance both to the Indian nations
and to French enterprise. He made a careful sketch of the straits,
based on his own observations and what he could learn from
the Indians. He must have tried to take soundings: His map
shows the water deepening from one fathom in St. Ignace harbor
to forty fathoms off the west shore of Mackinac Island; in the
Round Island passage, it indicates a sudden startling depth of
two hundred fathoms. His drawing shows a "sweeping current
moving both ways" through the straits, and it pictures 21 big
canoes pulling in whitefish near Mackinac Island.

In the dangerous year 1690, when Iroquois raiders murdered
Frenchmen on the outskirts of Montreal and English traders were
coveting strategic Mackinac, Governor Frontenac determined to
secure the Straits. To St. Ignace he sent Louis de la Porte, Sieur
de Louvigny, with 150 Canadian troops. There, near the Jesuit
mission, De Louvigny built Fort de Buade, named for Louis
de Buade, Comte de Palluauetde Frontenac—the Governor himself. This garrison, it was said, would protect the Jesuits and
the fur trade. But the Jesuits did not need protection, and the
fur trade was in no danger. Actually the military force was there
to impress the wavering Indians with the power of France and
to regulate the fur commerce. Every canoe cargo of merchandise
or peltry would be inspected, its license verified, its destination
approved—or such was the intention. But the soldiers soon took
to trading on their own, exchanging garrison stores for Indian
peltry, which they sold to unlicensed traders. Unlawful furs went

to English traders on Lake Superior, who shipped cargoes out of Hudson Bay. Some French troops deserted to become vagabond *coureurs de bois.* The trade was more lawless than before.

In 1694 a new commandant arrived. Antoine de la Mothe Cadillac began with a firm hand. The fort was cleaned up, the storehouses were overhauled and military routine gave order to the careless place. Cadillac scorned the Jesuits and harried the *coureurs de bois.* But illegal trade went on. A glut of peltry overflowed the warehouses on the St. Lawrence and ruined the market in France. Somehow all the King's regulations got lost in the wilderness.

In 1696 came orders to close the western posts. All trading licenses were revoked, and troops were withdrawn. The Indians were urged to bring their peltry to the St. Lawrence, as they had done when the trade first began. Cadillac's own voice was heard in this decision. From the little world of indulgence and misrule at St. Ignace he had gone to Paris, where he proposed the building of a fort at Detroit, astride the waterway between the lower and upper lakes. A French stronghold there would block the English from access to the upper country.

Back in the New World in 1701, accompanied by Alphonse de Tonty, younger brother of the man with the iron hand, Cadillac took an expedition to the Detroit River and built Fort Pontchartrain, named for the Colonial Minister. Inside the log stockade were soldiers' barracks, a church and a priest's house, a magazine, a commissary and trading houses. Supplies and trade goods came through the water gate above a boat landing. To this place Cadillac attracted Indians from St. Ignace and lower Michigan. Two thousand Huron, Ottawa and Potawatomi tribesmen built their huts on the Detroit riverbank—within reach of French blankets, kettles, matches, guns, powder, shot and brandy.

At the Straits, three hundred miles north, a remnant of the Indians remained with the mission priests and some lawless traders. But St. Ignace was dwindling. Illinois peltry, which formerly had come to Michilimackinac for transfer, now went down the Mississippi to New Orleans. With no licensed cargoes to sabo-

tage, the vagabond *coureurs de bois* scattered in the wilds. Silence settled on the place where Indians had whooped and
shouted, French fiddlers had twanged *La jeune Sophie* and *La
fille aînée* while the voyageurs danced with Indian women and
red and white men had gambled by leaping firelight. Snow fell
deep in the woods, and above the frozen bay the northern lights
streamed through the winter sky.

In 1706 the Jesuits gave up. They packed their altar pieces,
loaded the canoes and set fire to their weathered chapel. If they
looked back from their departing craft, they saw smoke going
up where Father Marquette's bones were buried. The paddles
dipped again on the long way to Quebec. In a few seasons, brush
would thicken, and the forest would close over the first
Michilimackinac.

. 7 .

A MAN FROM OLD MACKINAW

When the garrison was removed from St. Ignace in 1701, Detroit became the French capital in the West. But the lake currents still flowed through the Straits of Mackinac, fish still swarmed in the cold clear water, beaver still dammed the dark forest streams. And English traders from Lake Superior were reaching down to the Straits to divert the trade that Cadillac had hoped to draw to Detroit. The Straits could not be abandoned. Naturally, inevitably, without authority or system, a new settlement began at Michilimackinac—unlicensed canoes bringing illegal cargoes, a few French traders building huts and store-rooms, small bands of Indians gathering on the windy shore. This time the location was the south side of the narrows, directly across from ruined St. Ignace, at a point convenient for cargoes from Green Bay, L'Arbre Croche and other places on Lake Michigan. It was a blunted point, known to the Indians as "Pequote-nong" ("Headland"), at the location of the present Michilimack-inac State Tourist Park, a mile west of modern Mackinaw City. The shelving shore was open to all the winds that blew. Its people would know the sting of snow and sand, the chill of moving fog banks, the roar of restless seas.

In 1713 French officials saw need for a fort at Michilimackinac, though it was two more years before an expedition arrived. Out of the lead canoe stepped Constant Le Marchand de Lignery. A small company of soldiers and workmen followed him across the windswept beach, where a dozen trading huts were scattered in thin pine and birch woods. That summer, axes thudded at the forest edge, and on the point log walls went up. Around a trampled square the Frenchman raised a palisade of sharpened logs. Blockhouses were walled and roofed, and six iron cannon were mounted on bastion platforms. From its windy point, the second of the forts of Mackinac commanded the blue straits. (To lessen confusion, historians have referred to this post as "Old Mackinaw," while designating as "Ancient Michilimackinac" the earlier station at St. Ignace.)

To Old Mackinaw Indians brought furs to trade for guns, traps, knives, needles, fishhooks. They built brush huts where later a lighthouse would flash above the shore. The priests arrived, raising a cross beside Le Marchand's white and golden banner and lighting candles in a dim bark chapel. By 1722 there were thirty French families—of soldiers and officers—in the fort and thirty traders' families outside. The men of the garrison served three-year terms, and many signed again when the term was up. By 1750 one trooper had spent twenty years at Michilimackinac; another grizzled veteran, a one-time Parisian, had been there for thirty years. The soldiers received no pay but were issued powder and bullets, which they could trade for Indian peltry. Departing soldiers took packs of furs to the St. Lawrence markets.

On Mackinac Island, six miles across the water, a band of Chippewas had settled; they came regularly to the Michilimackinac trading houses. At L'Arbre Croche, thirty miles down the Lake Michigan shore, Ottawa tribesmen confessed their sins in the new mission of St. Ignace. To Fort Michilimackinac came fleets of canoes for council with the French commanders. Trade ebbed and flowed while tribal wars flared up and England and France, two Old World enemies, contested for the New World wilderness.

The Jesuits had planted their cross firmly at Michilimackinac. They held their own property there and a secure income; they controlled the blacksmith business at the straits, charging Indians and Frenchmen alike for the repair of guns, traps and kettles and the forging of spears and anchors. In the fort yard they built a timber church big enough for the station's soldiers, traders and Indians.

Charles de Langlade is a memorable man, who stands out bold and clear against the changing fortunes of Michilimackinac. He was in the midst of Old Mackinaw's trade and traffic, of Indian troubles and treaties, of frontier war and commerce. Some historians say that he struck the spark that inflamed North America in the French and Indian War. At the end of an adventurous life, he became the patriarchal "Father of Wisconsin."

In France the Langlades were a noble family, with an ancestral home at Castle Sarrasin in Basse Guyenne. In Canada they began as army officers and became frontier traders. It was in a Mackinac trading house that Charles de Langlade was born in 1729. His mother was an Ottawa woman, sister of the chief Nissawaquet, called "La Fourche" by the Canadians. The boy grew up among Indians and voyageurs. He was taught religion and French history by the Jesuit Father du Jaunay, but his real training came from his Ottawa uncles.

Wars in the wilderness were sporadic and confused—tribe against tribe, red man against white and red and white men against each other in various alliances. In one contest the Ottawas clashed with a southern tribe allied with the English, and the French commander urged them on. La Fourche, the Ottawa war chief, had a dream in which he saw his small nephew Charles de Langlade accompanying his warriors into battle and returning in canoes laden with bloody trophies. Soon afterward he took the ten-year-old down the Mississippi on a campaign against the Chickasaws. To the boy the battle was an exciting game, full of shrill whoops and flashing hatchets. Back to Old Mackinaw they came with scalps to hang in their doorways. So Charles de Langlade became a talisman for the Ottawas; he went with them on many warpaths.

At this time the Fox tribe (Outagamis) was settled on the west bank of the Fox River forty miles above Green Bay. Though the Ottawas also claimed that river, the Foxes levied a toll on every canoe that passed their village. They kept lookouts on the hill, and at sight of travelers they lighted a fire—a signal that the canoe must stop and pay tribute. This irked the French proprietors. From Michilimackinac they armed the Ottawas and sent them under Charles de Langlade to break the blockade.

Langlade, grown to manhood, was a natural leader, a bold and magnetic soldier. Straight and solid as an oak, he wore around his bronze neck the silver chain and crucifix of a good Catholic. He had dark and darting eyes under a black, unbroken line of eyebrows. Normally quiet, his voice could boom out like a cannon. Among the Indians he had a warrior's name—"Akewa-ugeketauso."

In the vast, sparsely populated country of the lower lakes a bigger contest was growing. French traders from Detroit were contending with English traders, who led packhorses over the Pennsylvania mountains. By 1750 the English had thrust a wedge between Canada and Louisiana, and they meant to drive it deeper into the French trading empire. With shorter trade routes and no winter freeze-up, they could sell goods more cheaply than the French could—though one English trader sold needles for a dollar apiece, telling the savages that the man who made needles had died and the supply was going. English rum was sold for half the price of French brandy and had the same effect; at a British post an Indian could get drunk for a muskrat skin—at a French post it required a beaver. The French traders gave but a pint of powder for a buckskin, whereas the English gave a quart.

To Quebec went reports of Indian violence. A Wabash trader who offered a Huron one bullet and one charge of powder for a beaver skin got a hatchet stroke in his head. A French sentry was killed at the gate of Fort Miami (the present Fort Wayne); his scalp was hung on a Huron lodge at Sandusky Bay. A few months later the commander at Detroit informed the Canadian governor that Miamis and Ouitenons were seizing Frenchmen and their property. From Illinois came word that the Shawnees and Miamis were plotting an attack on French posts in the upper country.

To encourage settlement in the West the French governor had offered a farm and all equipment to any family that would settle

in Detroit. But the French were not much interested in frontier
farming; the plan attracted just 46 families. In another effort
to affirm French proprietorship, the Governor sent an expedition
into the Ohio country, under command of Pierre Joseph de
Céloron de Blainville. A Canadian by birth, Céloron had been
a successful commander at both Michilimackinac and Detroit;
he was respected by French traders and generally liked by the
Indians. His purpose was to win back the tribes to a French
alliance, and he seemed the right man for this military-diplomatic
mission.

With 200 French troops and 35 Indians, Céloron left Montreal
in the summer of 1749. Ahead of this brigade went a half-breed
agent, Chaubert de Joncaire, to tell the tribes that Ononthio's
men were coming. ("Ononthio," meaning "Great Mountain"
in the Iroquois language, was a term all the western tribes used
to designate the French governor.) When Céloron arrived in
the Ohio towns, the chiefs were willing to accept his presents,
but they would make no alliances. In some villages he found
British traders, whom he warned to leave the country. He had
been ordered to seize British stores and caches of peltry, but
the traders were too well entrenched to permit that. The French
commander could only make his speeches and march on.

In western Ohio on the Miami River lay the Miami town of
Pickawillany. Its chief was known to the French as "La
Demoiselle," but the English knew him better. They called him
"Old Britain," and they made his town a center of English trade.
After visiting a Shawnee camp on the Ohio River, Céloron led
his men up the Miami Valley, intending to disrupt the trade
at Pickawillany and disperse the English traders. The French
force arrived at Old Britain's town at the end of summer and
found that the British agents had returned to Pennsylvania with
laden pack trains. Céloron stayed there for five days but had
only one uneasy meeting with the chief. He refused the French
presents—four kegs of powder, four bags of bullets, four bags
of paint and a box of assorted needles and thread—and then
he got them anyway; the dry September streams would not float
canoes, and Céloron had to leave his gifts behind. Marching

his men overland to the northward-flowing Maumee River, he
built new canoes and headed for Lake Erie. His expedition had
traced the bounds of the present State of Ohio and had found
it lost to France. "All I can say," his report concluded, "is
that the nations of these localities are very badly disposed toward
the French and are entirely devoted to the English. I do not
know in what way they could be brought back."

These events hundreds of miles distant were felt at Michilimackinac, as a storm on Lake Huron sends tremors to the farthest
shores and harbors. At Old Mackinaw Charles de Langlade (he
had become a cadet in the French army three years earlier)
thought of a grim way to reclaim the Ohio Indians from their
English alliance. In the spring of 1752, he set out with 250 Ottawa and Chippewa warriors and a dozen French soldiers for
the Ohio country. Over the beach whooped the paint-daubed
tribesmen, wearing headpieces of stag horns and necklaces of
bears' teeth, and over the trampled sand they trailed belts of
eagle feathers. Their canoes were painted for war, and in them
were spread the war mats painted with wolves and bears. Pushing off the craft, they lined up facing the shore. With sunlight
burnishing his paint-striped body, the war chief shook a gourd
rattle, invoking the manitou for a favorable journey. *Che! Che!*
chorused the warriors. From the shore, where the French looked
on, old men exhorted the warriors to fight well, to be wary in
the enemy's country, to spy out their camps, to attack with
stealth and swiftness and to come home victorious. Over the
water the chief shouted a farewell, asking the village to avenge
them if they did not return. Then, in a chorus of yells, paddles
were thrust into the current. Around the point the canoes vanished on the long war journey. In his baggage Charles de Langlade had a rough map of the British posts in the Ohio country.

On the morning of June 21, 1752, Pickawillany was a quiet
town. Breakfast was over, and the Indian women were hoeing
the cornfields north of the village. Some old men sat against
the shady side of the lodges. La Damoiselle—alias Old Britain—
the Piankeshaw king, was there, smoking a clay pipe in his doorway, but the warriors were away on a summer hunt. In their

huts outside the stockade were eight English traders. The morning air was still, and from the willow trees along the creek came the turtledoves' languid, monotonous song.

With sudden cries of alarm, the women came running from the cornfields. Gunfire slammed into the town. Dogs and children scattered before a band of shooting, shouting warriors. Five of the English traders and twenty Indian men and boys got into the fort and closed the timber gate. Three traders came out of their huts too late; they could only surrender to the whooping Indians. From behind trees and huts the invaders fired musket balls through the gaping stockade.

After six hours of siege, the raiders had killed fourteen Indians, including Old Britain himself. In mid-afternoon the firing ceased, and Langlade offered to leave the town if the Piankeshaws would deliver the English traders. The besieged old men were willing; they had no water inside the stockade, and the hot June sun was beating down. Two of the traders were hidden in the fort; the other three surrendered. One of them had been wounded. He was stabbed to death by the northern warriors.

Before they left the place, the raiders feasted. Old Britain was boiled and eaten, and they dismembered the dead trader and ate his heart. They pillaged the fort, burned some lodges and stripped the trading post of all its goods. Then, loading their canoes with plunder, they paddled northward. While most of his two hundred tribesmen went back to Michilimackinac, Langlade took five English prisoners to Governor Duquesne at Quebec. It was a gratifying present for the new French commander-general. He rewarded Langlade with an annual pension of 200 francs and sent him back to Old Mackinaw in a French dress uniform.

The unrest of the time went like a wind through the northern wilderness. The next summer, 1753, a general council was called at the Straits, and tribesmen trooped in from all directions. On the beach at Old Mackinaw sounded voices of all the northwestern nations, from the Sioux, Assiniboins and Pawnees of the Canadian prairie to the Kickapoos of Illinois and the Weas of the Wabash. The campfires of 1,200 warriors flickered along the shore. Though the French had called the tribes together, Commander de Beaujeu sent his interpreters to listen. The Indians were restive, and the French officers were watchful. They kept the fort cannon loaded with grape shot and the garrison under arms. Double sentries manned the sally ports.

With a thousand warriors assembled on the point, where visitors now picnic in the sunset, the French commander spoke:

> I was sent by your Father Ononthio [Great Mountain] to tell you that he loves all his children, and wishes to give them a token of his love by the presents that I was charged to bring you in his name. But I am also instructed to let him know your views about pledging yourselves to raise the hatchet and to go with your French brothers to fight the English. For your father Ononthio has heard that you have listened to evil counsel, causing you to turn your arms against your French brothers, who are as numerous as the leaves of the trees. Those you see around me here are only a small branch of the great tree.

Around the gathering the words were repeated by the interpreters. The chiefs stood up. One after another they declared themselves ready to march at the order of their father the Great Mountain, and they would send their young men to war against the English who had deceived and cheated them. The commander thanked them for their speeches and had tobacco passed around to all the tribesmen. They formed a giant huddle and joined in a thousand-voiced war cry. Then to the rhythm of gourds and rattles they danced, while the daylight faded and campfires leapt in the dark.

There were two more noisy sessions, with interludes of the puffing of pipes and the presenting of ceremonial beads and belts. Then the tribes gave demonstrations of ambush and attack. In this pantomime, a stealthy warrior crept upon an unsuspecting enemy. After a short pursuit he overtook the victim, cut a circle with his knife blade and attached a phantom scalp to his belt while quavering the war cry. With that trophy, he sped away ahead of his pursuers. Another actor appeared; darting from one tree to another, he made a sudden foray against the enemy and made good his escape. In further pantomime, a warrior paddling a canoe raised a hand to shield his eyes; he beached his craft and hid in brushy cover to surprise his adversary. Discovered and cut off from his canoe, he dashed into the woods. Turning there, he fell upon his pursuer with whoops of triumph.

During the days of council, the warriors consumed great quantities of French provisions, and the commander was eager to disperse the gathering. In a final session, presents were distributed—powder, knives, shirts, blankets, cloth and ribbon. The next day the canoes scattered over the water, and that night the fires winked out on the long curve of shore.

Seasons passed at Old Mackinaw—the siege of winter and the surge of spring. In the fullness of the next summer, 1754, in the timbered chapel of Stc. Anne de Michilimackinac, Charles de Langlade was married. The bride who knelt beside him in the candlelight was Charlotte Amboisène Bourassa, a slender, dark-haired girl with fair skin and fine, clear features. The daughter of a wealthy trader, she had been educated at Montreal; she spoke pure French, worked delicate embroideries and danced the minuet and the quadrille. She had returned to the Straits in the springtime, fresh as a windflower at the edge of the woods. Langlade must have been a reluctant warrior when word came the next spring that armies were marching toward Fort Duquesne on the upper Ohio.

Early that year an English fleet with two regiments under General Edward Braddock had sailed out of Queenstown harbor for Virginia. With these 1,400 British regulars and 500 colonial troops, Braddock meant to drive the French out of Fort Duquesne, which they had built on the site of the present Pittsburgh. After drilling his combined force at Fort Cumberland, Braddock marched into the Allegheny wilderness in June 1755.

At far-off Michilimackinac, Langlade had been gathering Ottawa, Huron and Chippewa tribesmen to take up the hatchet against the English. With two hundred warriors in a fleet of canoes, he headed southward, paddling from dawn till dark in fine June weather. Early in July they arrived at Fort Duquesne and reported to De Beaujeu, the French commander, a brother of the captain at Michilimackinac.

Indian scouts reported Braddock's army advancing in three columns toward the Monongahela River. Commander de Beaujeu decided to intercept them there. Along with six hundred Frenchmen and Indians, Langlade's warriors marched to the Monongahela and concealed themselves in dense ravines along the river. They were waiting when the English arrived and broke ranks for their noon rations.

Langlade wanted to attack at that moment, but Beaujeu hesitated: The British outnumbered them more than two to one. Langlade persisted—they could not halt the British in open battle, but they could stun them now from ambush. When the commander agreed, word went from thicket to thicket, and rifles were aimed at red coats through the trees. The attack burst like a thunderclap. In this battle of the wilderness, the British never saw their enemies; seizing their muskets they fired blindly across the river. Crouching in trees and thickets, the shadowy Indians cut down the British regiments. Braddock fell, and, while his troops scattered, the Indians charged after them with tomahawks and scalping knives. In the midst of victory, Beaujeu was killed, but the French and Indian losses were small.

The war had begun with a heady French victory, and Langlade returned to Old Mackinaw with an ensign's commission. He was back in the heart of the conflict while the British power slowly grew. He defeated Rogers's Rangers on Lake Champlain in 1757; he aided in the attack on Fort William Henry. But in the battle of Quebec, on September 13, 1759, he saw his two half-brothers killed on the Plains of Abraham. He left Montreal a few days before it surrendered to General Amherst.

Back to Michilimackinac he brought the heavy news of French surrender. During the century and a half since Nicolet had passed the Mackinac Straits, France had claimed a wilderness empire. By 1760 there were barely 60,000 Frenchmen in the New World, but they had given names to lakes, bays, falls and rivers, as well as to military posts, trading stations and religious missions over nearly half the continent. The map of the western wilderness was as French as Normandy. Now with the surrender at Montreal, it all passed to the English King.

At Michilimackinac Captain Louis de Beaujeu did not wait for orders to abandon the post. He embarked his garrison—4 officers, 2 cadets, 48 regulars and 78 militiamen—in a fleet of canoes and pushed off down the eastern shore of Lake Michigan. The destination was the French settlements in Illinois. There, deep in America, the Frenchmen would wait for word (which never came) of French recovery of the lost dominion.

As second-in-command, Charles de Langlade ruled the empty post, where a few French traders remained among the Indians. He delivered Michilimackinac to the English when Captain Henry Balfour arrived at the end of September 1761. Always a realist, Langlade then put on a scarlet tunic, with a Moroccan sword belt held by a silver buckle, and became a British man. He had survived the fall of New France, and he would outlast the English regime at the Straits. Late in life he recalled that he had fought in 99 battles and wished for just one more. Under the flag of a new nation he would live on his own land at Green Bay, where he established the first settlement in Wisconsin.

PART TWO: THE BRITISH

It is the most respectable situation I ever saw, besides convenient for the subsistence of a garrison, the safety of troops, traders and commerce.

MAJOR PATRICK SINCLAIR

. 8 .

TALE OF AN OLD TRADER

The first Englishman to arrive at Old Mackinaw was not a soldier but a trader; commerce went ahead of government. In 1760 Alexander Henry, a restless young man from New Jersey, passed his 21st birthday on the St. Lawrence, with his mind on the future. He nearly died that summer when his boat was swamped in the Rapides des Cèdres. In numbing water he clung to the upturned craft until a member of General Amherst's staff pulled him to shore. On the surrender of Montreal, Henry went into the trading business. That winter, while taking refuge from a snowstorm in an Indian camp, he was attacked by a drunken Indian; he barely escaped down the ice-strewn St. Lawrence in a leaky canoe. He had a charmed life if not a sheltered one.

At Les Cèdres Alexander Henry heard from a veteran French trader of the rich fur trade in the upper country; the man went on to say that "Michilimackinac was richer in this commodity than any other part of the world." These words turned Henry's future in a new direction.

After five years of war, the warehouses of Montreal were empty. Henry went to Albany and loaded a string of boats with English trade goods, including a stock of barreled rum. Back on the St. Lawrence, by way of Lake George and Lake Champlain, he outfitted his voyageurs at La Chine. Beside the rapids stood Ste. Anne's Chapel, an outpost of prayer in the wilderness. The boatmen made confession there and left small offerings for Ste. Anne, "who protects all voyageurs." Then they took on the regulation rum, eight gallons to a canoe—one gallon for each man in the big trading craft—and all got drunk. After a noisy farewell they dipped their paddles. With whoops and yells sub-siding into a gay Norman song, they began the long journey.

Six hundred miles and 36 rugged portages later they were at the head of Georgian Bay, stopping at an Indian village. When the tribesmen learned that the *patron* of these French paddlers was an Englishman, they told Henry's men that he would cer-tainly be killed by the Indians at Michilimackinac. With that prospect, they reasoned, they had a right to share in the plunder of his cargo, and so they demanded a keg of rum. Henry "judged it prudent to comply." He also took heed of the warning and garbed himself as a Frenchman, replacing his broadcloth tunic with a blanket coat and a tasseled red wool cap. "The next thing," he recalled years later, "was to smear my face and hands with dirt and grease; and this done I took the place of one of my men and when Indians approached used the paddle with as much skill as I possessed." As he knew but a few French words, he used lively French gestures and said little.

At Mackinac Island, where there was a village of a hundred Chippewas, Henry stopped without detection. More confident then, he took his brigade across the strait to Fort Michilimacki-nac, where Charles de Langlade was in charge. Though the French garrison was gone, there were still some French traders without much to offer the restless Indians. Henry rented an empty house next door to the Langlade place, where he tried to stay secluded. But his men betrayed him, and the French traders beat a path to his door. They wanted his trade goods, and they urged him for his own safety to go to Detroit.

But Henry was there to stay. Word of his identity went across the water, and the Chippewas from Mackinac Island came to threaten him. Sixty warriors, headed by Chief Minavavana, marched to his house, each waving a tomahawk and a scalping knife. Their faces gleamed with grease and charcoal; their naked torsos were striped with clay. They crowded into the house and sat silent on the floor while Henry waited. Finally the chief rose and addressed the trader, charging him with all the policies of the British:

Englishman, you know that the French king is our father. He promised to be such, and we in return promised to be his children. This promise we have kept.

Englishman, it is you that have made war with this our father. You are his enemy; and how then could you have the boldness to venture among us, his children? You know that his enemies are ours.

Englishman, although you have conquered the French, you have not conquered us. We are not your slaves. These lakes, these woods, these mountains were left to us by our ancestors. They are our inheritance, and we will part with them to none.

Englishman, our father, the King of France, employed our young men to make war upon your nation. In this warfare many of them have been killed, and it is our custom to retaliate until such time as the spirits of the slain are satisfied.

As an interpreter put all this into English, Henry must have wondered why he had not turned back from Georgian Bay. But the harangue ended with a surprising softness. The spirits of the slain, the chief explained, might be satisfied in either of two ways: by the spilling of English blood or by the receiving of English presents.

Englishman . . . you do not come armed with an intention to make war; you come in peace to trade with us and supply us with the necessaries of which we are in much want. We shall regard you therefore as a brother; and you may sleep tranquilly without fear of the Chippewa. As a token of our friendship we present you with this pipe to smoke.

After a ceremony in which everyone present blew three puffs of smoke, Chief Minavavana made a request. For himself and his men he asked for a taste of "English milk," to see how it differed from the French product. Henry promptly offered a cask of rum, and the Indians went home happy.

Thus established, Henry took inventory of his goods, hired some Canadian interpreters and canoemen and prepared to send his cargoes to farther posts on Lake Michigan and Lake Superior. Already two other English traders had arrived from Montreal— Stanley Goddard and Ezekiel Solomon—and Henry was anxious to keep ahead of them. But at that point, late in the summer of 1761, a band of Ottawa warriors came up from L'Arbre Croche. They swarmed through the fort, billeting themselves in barracks and houses and looking vainly for plunder. In the commandant's house, a group of chiefs set up a council room and summoned the traders. They demanded a credit system— every warrior should receive trade goods to the value of fifty beaver skins, which would be delivered next season. The protest-ing traders were given a day to think this ultimatum over. The next morning, to their astonishment, they saw the Ottawas piling into canoes and paddling for L'Arbre Croche.

The reason was soon evident. By noon the straits were black with boats; a British commander was arriving with three hundred troops of the 60th Regiment. On October 1, 1761, while knots of Indians watched in grim silence, the flag of England rose over Fort Michilimackinac.

As though they could read the future, the Indians hated and feared the English. The French empire in America left the tribes in possession of the continent, but British occupation meant the spread of settlement and occupation. New France had scattered forts and missions in the wilderness, dominating the Indians but not displacing them. The English-speaking people would drive them out.

At the head of the British troops arriving at Old Mackinaw was Captain Henry Balfour. After a few days' rest, he took most of his men on west to establish garrisons at other stations. He left Lieutenant William Leslie of the 60th Regiment—the Royal Americans—to hold Michilimackinac with a force of some thirty men. It was a hardship post, dealing with surly Indians and re-sentful French traders. After a year the young commander asked to be relieved from "this disagreeable station." In time a new order came, but Leslie was not that lucky; he was reduced to second-in-command under Captain George Etherington—on whom disaster fell. By compliance linked with dignity, as Park-man observed—caressing with one hand while the other grasped a sword—the French could maintain themselves in exposed places where an English garrison would have been cut off in

a twelvemonth. The English had longer than a year at Old Mackinaw, but not much longer.

The French and Indian War had centered on the country between the St. Lawrence and the upper Ohio. But one man saw
that the whole Northwest was at stake. He was not French or
English, but Ottawa. The Ottawa warriors, whose forest home
stretched from Lake Huron to Lake Michigan, were banded in
a loose confederacy with the Chippewas and the Potawatomis.
The influence of their war chief Pontiac extended far beyond
the council fires of his own people.

Pontiac had a shrewd, bold mind and a smoldering hatred
of the English. Though it was later said that he led a band of
warriors against Braddock's army in Pennsylvania, he first
appeared in English records when he met Major Robert Rogers
beside the gray waters of Lake Erie. It was November 1760,
and Rogers was on his way to take possession of Detroit and
Michilimackinac. Well along the Lake Erie shore, he pulled his
fifteen bateaux into the mouth of the Cuyahoga River, later the
site of Cleveland. To the English camp came Pontiac with a
band of Ottawas, wanting to know on what authority Rogers
had entered that country. Rogers explained that the French had
surrendered the posts and that he was on the way to take possession; the English, he added, meant to bring peace and order
to the interior. Pontiac seemed to accept that statement; he
smoked a pipe with the English captain. Rogers proceeded to
Detroit, where he took command. From there he started on toward the northern straits, but winter's ice turned him back.

In 1760 the Indians between the Ohio River and the Great
Lakes numbered fewer than the population of the present Sandusky, Ohio; altogether the tribes counted perhaps eight thousand warriors. British control might have seemed a simple task.
But the interior was a vast, vague land with a few forts separated
by hundreds of miles of wilderness and water. To these posts
were assigned a scant six hundred English troops. Instead of
winning Indian allegiance, they treated the tribes with contempt,
while British traders cheated and swindled them. Meanwhile

English settlers were moving into Indian lands along the headwaters of the Ohio.

Early in 1763 Pontiac's messengers went to all the western
camps and villages, carrying the war belt of black and purple
wampum and the red-stained tomahawk. Their mission was to
unite the tribes in a bold and stunning action. On a chosen day
in May, signaled by the changing of the moon, warriors would
attack every British post from Pennsylvania to the Straits of
Mackinac. When that day was over, no Englishman would be
left alive in the western country.

Inflamed by this audacious plan, the Indians somehow caught
Pontiac's craft and patience. Bands straggled in from their winter
hunt, pitching their camps around the British stockades, accepting a few twists of tobacco and some gunpowder and rum for
their winter catch of furs. They did not betray their smoldering
conspiracy.

In the western country were fourteen British posts. At each
of them the uprising was carefully planned. Pontiac himself
would lead the attack on Detroit, and other chiefs would be in
charge at other stations. At Michilimackinac the long winter de-
layed communication between the tribes; its massacre came three
weeks after the other forts had fallen.

On the tenth of May, while the rivers were brimming and
a spring wind rustled in the new-leafed forest, the stunning blow
fell on a dozen outposts. Fort Presque Isle on Lake Erie was
fired by flaming arrows. Fort Sandusky was overrun by its Wyan-
dot village. Fort St. Joseph on southern Lake Michigan was
rushed and ransacked by howling Potawatomis. Fort Ouitenon
on the Wabash and Fort Miami on the Maumee fell to whooping
raiders. At Fort Le Boeuf the blockhouse was burned, the Indians
danced in a cloud of smoke and ashes. Detroit alone withstood
attack, but a rain of bullets pelted the palisade, and a bitter
siege began. When word reached Michilimackinac three weeks
later, drums throbbed all night around the Chippewa campfires.

As though they heard that summons, other warriors came from
the village on Mackinac Island and from fishing camps down
the lake shores. At first it looked like good business for the merchants. All day Indians streamed into the trading houses. After

looking at silver armbands and brass buckles, they finally bought knives and hatchets and returned to their noisy camps. On the open field just east of the fort they held an endless game of baggatiway, played with webbed rackets and a deerhide ball. Charles de Langlade warned Etherington that the tribes were restless, but the sport looked harmless to the English captain.

In London the King had a birthday. At Fort Michilimackinac there were toasts to the King and the Queen, to the Governor General at Quebec, to the English future in this wild country; and the boom of cannon saluted the monarch four thousand miles away. Joining the celebration, the Indians staged a special ball game, one picked team against another, for a high wager. Among the tribes, this game of bat and ball was played in both sport and superstition: It might invoke fair weather or ward off disease or honor the dead. But on this holiday at Old Mackinaw it was played for a fiercer purpose, and it began one of the darkest days in frontier history. An eyewitness set it down years afterward from a seared memory, and so we have the whole grim story.

As Alexander Henry recalled it, the ball game was a kind of festival, with the white men invited as spectators and Captain Etherington himself putting a bet on the Chippewas, who were contesting with a team of the Sac nation. Henry did not watch the sport; he wrote some letters to go on a Montreal canoe that was to depart the next day. Outside his window the noisy game went on, players running and shouting, watchers surging along the sidelines. He did not see the Indian women gathered near the fort gate with hatchets hidden in their blankets. He did not see the ball lofted, as if accidentally, over the palisade and Indians racing through the gate to retrieve it. But a burst of war cries took him to the window, where he saw warriors snatching hatchets from their women and cutting down unarmed white men. Henry seized his fowling piece and listened for the roll of drums that would summon the garrison. All he heard was whoops and yells as four hundred savages slaughtered the troops while the French traders looked on. The uprising was against the English.

Next door to Henry's house was the home of Charles de Langlade, and the trader sought refuge there. Leaping the picket
fence, he ran into a room where the Langlade family was watching the massacre from its windows. An Indian woman servant
led him up a steep stairway to a garret. From that hiding place,
amid a heap of birchbark pails sticky with maple sap, he peered
through a chink in the wall at a scene of carnage: warriors scalping the dead and dying, Indian women plundering the King's
Storehouse, red men drinking English blood in a frenzy of rage
and triumph.

Then the hidden man heard Indians entering the room below
him. He had just crawled into the mound of birchbark pails when
four blood-smeared Indians broke into the garret. They grouped
in the dimness, close enough for Henry to touch them, and went
muttering down the stairs. When they were gone, the trader
fell asleep.

He woke to the sound of rain on the roof. Mme. de Langlade,
coming up to close a chimney opening, told him that most of
the Englishmen were dead and that the Indians were despoiling
the fort. Henry stayed in hiding. The next morning Indians returned to the Langlade house. Staggering with rum, they still
remembered that the English trader had not been found. A half-
naked Chippewa, smeared with grease and charcoal, dragged
him out of the garret and down the stairs. Outside Henry broke
free and ran into the fort, where his former Indian friend Wenniway called off the pursuer. Henry hurried back to his garret.

That night he was called downstairs to meet the English officers, Etherington, Bostwick and Leslie, who had survived the
massacre. After a consultation on the unlikely prospect of regain-
ing possession of the fort, all of them spent the night in the
garret. In the morning Henry was taken with three other civilian
captives to a canoe beyond the water gate of the fort. With
seven Indians and the four prisoners, each plying a paddle, the
craft was headed toward the Beaver Islands thirty miles out on
Lake Michigan. When a fog closed in they changed course, following the shoreline toward the Ottawa town of L'Arbre Croche.
At Waugoshance Point the Indians gave a war whoop that was
answered from the fog. As the canoe neared the dim point, a

band of Ottawa warriors splashed into the water and dragged
the prisoners ashore. The seven Chippewas paddled on
southward.

For the bewildered white men it was touch and go. While
they despaired of their lives, the Ottawas pumped their hands,
declaring friendship. The Chippewas, they said, had meant to
kill and devour their captives on Big Beaver Island; now the
Ottawas put them in a canoe and headed back to Michilimackinac. Other Ottawa warriors followed, enough to outnumber the
Chippewas at the fort. "We had changed masters," Henry observed, "but were still prisoners." At Fort Michilimackinac they
were kept in the commandant's house with an Ottawa guard
around it.

Next day a noisy council of Chippewa and Ottawa tribesmen
argued about the captives. When the Chippewas agreed to share
the fort plunder with them, the Ottawas gave up the four Englishmen, who were then marched to the Chippewa camp on the
sandy point. They were thrown into a lodge, where they found
fourteen English soldiers tied to a center pole. Henry was left
untied, but he spend a miserable night huddled in a ragged shirt
that was his only clothing. For two days he had not eaten. In
the morning he was given a slab of bread cut with a bloody scalping knife. Dried blood softened with spittle was smeared on the
bread, and the captives were told to eat the blood of their
countrymen.

This dark morning was suddenly brightened when the Chippewa chief Wawatam came in. An avowed "brother" whom
Henry had befriended in seasons past, he sat down beside the
scowling chief Wenniway while the two smoked pipes in silence.
No words passed, but when Wawatam arose he spoke to the
helpless Henry. "Take courage," he said as he strode out of
the lodge.

An hour later Wawatam and his Chippewa wife returned with
armloads of blankets, shirts and implements, which they laid
before the scowling Wenniway. "See there," said Wawatam,
pointing to Henry, "my friend and brother among slaves, himself
a slave! You all well know that long before the war began I
adopted him as my brother. . . . He is my brother; and because

I am your relation he is therefore your relative too: and how, being your relation, can he be your slave?"

Wawatam then reminded the war chiefs that he had not revealed the plot to attack the fort; he had even left the fort on the promise that Alexander Henry would be protected and delivered safely to him. This promise he now claimed, and not with empty hands; he offered the goods heaped on the floor to buy off any claim that any man had on his brother, the prisoner.

So soon after their bloody orgy the warriors were grave and formal. They smoked in silence. Then the chief arose and replied. He granted the truth of Wawatam's statements and acknowledged the promise that had been made. At the time of the assault, he declared, he had searched for the trader but could not find him. The next day the Englishman was found, but the warriors, drunk with rum from the fort, had disregarded the order to deliver this man. "I am very glad," he concluded, "that your friend has escaped. We accept your present, and you may take him home with you."

If Henry missed some of this speech in the Ottawa tongue, he could follow its tone and gestures. A moment later he was a free man, walking beside Wawatam to a lodge where food and drink were laid out for him. From this haven he looked out the next morning and saw the bodies of seven white men dragged toward cooking fires on the shore. After beheading one of the bodies, two Indians hacked it into four parts, which were thrown into steaming kettles. Wawatam was summoned to the feast, taking with him a dish and a spoon. When he returned, an hour and a half later, the dish contained a human hand and a chunk of flesh. It was a Chippewa custom, he explained to Henry, to make a war feast of slain enemies.

That evening a canoe arrived from Montreal, and its boatmen ran shouting to the fort. Instead of an English welcome they received an Indian beating and were marched to the bloody guardhouse; they would endure weeks of captivity before being ransomed by Montreal merchants.

The Indians decided to withdraw to Mackinac Island, where they could beat off any attack by the English. At noon on June

9th they broke camp, loaded their plunder and their prisoners and paddled across the straits. When a wind came up and waves threatened to swamp the canoes, a dog was thrown into the water for a sacrifice. Arrived at the island, the women unrolled mats and set up their lodges. When two Montreal canoes appeared off Bois Blanc Island, the Ottawas paddled out, waited behind a point of land and surrounded the traders. In the canoes was a stock of rum. That night the Indians began a frenzied celebration. Wawatam told Henry that it would be dangerous for him to remain in the village, adding that "he could not himself resist the temptation of joining his comrades in the debauch." But first he led his friend through the steepening woods to a sandstone cliff with a cave at its base. Left there at nightfall, Henry broke off some pine branches for a bed, rolled up in his blanket and slept.

Before daybreak he was aware of some hard object under him. He drew out a bone, which he supposed was part of a deer. But daylight showed that he was lying on a heap of human skulls and bones. He left that place and wandered through the woods.

After a day without food he crept into a thicket; he could not bring himself to sleep again in the cave of skulls. Next morning Wawatam appeared. He took his ravenous friend back to the village where the tribesmen were sleeping off their intoxication. When Henry told about the cave of skulls, a band of curious Indians went to see the place for themselves. It was a new discovery for these people, who had often camped and sojourned on the island, and they tried to account for the dead. Some remembered their tribal story of a great flood and supposed that island-dwellers had taken refuge in that high cavern, where they were caught by the rising water. Others thought it marked the last stand of a band of Ottawas during a war with the Hurons. Henry's own theory, reflecting recent events, was that the cave had once been a receptacle of the remains of captives whose flesh was devoured at war feasts.

A few days later some canoes full of Indians arrived from Detroit, where they had fought the English in Pontiac's rebellion. To conceal his identity, Henry dressed like an Indian. With shaved head and greasy scalplock, face striped with clay and charcoal, a painted shirt, a collar of wampum, scarlet leggings and a blanket over his shoulder, he passed freely around the campfires. The success of this disguise led him to return to Michilimackinac, where he found his storehouse plundered. Now he had to subsist like an Indian.

With Wawatam and his band, Henry coasted down to L'Arbre Croche and on to the site of Ludington, where Father Marquette had died nearly a hundred years before. There, after Wawatam had sacrificed a dog to the local manitous, they made a camp for the winter. By then Henry was a skilled hunter and woodsman, wholly accepted by the Chippewas. He was out of danger, and he felt "the whispers of a lingering hope" that he would somehow again become his own man.

Late in April, laden with dried venison and peltry, Wawatam's band returned north to Michilimackinac. The place was quiet; around the houses of two French traders lay a scatter of Indian lodges. With a hundred beaver skins and some lesser peltry Henry had a winter's profit of $160. It was not enough, at the inflated prices of trade goods, to pay for an entire outfit of clothing, but he did buy two shirts, a pair of leggings and a blanket, along with some ammunition and tobacco.

All winter Henry had been cut off from the world. Then came a brigade of Indians from Saginaw Bay, recruiting warriors for the prolonged seige of Detroit. Seeing an Englishman there, they proposed to kill him and give the tribesmen a taste of English broth to arouse their spirits. Threatened again, Henry headed for Sault Ste. Marie, where the Chippewas had remained peaceful. That night the loyal Wawatam took his English friend over the water to St. Ignace—where in a later time the big car ferry *Wawatam* would steam across the strait. But when Wawatam's wife had a warning dream, the flight was halted. Next day, while the Indians pondered the next move, Henry climbed into a treetop on the point and saw a sail approaching from Michilimackinac. It was a trading canoe bound for the St. Mary's, with room for another paddler. Henry stepped in. When the canoe put off, Wawatam made a prayer to the Great Manitou to protect his white brother until their next meeting.

They did not meet again, but their friendship was recorded years later in Henry's *Travels*. It became a New World legend, a Damon and Pythias story of the wilderness. Now, two centuries after their parting, the red man and white man are remembered in the North Country. While the powerful *Wawatam* crunches a path through the frozen Straits, the big Canadian ice-breaker *Alexander Henry*, based at Port Arthur, clears the frozen channel above the Soo canal.

Ahead of Alexander Henry were years of further adventure. He searched for copper on Lake Superior and traded for furs on the Winnipeg prairie, the Athabasca River and the shores of Hudson Bay. Back from the wilderness in 1776, he made his home on the St. Lawrence. He became a Montreal merchant, making seasonal voyages to Europe and to the Indian country. His engraved miniature shows a sturdy, white-haired man with a high white collar and a white lace stock, but he had a weathered look until his death in 1824.

In Montreal the white-haired man recalled his adventurous youth, setting down with a natural charm and liveliness men and moments that were etched in his memory. His book was published in New York in 1809. It quickly became a famous account of frontier experience, and Parkman used it freely in his *Conspiracy of Pontiac*. In the twentieth century its validity was questioned by H. Bedford-Jones, who made a derisive picture of the author:

> Garrulous old trader, sitting with a jorum
> Close beside your elbow, and tobacco blowing free,
> Easy 'tis to picture you, spinning to a quorum
> Of pop-eyed New York burghers your tales of
>   deviltry!

But it is not easy to discount Henry's story, which is confirmed by fragmentary reports from various other sources. Some of his dates are doubtful, and his distances are inexact, but this tale of an old trader is a living chapter in the record of the upper country.

. 9 .

ROGERS AT MICHILIMACKINAC

Leaving the St. Clair River, the big Seaway freighters set their course N.N.W., laying a broad white wake over blue Lake Huron. Eighteen hours brings them to the northern straits. It was a longer journey in 1764. For three weeks a brigade of canoes and mackinaw boats worked northward, and, on September 22nd, Captain William Howard beached his boat at Fort Michilimackinac while the Jesuit priest and a few Indians and traders watched from a barren ridge of sand. A trader named Parant handed Captain Howard the keys to the fort, though a man could walk through the gaping palisade. When the fleet was landed, two companies of the 17th Regiment fell into line and marched through the water gate. With a roll of drums, the British ensign jerked up the flagpole in the weedy compound. After a year of desolation, English rule was returning to the scene of massacre.

In the shortening days of October, supplies arrived from Detroit. Four small cannon were hauled across the sandy flats; with a creaking of blocks and tackle, they swayed up to the bastion platforms. There were, complained Captain Howard, "no balls for the cannon, nor shelter for the mortar," but the empty guns were pointed toward the charred circles of old Indian camps on the shore.

That winter axes thudded in the pine woods, and trees crashed down. Thanks to a French trader who had three shaggy horses tethered in the sand grass, Captain Howard hauled timber to patch the palisade and bolster the bastions. Three sagging houses were pulled down; with their nails and lumber the men enlarged

74

two barracks halls. Meanwhile a gang of shovel soldiers leveled off the dunes outside the stockade. They cursed the cold wind and the stinging sand.

To this place in 1766 a new commander brought his hearty appetites, headstrong rule and bold ambitions. He would not last long, but none of the English captains did. There were ten of them in 35 years—a sequence of lackluster men with one arresting name among them, one man who is remembered. Balfour, Leslie, Etherington, Howard, *Major Robert Rogers*, Glazier, Turnbull, De Peyster, Sinclair, Robertson, Scott, Doyle.

Before he came to Michilimackinac, Robert Rogers's name was known in Albany and Montreal, in New York, Philadelphia and London. An audacious, versatile, magnetic and extravagant man, he had, before his thirtieth birthday, touched the heights and depths of fortune. A romantic hero of the French and Indian War, he had led his green-clad rangers to victories from Fort Ticonderoga to the St. Lawrence. In 1760 he served with Amherst at the capture of Montreal and was sent to receive the French surrender at Detroit. With two hundred Royal Rangers in fifteen bateaux he voyaged over Lake Erie. At the mouth of the Cuyahoga River, where two centuries later the towers of Cleveland would rise, he met Chief Pontiac with a band of Ottawa warriors. Rogers and Pontiac got on so well that the chief accompanied the expedition to Detroit. There on November 29, 1760, the French flag came down and "with a burst of triumphant yells" the colors of England rose against the wintry sky. Rogers would have gone on then to Michilimackinac, but ice-clogged waters blocked his way. In winter snows he marched his men through Ohio and Pennsylvania to a triumphant welcome in Philadelphia and New York. In his rumpled Ranger's uniform Rogers was a hero to everybody but his creditors. He had been personally and officially careless about expenditures and military vouchers, and then, in the shadow of these debts, he married a woman of expensive tastes. ("Buy the organ by all means, Dearest . . . when I go home I shall hear how fine you play.") When the English minister ignored his application for an Indian agency, he turned to writing. He planned a four-volume work that would narrate his own adventures while describing the vast new British possessions in North America; incidentally it would make "some proposals for the Discovery of the North-West Passage by land." Here was the restless, visionary, fate-tempting Rogers. He had demonstrated his ability to conduct long marches in the wilderness: Now he offered to span the continent in the old chimerical search for a water route to India.

His writing was soon interrupted by Pontiac's uprising, for Rogers the soldier was needed again. In the bloody spring of 1763 all the western posts except Fort Pitt and Detroit were captured, and those two strongholds were besieged by savage armies. Rogers went west with an expedition to relieve Detroit. In a farmhouse fortified with bales of beaver pelts he held off two hundred warriors. Eventually he led his men into the beleaguered fort.

With Detroit saved, he returned to New York where his creditors promptly clapped him into debtors' prison. He got out when his soldiers stormed the jail as if it were an enemy stockade. In search of "whatever may offer" he went to London where he wrote his *Journals of Major Robert Rogers* and *A Concise Account of North America*. Published in 1765, the books were resounding successes, and Rogers's spirits soared again. On the crest of this wave he petitioned the English Parliament for authority and funds to conduct an expedition of two hundred men "from the Great Lakes toward the head of the Mississippi and from thence to a river called by the Indians Ouragon which flows into a bay that projects northeastwardly into the country from the Pacific Ocean." That was the first printed appearance of the name that would become "Oregon," a name known on both sides of the Atlantic before there was any known feature to go with it.

English political and commercial ambitions were stirred by the proposal, but the French war had been costly and the treasury was low. Rogers blithely asked for £32,000 to search for a passage as vague as a myth. The ministers denied his request, but they gave him something that might start him on the way. He was appointed to command Fort Michilimackinac, at a salary of £15 a month, and to be Superintendent of the Indians "particularly to the westward of that post." Rogers grasped the offer. In that outpost he could learn more about the undiscovered country; he might even send out a private expedition. The English Admiralty, he remembered, had a standing reward of £20,000 for discovery of a water route across North America.

Back in New England, Rogers enlisted one of his old ranger captains, James Tute. In Boston he met another veteran of the French and Indian War, a man old enough to be his father, big, ponderous, soft-voiced Jonathan Carver. Beneath his sleepy manner Carver had restless desires and energies. A self-taught surveyor and map-maker he wanted to see the northwest wilderness and to correct the deceitful French maps and charts of the interior. He wanted to explore the Mississippi Valley and "to ascertain the breadth of that vast continent which extends from the Atlantic to the Pacific Ocean." That was a dream well known to Rogers. Without authority he added Carver to his staff.

On a flashing August day in 1766, from the rail of the schooner *Galdwin,* with his chattering wife on one side and the brooding Carver on the other, Rogers had his first view of the northern straits. It was a noble setting—the long, wild forest shores, the sandstone walls of Mackinac Island white as the cliffs of Dover above the restless lake, the wilderness gateway beckoning to the west. Soon Michilimackinac appeared, a weathered log stockade beyond a huddle of brush huts and flimsy houses. Betsey Rogers stopped chattering, but her husband exclaimed about this fortress between two empires—this bastion and beacon where the white man's dominion ended and the red man's realm began. His roving eyes caught the puff of smoke at the corner bastion; he raised a hand when the boom of the cannon came. Out poured a swarm of canoes. *Bo-jo! Bo-jo!* cried the Indians, and Rogers roared back their welcome. Through the water gate came a troop of soldiers, scarlet against the weathered palisade. They lined the wharf while Rogers strode ashore.

As commander of the troops and superintendent of the northwest tribes, he was the ruler of that place and all its realm of wilderness. He had orders from General Thomas Gage and Sir

William Johnson, the head of all Indian affairs, to confine trade
to the fort itself, so that the Indians would not be cheated and
debauched with rum. But these officials were far away from the
realities of the upper country. Rogers meant to make Michilimackinac the capital of an inland empire. He had big ideas,
bold expectations and no scruples anywhere.

Commander Rogers was soon in action. His Michilimackinac
journal begins "I set out," and the opening pages tell of a visit
to the Ottawa town of L'Arbre Croche halfway to Little Traverse
Bay on the Lake Michigan shore. The big man in buckskin clothing was at home with the chiefs and warriors. They told him
of bad birds flying from the west side of the Mississippi with
word that a French army was coming to dislodge the English
from Detroit and Michilimackinac. What was the truth about
this matter? Rogers told them that the French had not one inch
of ground on the west side of the Mississippi; they had sold
their western lands to the Spanish, "a set of people you well
know are mortal enemies to Indians in general." He declared
that there could be no French troops coming up the Mississippi
as long as its waters flowed. The English were in control, and
they would befriend the Indians. As a token of that friendship,
he passed out coats and shirts and twenty gallons of rum. He
left them with word that the Ottawas would be welcome at
Michilimackinac in the spring.

Back at the post, he had a visit from the Chippewas on Mackinac Island. They too told of bad birds flying about with word
that the French would soon be coming up the Mississippi to
take this fort. Rogers assured them of the English power and
good will. With gifts of coats, shirts, guns, shot, powder, twenty-
four pounds of tobacco and sixteen gallons of rum, they went
noisily back to their island.

Unlike his predecessors, the new commander sought and won
the good will of the tribesmen. All fall, bands of Indians were
welcomed to the fort with salutes of cannon, and when they
asked also to be saluted with the bottle Rogers complied. Even
begging Indians were listened to. "I have had a melancholy
winter," one of them said. "One of my sons is dead and all

my family are in tears for his loss. I hope you will give me something to wipe away the tears from my eyes and something to
bury the dead." Rogers gave him a stroud blanket and a linen shirt
to bury his son. A sick Indian arrived, "poor, hungry and naked,"
and told his melancholy story. Rogers noted in his journal, "I
gave him one half gallon of rum, one pound of tobacco, with
some victuals."

Meanwhile Jonathan Carver had set out on his travels. Leaving
the fort with a band of singing voyageurs in the fur brigade
of a Montreal trader, he followed the Green Bay and Fox River
route to the Wisconsin. At the portage he found the grass writh-
ing with serpents, and there a French trader named Pinnisance
told him the famous story that Carver solemnly recorded as an
example of the intelligence and docility of rattlesnakes.

> An Indian belonging to the Menominee nation, having taken one
> of them [rattlesnakes], found means to tame it; and when he
> had done this treated it as a Deity, calling it his Great Father
> and carrying it with him in a box wherever he went. This the
> Indian had done for several summers, when M. Pinnisance acci-
> dentally met with him at that carrying place, just as he was
> setting off for a winter hunt. The French gentleman was sur-
> prised one day to see the Indian place the box which contained
> his God on the ground and opening the door gave him his lib-
> erty, telling him while he did it to be sure and return by the
> time he himself should be back, which was to be in the month
> of May following. As this was but in October M. Pinnisance
> told the Indian, whose simplicity astonished him, that he fancied
> he might wait long enough when May arrived for the arrival
> of his great father. The Indian was so confident of his creature's
> obedience that he offered to lay the Frenchman a wager of
> two gallons of rum that at the time appointed he would come
> and crawl into the box. This was agreed on and the second
> week of May following fixed for the determination of the wager.
> At that period they both met there again, when the Indian set
> down his box and called for his great father. The snake heard
> him not, and the time being now expired he acknowledged that
> he had lost. However, without seeming to be discouraged he

offered to double the bet if his great father came not in two
days more. This was further agreed on; when behold on the
second day about one o'clock the snake arrived and of his own
accord crawled into the box which was placed ready for him.
The French gentleman vouchsafed for the truth of this story,
and from the accounts I have often received of the docility
of those creatures, I see no reason to doubt his veracity.

Carver had been instructed to map the Wisconsin River and
the Mississippi—he was the first Englishman to trace the shores
that the French had known for nearly a century—and to note
the Indian towns and their populations as far north as the Falls
of St. Anthony. There he would spend the winter, sending back
reports to Rogers by the spring fur brigades. At every Indian
settlement he was to announce a great-council gathering for the
next June at Michilimackinac. Two weeks behind Carver came
Captain James Tute with bolder orders. He was to ascend the
Mississippi and to winter with Carver at the Falls of St. Anthony;
in the spring they were to seek the Northwest Passage or, failing
that, "the great River Ourigon that falls into the Pacific Ocean
about the Latitude Fifty." For the first time in his career, Rogers
was sending men on a march he could not share. He must have
had some restless nights, poring over his maps of the Northwest
while the water pounded in the Old Mackinaw sands.

Carver at least had his desire; he was traveling into the vast
northwest, with undiscovered country ahead of him. After a stop
at Prairie du Chien at the mouth of the Wisconsin—a place
swarming with Indians, vagabond traders, dogs and half-breed
children—he paddled up the Mississippi in a single canoe
manned by a voyageur and a Mohawk Indian. They made slow
progress, and Carver had time to map the bluffs and islands,
to stop at Indian camps, where he announced the great council
that Rogers was planning and to ponder the ruins of Fort Beauhar-
nois above the wide waters of Lake Pepin, which the French
had erected half a century earlier. Just above the mouth of the
St. Peter's—the Minnesota River now—they had to leave their
canoe because the Mississippi was choked with ice. With a roving
Indian youth—"a prince of the Winnebagoes," Carver called

him—the old map-maker tramped sixty miles to the Falls of St. Anthony. To the thundering cascade the young Winnebago offered his pipe and tobacco, his arm- and wristbands, his bead necklace and his earrings. Carver looked on respectfully and then shared his own tobacco with his companion.

Returning to the St. Peter's, Carver fixed a peace pipe on the bow of his canoe and paddled two hundred miles up the westward-leading St. Peter's to the country of the Sioux. He arrived at a Naudowissy Sioux village on December 7th and spent five months with those people. As he acquired their language, he learned of their long enmity with the Chippewas, and he avidly recorded their grasp of western geography. "I have learned," he wrote with great satisfaction, "that the four most capital rivers on the continent of North America, the St. Lawrence, the Mississippi, the river Bourbon, and the Oregon or the river of the West, have their sources in the same neighborhood. The waters of the three former are within thirty miles of each other; the latter, however, is rather farther west. This shows that these parts are the highest land in North America; and it is an instance not to be paralleled on the other three quarters of the globe that four rivers of such magnitude should take their rise together, and each, after running separate courses, discharge their waters into different oceans at the distance of two thousand miles from their sources. For in their passage from this spot to the Bay of St. Lawrence; to the Bay of Mexico south, to Hudson's Bay north, and to the Bay at the Straits of Annian west, each of these traverse upwards of two thousand miles." It was a neat and enormous geography that took shape in a smoky Sioux lodge while snow dimmed the Minnesota hills.

In mid-April Carver journeyed downstream with a band of Sioux hunters whom he had persuaded to attend the Michilimackinac council. At Prairie du Chien he met Captain Tute, who was supposed to have wintered with the map-maker at St. Anthony's Falls. Carver joined Tute's party, consisting of eight voyageurs and two Chippewa guides, and in line with Rogers's orders they struck up the Mississippi toward distant Fort La Prairie in the Saskatchewan country. As they went north

toward the enemy Sioux, the guides were uneasy. At the mouth
of the Chippewa River, which leads toward Lake Superior, they
refused to go on except by way of that side river. The white
captains, already short of food and without trade goods, had
no choice. They decided to head for Grand Portage on the northwest shore of Lake Superior, where they could restock their
canoes with supplies Rogers had promised to send from Michilimackinac.

Paddling up the Chippewa through singing, stinging clouds
of mosquitoes, Carver was in a border country between the Chippewa and the Sioux. It became the controversial "Carver's
Tract," which proved to be a more lasting puzzle than the mysteries of western geography. In Washington in 1825, the Congres-
sional Committee on Private Land Claims pondered a petition
for "Carver's Grant," described as extending on the east side
of the Mississippi River from the Falls of St. Anthony to the
mouth of the Chippewa River, from there eastward 100 miles,
thence northward 120 miles and back westward to the starting
point. "This grant," the petition stated, "was made to Captain
Jonathan Carver on the first day of May, 1767 by two chiefs
of the tribe of the Naudowissies, in consideration of distinguished
services rendered by him while in their country." It added

> that Captain Carver went to England in the year 1770 and so-
> licited the king to ratify his said grant; and that His Majesty
> and the lords of his council in the year 1775 granted his petition
> and ordered him to return to America and take possession of
> his land thus conveyed to him; but before the necessary prepara-
> tions for his departure could be made the information of the
> Battle of Bunker's Hill was received, which entirely frustrated
> his intended enterprise . . . that Carver died January 31, 1780,
> leaving a widow and seven children. Dr. Samuel Peters in the
> year 1806 purchased from the heirs of Jonathan Carver all their
> right to the said tract of country and obtained a deed therefor.
> The deed was signed by the two chiefs, one by the sign of
> the snake, the other by the sign of the tortoise. The original
> deed, left with Dr. Lettsom of London, was supposed stolen
> and is lost.

The claimant, Dr. Peters, had gone to Minnesota, where the heirs
and successors to the two chiefs declared the deed good and
valid. Now the congressmen had to decide. To complicate the
puzzle there was no mention of the land grant in Carver's lifetime. But the 1781 edition of his *Travels*, a year after his death,
included an account of an Indian council in Big Cave below
St. Anthony's Falls, where with due ceremony the gift was given.
Congress finally denied the petition and annulled the alleged
grant.

In the grim season of 1767 Carver had other problems. Bleed-
ing from black flies the party made a long, swampy portage to
the Bois Brûlé, which took them to Lake Superior. On July 19
they reached Grand Portage but found no canoes from Michilimackinac. Two weeks later an Old Mackinaw trader arrived with
a letter from Rogers. Assuming that "you must have goods
enough with you to complete your expedition," it instructed Tute
and Carver to go on to Fort La Prairie and the Pacific. But
the Pacific had lost its lure for Tute and Carver. With one empty
canoe and some hungry voyageurs, they headed back to Mackinaw. At the end of August the disgruntled explorers reported
to an exasperated commander. Carver would later boast of "having been fourteen months on this extensive tour, traveled nearly
four thousand miles and visited twelve nations of Indians," but
for Rogers he had accomplished next to nothing.

At Michilimackinac Rogers was having troubles and triumphs.
He had won the traders by freeing them from regulation, but
he was in debt to them for presents he had lavished on the
Indians. His great council had drawn tribesmen from all directions; thousands of Indians had pitched their camps in the Mackinac woods and along the curving shore. First came the Ottawas
from L'Arbre Croche and Grand River, then Potawatomis from
St. Joseph, Chippewas from Lake Superior, Menominis from
Green Bay, Puans from Lake Winnebago, Outagamis from the
Fox River, Sauks from the Wisconsin and Sioux from lands beyond the upper Mississippi. In a reek of raw peltry, they traded
skins of tobacco, corn, cloth, flags and guns. While the rancid
pelts were sorted, beaten, cleaned and baled for shipment to

Montreal and Albany, Rogers smoked, feasted and counciled with
his visitors. There was a peace council to end the war between
Sioux and Chippewa, and there were repeated trade councils
to bind all the tribes to British commerce. After many speeches,
Rogers spent a whole day doling out blankets, guns, powder,
lead, ornaments, tobacco—gifts that the commander had
acquired on credit from the traders. Finally "some refreshments
were distributed," and the canoes pushed off. With whoops and
cries, the tribesmen scattered over the water.

In his headlong way Rogers had outlined a trade that would
web from Old Mackinaw to distant places. He listed the savage
towns and camps, the furs that could come from them and the
cargoes needed to support the trade. Here was another Rogers,
a calculating, carefully figuring man, reckoning costs and profits
of the wilderness commerce. He reasoned:

> If the trade be confined to Michilimackinac, few if any
> Indians from the west of Lake Michigan or from the south
> and west of Lake Superior would ever visit the post at
> all, some because they are at such a distance that they cannot
> possibly do it, and others because they can be supplied at home
> with every article they stand in need of . . . for it is certain
> that if we do not send a supply to those Indians the Spaniards
> will . . . . This loss would be of the utmost moment, but it
> is not all, we should also loose their friendship, and their attach-
> ment to the French and Spaniards would become stronger so
> that we should have them for our most dangerous and impla-
> cable enemies.
>
> Secondly we not only wholly lose the trade of such numbers
> of savages by a confinement of trade to Michilimackinac, but
> those nations, tribes and bands that will continue to supply
> themselves from that post will not trade near so largely . . . [as]
> they would do were traders allowed to visit and supply them
> at their hunting grounds and winter quarters. The reason of
> this is plain: the presence of the trader with a supply of such
> articles as the savage wants excites and encourages him to
> greater industry and assiduity in hunting. It animates men,
> women and children to exert themselves to the utmost for the

procuring of what they can upon the spot immediately barter for such things as will be useful or ornamental to them.

As he went on with his argument, Rogers combined the profit motive with commiseration.

Besides, as the savages are mostly poor they are not able to supply themselves with large stores of such things as are absolutely necessary not only to their hunting but even their subsisting with any comfort, so that in case of any emergency or accident they must often suffer great inconveniences if traders are not among them or near at hand to supply them afresh, for instance the losing or breaking of a hatchet or two or three knives and the like may lay a whole family under great inconveniences for six or eight months together, the spoiling of a small quantity of gunpowder, the breaking a spring of a gunlock, etc. may be the means of destroying a whole season's hunt and of distressing and starving a numerous family. Whence 'tis easy to infer that confining the trade to the post of Michilimackinac will greatly diminish our trade even with those savages that will still depend upon it for their supplies, for the savage can trade only in proportion to his industry, skill and success in hunting.

In an eloquent summary the commander pictured Michilimackinac as the strategic outpost of British influence in America.

It ought to be a barrier to all that may come westerly, north-westerly or southwesterly to the Pacific Ocean—it ought to be a beacon from which a most extensive and as yet unknown territory is watched and observed—it ought to be a store-house fraught with all manner of necessaries for the constant supply of almost innumerable bands, tribes and nations of savages.

After this lengthy preamble, Rogers made a startling proposal—that Michilimackinac be made an independent province, outside the regulation of the eastern officials, with its commander in sole charge of the traders and the Indians and with a company of rangers at his command. When this blueprint for

the independence of the vast interior reached New York and
Montreal, Sir William Johnson called it "a scheme for establish-
ing a needy man of bad circumstances and worse principles in
the first authority."

In all his reasoning Rogers had said not a word about the
controversial matter of the traffic in rum. To Michilimackinac
in the summer of 1767 came Lieutenant Benjamin Roberts, an
agent and inspector for Sir William Johnson; he was sent to
watch the sale of rum, the conduct of the Indian trade and the
commander's high-handed rule.

One midnight in mid-August Roberts was awakened by the
clump of feet and muffled voices. Some of the "vagabond
traders" of the place were smuggling rum out of the fort's commissary. Roberts heard enough to deduce that the men were
in Rogers's service, stealing the rum at his orders; he watched
them load it into canoes and set off across the straits. The next
morning Roberts took a detail of men and found 41 kegs cached
in the woods at Point St. Ignace. He brought back the cargo
and was met by the commander. Roberts meant to return the
rum to the commissary, but Rogers ordered it put in the King's
Storehouse; if unclaimed it would be used, he said, to reward
the troops for extraordinary labor. The argument led to a chal-
lenge, and before a crowd of onlookers Roberts accused the commander of treason. Rogers then ordered Roberts locked in the
guardhouse. So ended the quarrel over rum, but Rogers's troubles
were just beginning.

In New York General Gage, Commander in Chief of British
forces in North America, had heard of Rogers's extravagance
and disregard of orders. Then came other reports, stating that
Rogers meant to establish an independent Northwestern province, which would be ruled from Michilimackinac. Early in December, Ensign Robert Johnston arrived at Michilimackinac from
Detroit with orders to place Rogers under arrest "for High Treason, or being a traitor to his King and Country." The orders
were delivered to Captain Spiesmacher, second-in-command,
and Lieutenant Christie. With the fort gates closed and the men
under arms, Spiesmacher asked to confer with the commander.

While they talked in the middle of the compound, a file of armed men marched up. Spiesmacher then read his orders and placed Rogers under arrest. The commander's quarters were searched for incriminating papers, though all that was found was "his plan of Lake Huron, St. Clair, Superior and part of the River of Mississippi, the Journals of the detachment he sent to find the Northwest Passage, and a few Indian speeches." Meanwhile Rogers and his wife were kept in another house under guard. A week later they were returned to their own quarters, where they would be confined until the schooner came from Detroit in the spring.

In the long, bleak winter Rogers was shunned by the officers, though the men still offered little friendly services. Some puzzled Indians came to see him, and their mutterings led Spiesmacher to deny Rogers further visitors. When he heard a rumor that Rogers had plotted with the Indians to get him away, Spiesmacher put the prisoner in irons and moved his wife to another dwelling. With horse fetters on his legs, the brawny major clanked back and forth across his drafty room. When an iron clangor sounded, he could see a glowing in the forge across the trampled snow. Stoically he wrote to Gage, asking for a speedy trial. Accustomed to marching and lively exercise, he explained, his health was suffering from confinement.

The long winter passed, and through his window Rogers saw the drifting white clouds of spring. On the 21st of May the schooner *Gladwin* anchored off the point. When its cargo had been discharged, boats took the passengers aboard. Still in irons, Rogers was put into the creaking hold; he would lie on ballast stones during the ten-day voyage to Detroit. Over his head footsteps sounded. His wife never looked back as Michilimackinac dropped over the horizon. Jonathan Carver paced the deck while his mind went to the outpost where Rogers's empire had become Rogers's folly.

In Montreal Rogers was acquitted of the charge of treason, though not restored to office. Ruined in America, he went to London, where nine creditors had him committed to debtors' prison. Also in London, walking the gray streets with a woods-

man's loose stride, was Jonathan Carver. The two men met on
Rogers's release. The old excitement flickered in their eyes as
they drew up a petition to Parliament for aid in finding the
Northwest Passage. They proposed to ascend the St. Peter's River
to its source, where they would make a thirty-mile portage to
the "Great River Ourigan," which flowed to the Pacific. No one
seemed interested in this heroic project. Another petition fared
better; through the influence of Lord Dartmouth, Rogers was
granted the retirement pay of a major. A broken man of 43,
he returned to America where the Second Continental Congress
was convened in Philadelphia.

The rest for Rogers was all downhill. During the Revolution
he tried to ally himself first with the loyalists and then with
the patriots, but neither side wanted him. His wife divorced
him. He was banished by statute of New Hampshire; like an
exile he returned to England with the defeated British army
at the end of the war. After another term in debtors' prison,
he lived with the fading comfort of alcohol in a shabby lodging
house in south London. He died there in ignominy on a soft
spring day in 1795.

In England Carver had turned to writing. Deaf to the murmur
of London outside his window and to news of the Revolution
in America, he recorded his *Three Years' Travels Throughout
the Interior Parts of North America for more than Five Thousand
Miles, containing an account of the Lakes, Islands and Rivers,
Cataracts, Mountains and Minerals, Soil and Vegetable Produc-
tions of the North West Regions of the Vast Continent; with
a Description of the Birds, Beasts, Reptiles, Insects and Fishes
peculiar to the country. Together with a Concise History of the
Genius, Manners and Customs of the Indians inhabiting the lands
that lie adjacent to the heads and west of the River Mississippi;
and an Appendix describing the Uncultivated Parts of America
that are the most proper for farming Settlements. By Jonathan
Carver, Captain of the Provincial Troops in America.*

Though its geography was muddled and its facts were mixed
with fancy, the book had the feel of the vast, wild country and
vivid pictures of the savage tribes. For Carver this success came

too late; he died in poverty in 1780, just before the book caught on. It fascinated European readers, going through thirty editions in six languages. From its pages Chateaubriand drew his romantic descriptions of Indian life and Schiller found the material for his famous "Indian Death Dirge." After reading the *Travels*, the American geographer Jedediah Morse applied the name "Oregon" to a westward-flowing river, and young William Cullen Bryant used it in his somber poem "Thanatopsis." The word that Carver had heard from Rogers when they looked west from Michilimackinac became a part of the future of America.

. 10 .

THE ISLAND FORT

On the rocky coast of Caithness at the northernmost point of Scotland, Sinclair's Bay curves between Noss Head and Duncansby Head by John O'Groat's house. For centuries the leading name in Caithness County has been that of the Sinclair, or St. Clair, family. There in the same year, 1736, were born two men who would have civil and military command of Michilimackinac, four thousand miles away. Arthur St. Clair became a general in the American army, a member of the Continental Congress, and the first governor of the Northwest Territory, which extended from the Ohio River to Lake Superior; his huge domain included the Straits of Mackinac, which he never saw. His distant cousin Patrick Sinclair, serving on the British side, became commander of Michilimackinac and lieutenant governor of the upper country during the final years of the Revolution. His work still stands, for he was the builder of the fort on Mackinac Island.

After his youthful schooling, Patrick Sinclair entered military service. At the age of 22 he was commissioned ensign in the famous Black Watch Regiment, the 42nd Highlanders. He served in the West Indies, taking part in the attack on Guadeloupe, and in 1760 he fought with Lord Jeffrey Amherst and Major Robert Rogers at the capture of Montreal. From there he went into the Naval Department on the Great Lakes. He had charge of boats serving the Indian trade—schooners, sloops, snows (the almost forgotten "snow" was a two-masted, square-rigged vessel, a freshwater brig), bateaux and canoes. As captain of the eighty-ton schooner *Gladwin*, he brought aid to besieged Detroit. In 1764, on a voyage to Michilimackinac, he took the first sailing

90

vessel over Lake Huron since the one-way passage of the *Griffin* 85 years before. In 1766, as master of the *Gladwin*, he brought Robert Rogers and Jonathan Carver to the post at the Straits. Between voyages Captain Sinclair carried on a marine survey; he took the first soundings of the river mouths, bays and harbors between Lake Erie and the Straits of Mackinac.

By the Quebec Act of 1774, the English Parliament created the Province of Quebec, extending from the Gulf of the St. Lawrence to the Ohio River and the Mississippi. Its four huge western districts were to be governed from the frontier posts of Detroit, Michilimackinac, Kaskaskia and Vincennes. In London on April 7, 1775, eleven days before Paul Revere's ride, Patrick Sinclair was commissioned by George III Lieutenant Governor and Superintendent of the post of Michilimackinac. His authority extended over the territory of all the Indians who came there to trade.

Governor Sinclair sailed from Glasgow early that summer, but it took him four and a half years to reach his wilderness station. Arrested by American officials in New York, he was returned to England the next year. He did not get back to America until the fall of 1777; that winter he spent with Lord Howe in Philadelphia. He sailed north to Halifax the next summer, and it was another year before he made it to Quebec. In June of 1779 he presented his commission to Governor Haldimand, who briefed him on conditions in the upper country.

Meanwhile Michilimackinac was in the charge of Major Arent Schuyler de Peyster, who found the place tedious and trying. For distraction he wrote verses and kept pets—a tame swan, a spaniel and a striped squirrel named Tim. During the American Revolution, Britain's energies and attention were focused on the eastern colonies, and the western posts were all but forgotten. At the end of a long and uncertain line of communication, Mackinac received scant supplies and few dispatches. When news came that George Rogers Clark's Virginians had captured the Illinois posts of Kaskaskia and Vincennes, De Peyster began to wonder what was happening beyond his horizon of woods and water.

Rumors spread among the Indians, the traders and the voyageurs, even among the men of the garrison. One story said that Clark's men had advanced to Milwaukee, where they were building boats to attack Michilimackinac. Another tale had Clark attacking Detroit and cutting the lifeline of the upper country. "The whole country is in the greatest confusion," De Peyster reported, "being at a loss to know which route the rebels will take next." Meanwhile he reinforced the stockade and fenced the soldiers' quarters with pickets against a surprise attack by Indians trading within the fort. To Quebec he sent appeals—which in those uncertain times might never be delivered—for more troops and more arms, for rum to bribe the Indians and rations to stock his commissary. General Haldimand replied that the Michilimackinac garrison should be self-sufficient, living off the country.

Ever since Major Rogers's inglorious departure, the fort had been disintegrating. West winds dashed lake water against the stockade and left the pickets loose and leaning. The sand hills shifted with every storm, and details of troops were kept shoveling—twelve at a time, as there were only twelve shovels in the storeroom—in a futile contest with the dunes. Sand reefs built up in the bay, so that boats had to anchor off shore, lightening their cargoes in canoes and skiffs.

Life at the fort was mostly monotony. Half the garrison was illiterate, and the men had nothing to talk about but the rank Chippewa women, the traders' rum, mosquitoes in the woods and the catch of whitefish in a pitching mackinaw boat. Except for parade they dressed in greasy buckskins and wore their hair in pigtails. Drunkenness was common, though it was punished at the whipping post. For attempted desertion—in a wilderness with no place to go—one man was sentenced to a hideous flogging of a thousand lashes. Another set himself adrift on an ice floe; after nine days he floated back, famished and half frozen.

Winter was a long season, with the straits locked tight from December to April. Over the white waste moved a gray scud of clouds, and the night wind brought the rumble of drift ice far out in Lake Michigan. Sometimes a dog fight enlivened the fort yard, though this diversion was less frequent than the ugly altercations between sergeants and soldiers. On Sundays the troops were marched to church; for missing this muster a soldier was confined in the black hole. Officers stole rum from the storehouse commissary and sold it to the Indians. One ensign was caught filling empty barrels with boiling water to make up the "leakage"; the keg-flavored water was then sold to the troops at the cut rate of 18 shillings a gallon.

In 1780 the English trader John Long spent the Mackinac winter with a Chippewa family, preferring that arrangement to life inside the fort. Since the massacre seventeen years earlier there had been a regulation barring Indians with firearms from the fort and ruling that no Indian women could be kept overnight inside the stockade. To get around this last order, at the urging of some friends in the garrison, trader Long tried a ruse that almost worked. One day he accosted two soldiers on the beach, asking if they could spare time to roll a large hogshead of beer from the Chippewa Point landing place to the fort. The men agreed, laboriously trundling the barrel up the loose sand ridge. At the fort gate they met the officer of the day. The sweating men explained the arrival of beer. That pleased the officer, who looked with new interest at the trading sloop in the bay; he passed them in. Just inside the gate one soldier stubbed his foot on a stone and let go the barrel, which got away from his companion. Picking up speed it bounced and bumped across the parade ground. When it banged against a barracks wall the head dropped out—spilling two giggling Indian girls. They were still reeling with dizziness when the officer arrived. The girls ran for the woods, and trader Long was summoned by the commander. After being threatened with arrest and a trip to Montreal in irons, he was let off with a reprimand. Concluded John Long, "I did not choose again to risk the commanding officer's displeasure."

For the resident traders at remote Mackinac, life was far from primitive. They had Negro and Indian slaves, well-stocked cellars and pantries, the society of their neighbors and the officers at the fort and a profitable traffic with the tribes. Spring and fall were enlivened with the arrival and departure of their voyageurs.

Summer brought trips to Detroit, Niagara or Montreal. In winter there were long evenings by the fireside and weekly dances in the fort.

In those years the leading trader at Old Mackinaw was John Askin, who had come to America from Ireland as a youth of nineteen. After service in the French and Indian War, he became one of the first British traders in the upper country. He settled at Michilimackinac in 1764, soon after the massacre, and remained there for sixteen prosperous years. A wholesale trader, he had his own sloops and schooners, which brought cargoes to supply other traders, as well as to outfit his own agents and voyageurs. When he first arrived at the Straits, Askin took an Ottawa woman into his cottage. She bore him a son and two daughters, who were equally at home in the Indian camps and the traders' houses.

John Askin's intermittent diary sketches the life of a landed proprietor busy with his cottage garden and his inland farm, as well as of a frontier merchant.

1774

April the 16th the lake first broke up a little.

19th. I set the first potatoes. Same day the first wild ducks was brought to the fort.

20th. I began to harrow my ground at the farm.

22nd. Sowed some pease at the farm. . . .

23d. The large boat taken out of the fort by my man. Mr. Boyez sowed pease.

26th. The lake now passable in boats.

27th. Some ice returned. Sowed buckwheat at the farm and set the first potatoes there.

28th. M. Ainsse went in a boat for the Grant Traverse or to meet the Ottaways. Sowed parsnips and set potatoes at the farm. Also sowed oats.

29th. The first Indians arrived from the other side in a canoe. Planted onions for seed, also beans, squash seed, and cucumbers.

A view of early Mackinac from a sketch made in 1820, and published in *Ethnological Researches Among the Red Men,* by Henry R. Schoolcraft.

Champlain's map of 1632 showed Lake Huron (mer Douce) and Lake Superior (Grand Lac) but no Lake Michigan.

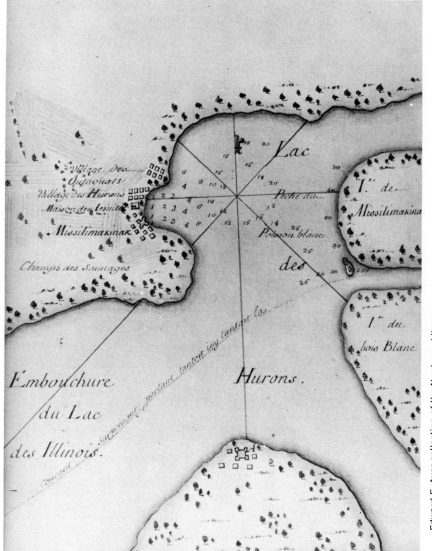

French map of the Straits of Mackinac, about 1717.

Marquette and Joliet at Chicago, August 1673

Father Jacques Marquette.

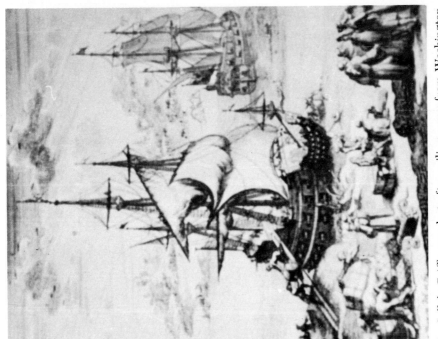

La Salle's *Griffin* was lost after sailing away from Washington Island, September 1679, through a storm-swept northern Lake

Mackinac Island Village and Fort with Chippewa Indians encamped to receive their annual payments, September 1842.

Fort Michilimackinac, Mackinaw City, with Mackinac Bridge in the background.

Major Robert Rogers, Commander of the fort at Old Mackinaw, 1765-1768.

Alexander Henry (1739-1824) survived the massacre at Old Mackinaw, 1763, and prospered for half a century in the Indian trade.

Restored Church of Ste. Anne de Michilimackinac, Fort Michilimackinac, Mackinaw City, Michigan.

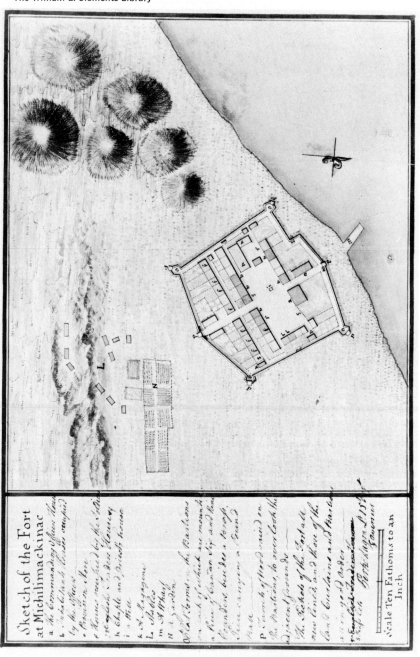

Map by Lieutenant Perkins Magra in 1766 shows Fort Michilimackinac with its outlying wharf (*m*), garden (*N*), stables (*L*) and sand hills rising from the Lake Michigan shore.

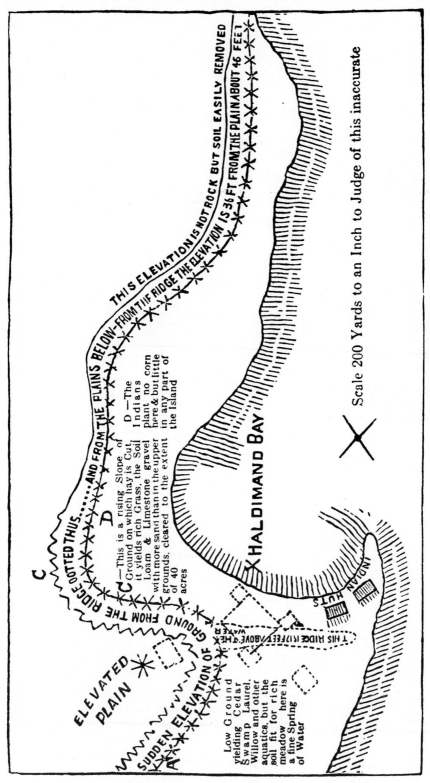

Outline of Fort Mackinac as planned by Sinclair in 1779.

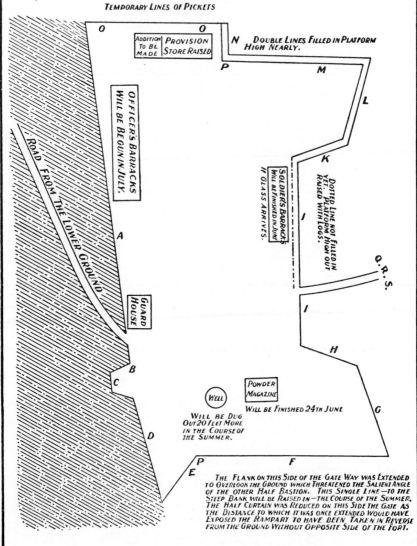

FORT·MICHILMACKINAC

SKETCH OF THE FORT ON MICHILMACKINAC ISLAND

TEMPORARY LINES OF PICKETS

O · · · · · · · · · · O

ADDITION TO BE MADE | PROVISION STORE RAISED

N · · DOUBLE LINES FILLED IN PLATFORM HIGH NEARLY.

P

M

L

OFFICER'S BARRACKS WILL BE BEGUN IN JULY.

ROAD FROM THE LOWER GROUND

A

SOLDIER'S BARRACKS WILL BE FINISHED IN JUNE IF GLASS ARRIVES.

DOTTED LINE NOT FILLED IN YET. PLATFORM HIGH OUT RAISED WITH LOGS.

K

I

Q.R.S.

GUARD HOUSE

I

H

B

C

WELL

POWDER MAGAZINE

WILL BE FINISHED 24TH JUNE

G

WILL BE DUG OUT 20 FEET MORE IN THE COURSE OF THE SUMMER.

D

P

F

E

THE FLANK ON THIS SIDE OF THE GATE WAY WAS EXTENDED TO OVERLOOK THE GROUND WHICH THREATENED THE SALIENT ANGLE OF THE OTHER HALF BASTION. THIS SINGLE LINE —TO THE STEEP BANK WILL BE RAISED IN —THE COURSE OF THE SUMMER. THE HALF CURTAIN WAS REDUCED ON THIS SIDE THE GATE AS THE DISTANCE TO WHICH IT WAS ONCE EXTENDED WOULD HAVE EXPOSED THE RAMPART TO HAVE BEEN TAKEN IN REVERSE FROM THE GROUND WITHOUT OPPOSITE SIDE OF THE FORT.

Sketch of the fort on Michilimackinac Island by Sinclair in 1781.

Officers' Stone Quarters, Fort Mackinac, showing picture of Dr. William Beaumont and monument erected in his honor.

One of the old Block Houses, Fort Mackinac.

A daily dress parade scene during the occupation of Fort Mackinac was admired by children and the island tourists in the 1880s.

Fort Mackinac, Mackinac Island, Michigan 1965.

30th. Sowed onions and spinach seed.

May 1st. The land gate shut.

2d. Began to plow. A very hard frost this night and a strong west wind.

3d. . . . Agreed with Elizabeth Staniford for my washing and all my family's—for 8 shillings per week.

6th. Sowed pease and set potatoes. Several showers of snow today. Lyons and Oakes arrived from a hunting party. An Indian canoe came from the opposite side.

7th. Sowed oats and set potatoes. Fair weather. Westerly wind.

8th. Hired Chabotte from this day to the arrival of the company's canoes from the Grand Portage for 100 pounds in peltry, or 200 pounds in Montreal, also 1 pair trousers, a shirt and pair of leggings. He obliges himself during said time to work faithfull whether on a voyage or otherwise employed.

In 1722, during a business trip to Detroit, John Askin married the daughter of a French merchant. At Old Mackinaw he enlarged his house and reared a second family of nine children. His wife's brother, Jean-Baptiste Barthe, became a trader at Sault Ste. Marie in something like a partnership with Askin.

In the late 1770s John Askin headed a household of twenty, including six Negro slaves and several Indian servants. Set back from the windswept shore he had a farm with oxen, horses, milk cows, swine and poultry. His blacksmith shop kept his own implements repaired and was visited by a steady stream of Indians with broken guns, spears, knives and kettles. In the harbor or on the way to distant places were his schooner *Welcome*, his sloop *De Peyster* named for the fort's commander, his keelboat, his Mackinaw boat and a dozen big trading canoes. He could ride in two-wheeled carriages in summer and in sleighs and carioles when the straits were frozen. He even had a sedan chair, like the gentlemen of London and Paris; carried by his Negroes Jupiter and Pompey in that upholstered rig, he must have arrived impressively at Indian camps and councils. On long winter evenings, when the wind howled across the icy straits and snow drifted over the dune, John Askin could fill his pipe and read the *Spectator* essays, the *Letters* of Lord Chesterfield or the wit and wisdom of Molière. With four hundred volumes in his library, he was a man of the world as well as of the wilderness.

Four and a half years after his appointment, Patrick Sinclair arrived at the Straits, much to the relief of Major De Peyster, who had had enough of remote Michilimackinac. In a tone of self-approval, he reported ridding the place of dishonest and disloyal traders. One of them, an ex-voyageur named Pero, had fled with a canoe full of gunpowder and brandy. When De Peyster sent a boat after him, Pero touched his pipe to a barrel of powder, blowing himself and his cargo to pieces. Now, writing to General Haldimand, De Peyster hoped that he could settle into "a quieter state." He had his wish: After an uneventful term as governor at Detroit, he retired to Scotland. In Dumfries he organized the Gentleman Volunteers, one of whose recruits, marching in kersey breeches, blue coat and round hat, was Robert Burns. Just a month before he died the ailing poet wrote some rueful verses "To Colonel De Peyster":

> —O, what a canty world were it
> Wad pain and care and sickness spare it,
> And fortune favor worth and merit
>   As they deserve.
> And ay a rowth—roast beef and claret!—
>   Syne, wha wad starve?

The new commander and the first official governor at Michilimackinac was a bluff, blue-eyed, forthright and impulsive man, whose firmness helped him to get on with both soldiers and Indians—though not with his superiors. Like a good Scotsman, Sinclair had not neglected to draw his £200 annual salary ever since his appointment in 1775. Arriving at Michilimackinac in the fall of 1779, he found a rickety fort overlooked by shifting sand hills. When the west wind blew, waves dashed the pickets, and spray rained on the parade ground. From that weathered, windswept place, he pointed his telescope at the white-walled island in its wide moat of water. Four days after his arrival he wrote to Quebec, proposing to move the fort to Mackinac Island. He pointed out the natural defenses of that location, its sheltered harbor for military and trading vessels and its abundance of timber and stone. Months would pass before he could have a reply, but Sinclair went immediately to the island to study the terrain. In his next letter to Quebec he enclosed a sketch of the island harbor—which he tactfully called "Haldimand Bay"—showing the "sudden elevation of ground" that rose from the first shelf of land along the shore. Of the location of present Turkey Hill he remarked: "This is a rising slope of ground on which hay is cut. It yields rich grass, the soil loam and limestone gravel with more sand than in the upper grounds; cleared to the extent of forty acres." The side of present Mahoney Avenue in the west end of the village he described as "low ground yielding cedar, swamp laurel, willow and other aquatics, but the soil fit for rich meadow. Here is a fine spring of water." A few Indian huts were marked on his map between the site of the present Iroquois Hotel and the Coast Guard signal station. He concluded, "It is the most respectable situation I ever saw, besides convenient for the subsistence of a garrison, the safety of troops, traders and commerce."

No word could come from Quebec until the ice went out in April. Meanwhile Governor Sinclair kept men on the island clearing forest, hauling logs, hewing pickets and puncheons. In February the Church of Ste. Anne de Michilimackinac in the fort yard was pulled down. Its logs and timbers were hauled over the frozen straits, and the church, measuring 25 by 45 feet, was erected again on the site of the present village post office on Market Street. (In 1827 the church was moved to a new location on Huron Street; the present church was erected there in 1873.) All winter the island echoed with the thud of axes, the crashing of trees and the jingle of trace chains. When the ice went out a landing wharf was built in the arc of the harbor.

In May came word from Governor Haldimand, approving the new location of the fort. One of Sinclair's letters had advised the Governor, "Be careful in the choice of an engineer, and don't send up one of your paper engineers fond of fine regular polygons." Haldimand's dispatch stated that no engineer would be sent; Sinclair could design his own island fortress. Sinclair had proposed to call it "Fort Haldimand," but the Governor appropriately held to the native name, ordering it called "Fort Mackinac." The old six-syllable "Michilimackinac" would not be heard again.

Sinclair had already consulted some Chippewa chiefs about a purchase of the island. The councils went on during the new season. For £5,000 the Indians agreed to surrender their claim to the place that had been a traditional council ground and a burial place for their dead. Finally in May of 1781, on behalf of all their people, five Chippewa chiefs made their marks on two deeds of title, one copy to be sent to Quebec and the other to be kept at Fort Mackinac. The deeds were signed by the totems of the chiefs and by Patrick Sinclair, "Lt. Gov'r and Commandant," Captain Mompesson, Lieutenant Brooks and Ensign McDonall; it was witnessed by six resident traders. At the end of this transaction, Governor Sinclair presented a wampum belt seven feet long to be kept by the Chippewas.

During the summer of 1780 the Michilimackinac traders pulled down their houses, salvaging the doors and windows. The latter were taken to the island and installed in new dwellings there. A government house was erected near the later Astor House on Market Street. On the height a ten-foot stockade of cedar pickets tipped with iron spikes enclosed a compound with blockhouses jutting from the corners. With chimneys and bunk space these bastions quartered the first troops sent across the water. Meanwhile a soldiers' barracks took shape, along with a storehouse, a guardhouse and a powder magazine. The first buildings roughly framed a central parade ground.

In midsummer of 1781 the King's 8th Regiment held the last parade at Michilimackinac. Down came the British colors. The troops embarked in keelboats, mackinaw boats and canoes for transfer to the island. Up the slanting fort road they marched, a line of scarlet across the white face of the cliff. On the new parade ground the British ensign was raised to the summer sky.

For Mackinac was occupied. For years the island community celebrated July 15th as the anniversary of removal.

While work continued—on barracks, storerooms and officers' quarters—some Indians had second thoughts about the island they had sold. When he heard rumors of a Chippewa threat to reclaim the place, Sinclair sent an urgent message to Detroit. With fair winds the brig *Dunmore* made a record run; in eight days the vessel was back with field guns on her deck. As she entered the half-moon harbor a cannon thundered, and echoes came back from the cliff. With men and horses straining, the guns were hauled up the fort road (steeper than the path today) and planted at the bastion corners. The Indians looked on in silence. The first artillery voice had ended all their threats.

Now Mackinac Island was the capital of the upper country. The schooners *Felicity* and *Welcome* plied from Detroit, bringing military stores and trade goods. Across the straits, from St. Ignace, Round Island and Bois Blanc and down the channel from Detour and the St. Mary's, Indians came to the island trading houses. From Lake Superior, the Mississippi and the Wisconsin, the tribes came for their annual presents. In 1781 Governor Sinclair received for Indian bounty 991 pairs of blankets, 102 dozen calico shirts, 50 dozen linen shirts and quantities of laced hats, feathers, mirrors, knives, hatchets, medals, needles, thread, axes, razors, brass and copper kettles, tobacco, guns, powder, shot and some thousands of gallons of rum.

Far around the shore flickered the fires of the visiting tribesmen—Chippewas, Sacs, Menominis, Foxes, Ottawas, Winnebagos, Sioux. Under the cliff, soldiers tended military gardens. From the height came a clatter of mallets and hammers where limestone walls were rising around the fort yard. And across the strait Michilimackinac was lifeless, its broken pickets jutting from the sand. It would remain an empty place, brush creeping down from the woods and sand blowing over the ruined timbers and foundations, until the twentieth-century reconstruction of Old Fort Michilimackinac.

In deep woods a little east of the Sugar Loaf Road there remains the old ruined lime kiln, built by Sinclair's men when

Sugar Loaf was still an Indian mystery. The broken furnace, six feet deep and fifteen feet across, has held the snows of many winters since British workmen shoveled limestone onto a hardwood fire to make mortar, whitewash and plaster. The walls of the fort were as white as the island cliffs and as enduring. Not an alien structure, the stronghold seemed to grow out of the earth, following the natural contours of the island upthrust. No other fort in America was as native and natural as the white-walled post above the crescent harbor.

On his £5,000 island—his payment amounted to about $3 an acre—Governor Sinclair spent many times as much to build his enduring fort. But not without resistance. He had to keep pleading for workmen and materials, and he waited impatiently for his successive drafts to be approved. One of his sketches shows an officers' barracks with the notation "will be begun in July," a provision store with an "addition to be made" and a soldiers' barracks that "will be finished in June *if glass arrives.*" In the month of July 1781 his drafts exceeded £60,000, and some of them were protested in Quebec. The next summer, when heavy drafts continued, Governor Haldimand sent three officers to examine Sinclair's accounts. They found careless bookkeeping, and they also learned that Indians had been giving furs to the commander, who in return increased their presents from the British government. Because of delayed and damaged cargoes, Sinclair had sometimes purchased traders' goods on credit for distribution to the tribes.

In September of 1782, while the investigators were still asking questions, Patrick Sinclair resigned his command and sailed for Quebec. His successor was Captain Daniel Robertson, who completed the massive walls and the stone and timber buildings. By the time of his death in 1787, Fort Mackinac was one of the strongest points in America. Its fall from British hands would not be by attack but by the terms of a treaty.

While commanding at Mackinac, Captain Robertson freed a Negro slave named Bonga, who then married a Chippewa woman and kept an island tavern, where his young son Stephen mingled with the Indians and voyageurs. Stephen Bonga grew up to be an agent for the American Fur Company, trading in the wilderness at the far end of Lake Superior. A picturesque figure, with a broad nose, a grizzled goat beard, a fur cap and pine staff, this Negro-Chippewa half-breed called himself "the first white man at the head of the lakes." Robertson himself left no memory except that of his "folly"—the death he stumbled to after drinking too much rum from his commissary. Even that memory blurred; Robertson's fall was somehow given to "Robinson," and it is "Robinson's Folly" that has marked the sheer southeast cliff of the island ever since.

Robertson was succeeded by Captain Scott, who seems to have governed in harmony with both white and red men. The final British commander was Captain William Doyle of the King's 24th Regiment. He complained about the drafty barracks but not about the defenses of the fort. It was as strong as ever. From a yawning ditch rose the solid walls, the stone and timber blockhouses pierced for musketry, the iron-barred sally ports, the gun platforms with cannon pointing over the settlement and the harbor.

This stronghold, with the flag of England flying, had been surrendered at the end of the Revolution. It was part of the huge territory ceded to the United States in 1783, when it was determined that the international border should follow the middle of the Great Lakes and their connecting rivers. But the fur trade was profitable, and Mackinac was far away. President Washington had sent Baron Steuben to Governor Haldimand to receive surrender of the Great Lakes posts. Haldimand replied that he had no instructions from London. John Adams, the American minister in London was put off by the English government, while Canadian merchants pushed the trade at Mackinac. Though the Treaty of Paris secured all the upper lakes country for the United States, with the boundary lines of today, it was thirteen years before the American occupation of the island fort.

In 1792 in his stone quarters on the hill, Captain William Doyle, in the presence of Lieutenant Edward Charleton of His Majesty's 5th Infantry, generously wrote out for trader John Johnston a grant of land on the American side of the Sault—three

hundred feet along the St. Mary's River running back to a distance comprising forty acres, bounded on the northeast by a
lot belonging to Antoine Landry and on the southwest by the
old Jesuit burying ground. None of them thought of the irony
of an English officer bestowing on an Irish trader, in the King's
name, territory ceded a decade past to the United States. The
English were still in possession.

At last, in 1796, President Washington reported to Congress
the British evacuation of the border posts of Oswego, Niagara,
Detroit and Michilimackinac. On October 2 the British flag came
down, and the American banner fluttered above Fort Mackinac.

TWO FLAGS IN THE WIND

On the tranquil summer morning of August 20, 1794, while the British flag still flew over Fort Mackinac, a battle raged on the Maumee River four hundred miles away. In a ruined forest where a storm had left a swath of fallen timbers, Mad Anthony Wayne's Legion of the United States met the warriors of the western and northern tribes. It took just sixty minutes for Wayne's crouching riflemen and his flanking cavalry to rout the Indians. Through the woods the warriors scattered. Hurrying northwest with the beaten Chippewas and Ottawas was the half-breed son of Trader John Askin of Michilimackinac and Detroit. The Askins were British loyalists as long as they lived.

The next spring Wayne called a treaty council at his stronghold of Fort Greene Ville, halfway between Lake Erie and the Ohio River. Three roads led into Fort Greene Ville, from the south, the north and the northeast—the wagon traces General Wayne had slashed from the Ohio to the mouth of the Maumee. A closer look would show the older paths of that country, the trails of the hunting tribes. Over the raw, new roads had come Wayne's army, some two thousand lean and weathered men from the frontier settlements. By forest paths, afoot and on horeseback, had come the chiefs and warriors of thirteen Indian nations. In the long days of June a fire was smoldering in the big council house at Fort Greene Ville, and the congress was gathering. With the Indians came white interpreters, traders and speculators. A few were there to help the tribes; others hoped to help themselves to government bounty.

John Askin, Jr., had fought with the northern tribesmen at

Fallen Timbers; then the chiefs asked him to accompany them to the council. "As the business they were going on," he explained, "was of great importance to them, they stood in need of a faithful interpreter and friend."

Askin left Detroit on July 2nd, with a canoe party of 27 Chippewa, Ottawa and Potawatomi warriors. At the head of the band were Chiefs Omissas, Mashipinashiwish and Opwagun and the toothy young prophet Chusco, "the Muskrat." They coasted Lake Erie and paddled up the Maumee past the site of the previous year's battle, still strewn with fallen trees, to the mouth of the Auglaize. There stood Fort Defiance, the northernmost of Wayne's border stations. Its commandant, Major Thomas Hunt, threatened to arrest Askin for having fought on the Indian side. This first encounter was enough for Askin, or so he pretended; he headed back toward Detroit, and the Indians followed. Seeing that the tribesmen would not go without their interpreter, the commandant sent a messenger after them. It was important, he said, for Askin to go to Greene Ville for the treaty council.

With the Shawnee chief Blue Jacket as its guide, the party paddled up the Auglaize River and made the portage to Loramie Creek. Near Loramie's Store, one of the early trading posts in the western Ohio country, they left their canoes. A day's march through the woods brought them to Fort Greene Ville. They arrived on July 21st.

In years to come Greenville would become a thriving county seat, with a shopping street called "Broadway" and a statue of justice over the courthouse door. But in 1795 it was a log stockade, closed by heavy gates and guarded by four square blockhouses. The southern and eastern bastions overlooked a meadow where garrison gardens striped the ground and cornflowers softened the stumpland. All around stretched the ancient woods. That summer Wayne's supply men drove herds of cattle and hogs to Greene Ville, and wagon crews unloaded pork, cheese, barley, coffee, tobacco, rice and whiskey. Eleven hundred tribesmen roamed the grounds, some of them limping with wounds received at Fort Recovery and Fallen Timbers. While sentries watched from the bastions, they wandered through the fort, climbing over supply wagons, peering into storerooms, crowding around the forges where blacksmiths hammered white-hot iron on ringing anvils. They raced their ponies in the pasture and held contests of strength and skill with Wayne's scouts and soldiers. At dusk fires flickered over the big meadow, and after supper the tribesmen gambled for salt, sugar, candles and tobacco, throwing colored plum stones on a blanket. They blew bark whistles and cane flutes; they beat gourd drums and danced in the firelight. Through a slow smoke of oak and hickory rose the savage cries.

On June 16th General Wayne touched a torch to the council fire and addressed the assembled Indians.

> I have cleared the ground of all brush and rubbish and have opened roads to the east, the west, the north and the south, that all your nations may come in safety, and with ease, to meet me . . . . The heavens are bright, the roads are open, we will rest in peace and love, and wait the arrival of our brothers. In the interim we will have a little refreshment, to wash the dust from our throats—we will, on this happy occasion, be merry, but without passing the bounds of temperance and sobriety. We will now cover up the council fire and keep it alive till the remainder of the different tribes assemble.

It was five weeks later, with Indians still straggling in, when Askin and his party arrived. They were met by one of Wayne's officers, with word that the General wished to see the delegation from the northern tribes. He led them to the fort and into the council house, where the Big Chief himself shook all their hands. Chief Amissas held up a belt of wampum given to the Chippewas at Fort Harmar six years earlier; he declared that he and his brothers had come to this Greene Ville council of their own free will and had brought this Englishman—John Askin—in order that they could have everything repeated and explained to them and not be ignorant of the council, as they had been in that earlier time at Fort Harmar on the Muskingum. General Wayne puffed the feathered pipe in approval.

The next day there was "no council." It was a field day, given to eating, chanting and dancing, the Indians engaging in foot races and horse races with the soldiers. On the following day, July 23rd, smoke went up from the council house, and the chiefs streamed in. But John Askin was halted at the gate; Wayne had ordered him excluded from the council. This time his Indians went without him, and that evening Askin learned that the tribes were divided and confused—one nation charging another with duplicity and deceit.

On July 26th Wayne read the proposed treaty. It contained ten articles, amounting to some 3,000 words. Article 3 described the boundaries of an extensive land cession in the Ohio country and stipulated the further ceding to the United States of sixteen strategic sites, including the mouth of the Chicago River and the posts of Detroit and Mackinac. The fire at Greene Ville was throwing shadows far away.

On July 31st, after a day of feasting, the chiefs were in good spirits. Wayne offered a beaded belt emblematic of the ten articles of the Treaty, and the Miami chief Little Turtle presented the calumet to the white leader in token of lasting friendship. In this access of good will the Chippewa Mashipinashiwish cheerfully consented to the ceding of the Straits of Mackinac and Mackinac Island. Then he made a further grant. Standing beside the ceremonial fire, he addressed the white men:

> You have asked of us the island of Michilimackinac and its dependencies . . . . You have also asked a piece of ground at the entrance of the straits to cut your wood on and for other necessary purposes; this is also granted to you, and I further add to it the Isle de Bois Blanc, as an instance of our sincere disposition to serve and accommodate you. You know, Brother, when the French formerly possessed this country we were one people and had but one fire between us; we now entertain the hope of enjoying the same happy relation with you, the United States.

A final effusion of friendship came from Omissas. Speaking for the three northern fires he declared:

> Elder Brother! You asked who were the true owners of the lands now ceded to the United States. In answer, I tell you

that if any nation should call themselves the owners of it they are guilty of a falsehood; our claim to it is equal; our elder brother has conquered it. Brothers! Have done trifling. Let us conclude this great work; let us sign our names to the treaty now proposed and finish our business. Elder Brother! If I can escape the snares of [the British] I shall ascend as high as the Falls of St. Mary's, and proclaim the good tidings to all your distant brothers in that quarter.

Though the treaty was not yet signed, John Askin saw his defeat: The Northern Indians had completely succumbed to Wayne's blandishments. He asked for a pass to return home, but instead of a pass he received a summons to the General's quarters. There Wayne confronted him with an intercepted letter from John Askin, Sr.; it had been sent from Detroit three days after the younger Askin's departure with the Indian delegation. The letter declared that the first article of any treaty should acknowledge that the Indians were sole masters of their lands. It continued:

But I am apprehensive that undue means may be taken to gain over the needy interpreters who have influence with the Indians to persuade them to sell or give up the right of selling their lands to the States . . . . As you have no favor to ask and are only with the Indians at their request to befriend them with your advice and to explain what they say, you need not care for the snubs or frowns of any man . . . . If any articles of agreement should be proposed to the Indians by the Americans which they or you do not clearly understand such as long conventions in writing, you should advise the Indians to ask leave to send a copy of it in here before they give an answer.

This letter, Wayne declared, incriminated Askin as a spy who deserved to be shot by the firing squad. To Askin's cool reply that it was a peace conference and he knew of no spies in time of peace, Wayne answered that he was in command and he would make the rules. (He then called troopers, who put Askin on a lead horse and headed south through the woods.) Two hours later they arrived at Fort Jefferson and delivered their prisoner to the commander. For ten days Askin lay in the guardhouse.

Meanwhile the ceremonies continued at Fort Greene Ville. On August 3rd, after all the chiefs had spoken and been answered, Wayne raked up the ashes of the smoldering fire and made his final declaration:

> I now deliver to you the wide and straight path to the Fifteen Fires, to be used by you and your posterity forever. So long as you continue to follow this road, so long will you continue to be a happy people. You see it straight and wide, and they will be blind indeed who deviate from it.

Translators repeated this to the Miami chiefs White Loon and Little Turtle; to the Wyandots, old Tarhe and the Half King's Son; to Buckongahelas and Queshowsky of the Delawares; to the Shawnees' Blue Jacket, Black Hoof and Red Pole; to Little Beaver and Little Fox of the Weas and Piankeshaws; to Chemung, Tapenebec and Okea of the Potawatomis; to La Malice, Augoashaway and Secan of the Ottawas; to the Chippewas' Little Thunder, Omissas, Mashipinashiwish and Opwagun. There was nothing for them to say.

According to the treaty terms, the Americans claimed all the country they had fought in and some that they had never seen. In addition to three-quarters of modern Ohio, the Indians would cede two large tracts in southern Indiana and a dozen scattered and strategic locations on the northern waterways. These locations included (Article 3, Section 13) "The post and island of Michilimackinac, and portions of the mainland adjacent thereto, also a piece on the mainland to the north to measure six miles on Lake Huron, or the Strait; also the Isle de Bois Blanc, the latter being an extra and voluntary gift of the Chippewa nation."

Nearly twenty million acres were ceded by the treaty, which also gave the United States the right to negotiate for further Indian lands and promised the Indians protection from intruders. For all this land the tribes received $20,000 in trade goods and a small annuity. In the future the United States would deliver annually $1,000 worth of horses and cattle, plows and harrows, axes and blankets to the Wyandots, Delawares, Shawnees, Miamis, Ottawas, Potawatomis and Chippewas; the smaller tribes, Kickapoo, Ouitenon, Eel River, Piankeshaw and Kaskaskia, would receive annuities of $500. It came to one-tenth of a cent an acre, plus yearly payments of $9,500 to the tribes.

The treaty covered two sheets of parchment twenty inches square. There was room for the names, totems and marks of 92 chiefs and the signatures of 27 officers. With the document signed and sealed, Wayne presented to each chief a bronze medal, shaped like a tear drop, showing President Washington handing a peace pipe to an Indian who had dropped his tomahawk. Then Wayne ordered a double round of whiskey, a feast of pork and beef and gifts for all the tribesmen. The treaty business was ended.

At Fort Jefferson, twelve miles away, John Askin lay in the guardhouse. On August 7th, four days after the treaty was signed, a messenger brought a pleasant note from General Wayne; it said that Askin was a free man, and it invited him to dine with Wayne at Fort Greene Ville. Askin declined the invitation and set out for Detroit. On the way he fell in with gift-laden Indians returning northward to their shrunken lands.

In Jay's Treaty, signed in London in 1794, the British had agreed to evacuate the northwest posts by June 1, 1796. In October of that year, American troops arrived at Mackinac Island— a company of infantry and a company of artillery and engineers under the command of Major Henry Burbeck. The British evacuated peacefully, and a new flag fluttered on the hill. A few seasons later a visiting inspector for the United States Army reported to the Secretary of War:

> Our fort at Michilimackinac from every consideration is one of the most important posts we hold in our western frontier. It . . . is an irregular work partly built with a strong wall and partly with pickets; and the parade ground within it is from 100 to 125 feet above the surface of the water. It contains a well of never failing water, a bomb proof used as a magazine, one stone barracks for the use of the officers, equal if not su-

perior to any building of the kind in the United States; a good
guard house and barracks for the soldiers and convenient storehouse for provisions, with three strong and convenient blockhouses. This post is strong both by nature and art, and the
possession of it has great influence with the Indians in favor
of the United States.

If it had great influence with the Indians, it had little effect
on their fur trade, which would not become significantly American until after the War of 1812. After the French flag had gone
from the Straits, many of the French traders remained, doing
business with the British merchants at Montreal. In 1784 the
Frobisher brothers joined with other Montreal men to form the
powerful North West Company, with resident agents—French
and half-breed—at Mackinac. Twelve years later, when the British flag was gone, the French were still there, cheerfully accepting a new government while they carried on the old wilderness
traffic. From Mackinac voyageurs set out for Lake Superior,
Green Bay and the Wisconsin and Mississippi Rivers. To Mackinac they returned, months later, to exchange bales of peltry for
fresh trade goods from the Montreal canoes.

The American fort overlooked a village as foreign as
Normandy. French merchants still sent their voyageurs to the
winter camps of the Indians, and French priests still said mass
for Indians and habitants in Ste. Anne's Chapel. In the log cottages were French rugs from Quebec and Ste. Anne de Beaupré
and gold-framed pictures of French convent scenes. A French
clock with a floral scroll might tick from a mantel; firelight would
show the fleur-de-lis on brass tongs and andirons. A sofa covered
with French brocade would have a folded buffalo robe at one
end and a French lace shawl at the other. Outside, along the
grass-grown harbor street, French lilacs, white and purple, sweetened the summer air. The settlement, according to one account,
contained 89 houses and stores. Most were log dwellings roofed
with bark, but some were said to be spacious and handsome.
All the houses, humble or otherwise, had fresh lime plastering
on the seaward side. It was a white village above a blue harbor.

From the fort boomed the sunset gun, and the flag came down.

French greetings passed in the twilight, a French song came from a voyageurs' campfire on the shore, a French fiddle twanged in a tavern. The hill was dark and silent under the stars.

The British had withdrawn from Mackinac Island—but not far. They had moved their garrison to St. Joseph Island, the nearest English shore, in the lower St. Mary's River. There, on the canoe route between Georgian Bay and Sault Ste. Marie, the North West Company had built a fur station in 1792 (its foundations still show in the scrub brush); now it became a military post in a rude stockade. A few tribesmen who were loyal to the British and some others who worked both sides of the straits brought their furs to St. Joseph and were there for annual handouts.

In June of 1798, a council of Chippewas was assembled at the makeshift fort, and the British gave them £1,200 in goods— about 3 cents an acre—in payment for the island. The presents included 700 blankets, 3,000 pipes, 432 knives, 4,000 gun flints, 180 hand mirrors. To celebrate the treaty, the English provided a bullock and fifty gallons of rum.

A few weeks later, in July 1798, a young officer of the Royal Engineers arrived from Quebec in the canoe of a Montreal merchant, bound for Lake Superior. George Landmann, a youth of eighteen with a fresh lieutenant's commission, had a large assignment. He was to build a wharf, a stockade, a blockhouse, a guardhouse, a powder magazine, an Indian council house, a bakehouse and a storehouse for Indian trade; for all this work he had no plans, no funds and no workmen. He found the garrison hutted up near the island shore a couple of miles from the location designated for the new fort. A log shack was allotted to him—it had neither floor nor chimney, and its single window was covered with greased paper. For a fireplace there was a stone slab under a two-foot smoke hole in the roof. Living like a Chippewa, Landmann set to work, bossing Indians, voyageurs and soldiers of the garrison. Three summers he spent on the island, returning to the St. Lawrence with the first snows. On one of his journeys he made an all-time record for canoe travel. With nine picked

voyageurs in a 25-foot canoe he made the run from St. Joseph
to Montreal in seven days and six hours.

Construction was slower. By 1800 the wharf and the stockade
were still unfinished, and there were not barracks enough to
house the troops. On a January night in 1802 fire broke out in
the bakehouse and threatened the entire fort. It was another
year before the bakehouse was rebuilt, and still longer before
the buildings were covered with clapboard to keep out rain and
snow.

To this desolate place in 1807 came John Askin, Jr., from Detroit. He had remained on the British side, and now he had
been appointed Indian translator and keeper of Indian stores
at the island post. He found St. Joseph a hungry place. "It's
an island abounding in rocks," he wrote, "and not a deer, bear,
racoon, moose, caribou or muskrat about it." The English had
taken hogs and cattle to the island, but the hogs had starved
to death, and the cattle had wasted. The Indians, Askin said,
lived entirely on fish; they made moccasins from the skins of
sturgeon and laced their snowshoes with skins of muskellunge.
During three days in November 1807, he handed out clothing
to three hundred Indians; that winter he issued rations to wrinkled old Ottawas who had known his father in better days at
Michilimackinac. "I never knew any set of poor devils," he wrote
to his father, "so wretched and miserable as the savages of
this place."

For its troops Fort St. Joseph was a Siberia. After five long
months of winter in 1809, two men deserted, hoping to make
their way to asylum at Mackinac, forty frozen miles away. Privates Myaugh and Kearey set out together, but on the second
day they separated. Myaugh gave out, and when he sank down
in the snow Kearey floundered on. The search party had no trouble following the halting tracks. Opposite Goose Island, a little
more than halfway to Mackinac, they found a dark form, like
a saw log, in the snow. It was Myaugh, frozen dead. Nine miles
farther they found Kearey. He seemed dead, but his pulse was
fluttering. They took him to an Indian shelter and then back
to St. Joseph. When spring unlocked the island both his legs

were amputated, and the fingers were gone from his hands. He never walked his post again.

That spring the regimental drummer reported to Captain Thomas Dawson a plot of mutiny: Rebellious soldiers planned to break open the King's storehouse, overrun the fort and take off in laden canoes. With the help of loyal Indians, Captain Dawson put the mutineers in irons. Some of them were kept in the guardhouse; others were isolated in remote Indian lodges. During this touchy time, a quarrel erupted between John Askin and his commander. Askin was removed from office, and then, when the Indians began to mutter, he was installed again.

For months at a time Fort St. Joseph was cut off from the world outside. Mail and newspapers came less frequently than did the rumors and reports of roving Indians. In 1807 tribesmen at the Straits were repeating the doctrines of the Shawnee Prophet, five hundred miles away. This fiery, fanatical, one-eyed brother of the war chief Tecumseh preached a return to primitivism and renunciation of the white man's trade and treaties. At St. Joseph, the Ottawas threw away their hats and coats, their mirrors and medals. All at once the trading posts were empty, and John Askin reported that a gathering of sixty Indians refused a gift of rum. It would not last long, but for a while the tribes were filled with a fervor for the old native life, an integrity they had lost to the white man's traffic. Their resistance would lead to the War of 1812.

Chanting old war songs, a band of Ottawas paddled southward toward Prophet's Town on the Wabash, where Tecumseh and the Prophet were uniting the western tribes. Meanwhile Canadian traders were arrested by the Americans at Mackinac, on suspicion of alienating Indians—"to have them ready in case war was declared by Great Britain."

From St. Joseph's in 1811 came the blanket coat that made the name "mackinaw" a household word throughout America. When winter began to howl around the fort, the quartermaster had no overcoats for the shivering troops; the last supply vessel of the season could not get through. Just two months earlier, in September of 1811, a new commander had arrived from a

long term of duty in India and Ceylon. Still dark with the tropical
sun, Captain Charles Roberts felt keenly the startling cold of
winds from Hudson Bay. From his empty warehouse he went
to the Indian storekeeper, John Askin, who had piles of Hudson
Bay blankets on his shelves. Captain Roberts wrote out a requisi-
tion, and Askin delivered the blankets. For a few weeks all the
women of St. Joseph, white and Indian, were busy cutting and
sewing blankets into short, belted coats, and by Christmas the
garrison was brightly and warmly clad.

The many-colored mackinaw coat proved ideal for active life
in the woods. Imitated by commercial tailors in years to come,
it even became the subject of a poem:

> When can its glory fade?
> Stout little coat of plaid,
> All the North wondered.
> Honor the coat they made
> Down at the old stockade,
> Still made by the hundred.

While the St. Joseph women were sewing blanket coats, the
Indians of the Wabash country were fighting American troops
in a cold November rain on the banks of Tippecanoe Creek.
With that battle—though war would not formally be declared
for seven more months—the War of 1812 began. Soon Captain
Roberts would have a new assignment for his mackinaw-clad
men. He would order them to capture Mackinac Island.

. 12 .

GUNS ON THE GREAT TURTLE

On July 8, 1812, a Montreal canoe was beached at Fort St. Joseph, and a messenger delivered a dispatch to the commandant. In his bare office, Captain Charles Roberts broke the seal and read the words of General Isaac Brock, British commander of upper Canada. War had been declared against the United States, and the commander at St. Joseph was directed to take "the most prudent means" either of offense or of defense.

Captain Roberts had a garrison of barely fifty men with an unheroic record of desertion, attempted mutiny and "unconquerable drunkenness." The Captain himself was racked with rheumatism and dyspepsia ("stomach and bowel complaint"). His fort was a rickety post on an exposed shelf or rock, with a few rusty cannon pointing at the water. It was indefensible, but Roberts was not thinking of defense. He immediately prepared to capture the fort-crowned Mackinac Island.

In the harbor at St. Joseph lay the North West Company's trading schooner *Caledonia*. Captain Roberts claimed the vessel for military duty and impressed its crew. He gathered guns and supplies from the St. Joseph traders and mustered the local voyageurs into a makeshift militia. With the help of John Askin, the fort interpreter, and John Dickson, a far-ranging trader who had married the sister of a Sioux chief, he gathered three hundred Chippewa, Menomini, Winnebago and Sioux warriors. Suddenly remote St. Joseph was a busy place—with Indians, traders and canoemen swarming around the weathered fort, quartermasters issuing blankets, guns and ammunition, soldiers piling equipment

115

on the beach, artillerymen hauling cannon to the wharf, white men and red men loading goods into bateaux and canoes.

A second dispatch came to Captain Roberts on July 12th, directing him to wait at St. Joseph for further orders. Waiting was difficult, with five hundred men eating out the commissary and the Indians chanting war songs night and day. Three days later a new dispatch freed the commander's hands: He was given authority to act on his own judgment. With that word Captain Roberts prepared to launch his expedition.

On the morning of July 16th, two iron cannon were hauled aboard the *Caledonia*. A line of men loaded powder and shot from the magazine. With a roll of drums the soldiers marched aboard. Voyageurs crowded into bateaux, and Indians pushed off their war-painted canoes. From the Caledonia's quarterdeck Captain Roberts gave the signal. Lines were cast off, and sails went up in the summer wind. With whoops and yells from the Indians, the invasion fleet got under weigh. Soon they were through the narrow Detour Passage, setting course for Mackinac Island 35 miles distant.

It had been a quiet summer on Mackinac Island. The expected trading schooners had not come up from Lake Huron, and the island had had no news of the impending war. For days at a time the fur posts were deserted. Occasionally a vessel with baled peltry from Chicago made a flurry of business in the harbor and the trading houses. Some Indian families came to claim their presents from the United States. But the long days passed with no canoe caravans whooping across the water. The British traders, already moved out of Mackinac, were diverting the traffic to St. Joseph and Sault Ste. Marie.

At Fort Mackinac, young Lieutenant Porter Hanks, who had taken command on the death of Captain Louis Howard a year before, had a garrison of 61 men. They drilled on the parade ground, cultivated the fort gardens between the harbor and the hill and gossiped with the townspeople. On their brief visits, the Indians had little to say. Their silence made Lieutenant Hanks vaguely apprehensive, even before his interpreter told him of a rumored gathering of warriors at St. Joseph. At this report, Hanks called some citizens together to discuss the safety of the island. They decided to send an observer to St. Joseph.

The most appropriate man for this mission was Captain Michael Dousman, a trader who had long associations with the Indians and the English. He could make inquiries about canoe cargoes his voyageurs should be bringing from St. Joseph; incidentally he could bring back information about military preparation there. He set out that evening, July 16th. No one on Mackinac Island knew that England and the United States were then at war.

Dousman traveled in his own canoe with his own voyageurs. They pushed off in the sunset, paddling eastward while the sky and water darkened. Behind them a few beach fires dwindled, and overhead shone Cassiopeia and the Northern Cross. It was a clear, still summer night, a good night for travel; the voyageurs would have their *patron* at St. Joseph soon after sunrise. According to one report, Michael Dousman had stretched out in sleep when the startled paddlers saw dark shapes and glimmering lights ahead. Dousman awoke to a chorus of shouting voices. He made out shadowy figures in small craft around him, and then he saw the looming sails of a schooner. In midnight darkness, on vast Lake Huron, he had blundered into the path of the British expedition.

Hauled aboard the schooner *Caledonia,* Dousman soon found himself facing Captain Roberts, who told him that England and the United States were at war and demanded information about the defenses of Mackinac Island. Though a prisoner, Michael Dousman was among friends and comrades—for years he had known John Askin and Robert Dickson and other English partisans. He talked freely of the weakness of the island garrison. He told of the Americans' ignorance of the war and their uneasiness about the Indians. While the invasion fleet moved on toward the island, Captain Roberts offered Dousman a parole (word of honor was binding in the eighteenth century) if he would promise not to alert the garrison. In a humanitarian concern for the safety of the island people, Roberts sent him ashore to warn the townsmen of the danger of Indian massacre: Once fighting began it would be impossible to hold three hundred warriors in check.

Somewhere off the north shore of the island, Dousman was put off in his canoe. Soon he was going from house to house in the village sending the citizens to his distillery at the western end of the settlement. Within its stone walls, they could be safe from berserk savages.

Meanwhile the British force was landing on a sandy beach on the island's northwest shore, two miles behind the fort, which faced the harbor. From the sea, Fort Mackinac was a Gibraltar, but it was mortally vulnerable from the rear. Behind the ramparts rose a wooded height (the side of later Fort Holmes), which commanded Fort Mackinac as that fort commanded the crescent harbor. To occupy this central height was Captain Roberts's objective.

It was three hours after midnight when the troops went ashore at British Landing. While artillerymen hauled their cannon over a faint Indian trail, the army toiled through tangled thickets. Two hours remained before sunrise. Through a dense black forest moved the grunting, muttering, cursing invaders. It was slow progress, groping through dark woods, climbing sudden ridges, staggering under loads of powder and ammunition, hauling at carts and cannon. Beyond the first rim of hills, the land leveled off in open fields and pastures, but another height loomed against the stars. The creak of ropes, the clank of iron wheels, the thud of axes chopping out a path for the wheeled artillery—it could not be a stealthy advance. But the sleepy sentry at Fort Mackinac was well out of hearing, and the fort guns were pointed at the harbor. When the sky began to pale, the British held the heights.

Through the fort, before the bugler's reveille, went a stir of agitation. The army surgeon, who lived in a cottage under the hill, had been aroused by the flight of the villagers at Michael Dousman's warning. When he learned of the British landing, he hurried up the fort road and was passed by the sentry through the sally port. Pounding on the door of Lieutenant Hanks, he told the sleepy commander that the British were at hand. Suddenly wide awake, Hanks sent an officer to reconnoiter the village. When he returned with word that the citizens had fled to Dousman's brewery, Hanks mustered his men. He stocked the blockhouses with ammunition, charged his field pieces and waited. Gray dawn brightened to radiant summer daylight, with gulls circling over two quiet schooners in the bay. From the southwestern blockhouses Hanks looked down upon a deserted village—not a curl of breakfast smoke from the chimneys, no movement in the grassy streets. But there was movement elsewhere. On the northern ridge, Indians and soldiers swarmed through the woods, and through his telescope Lieutenant Hanks looked into the mouth of a sixpounder planted on the island's highest point. Out of the woods came a white flag of truce. At the north gate of the fort, an officer met the British messenger. Moments later Hanks was reading Captain Roberts's demand for the surrender of the fort and island to His Britannic Majesty's forces.

With four men in the sick bay, Hanks had 57 effective troops and officers. Against him on higher ground were ten times that many British soldiers, militiamen and Indian warriors, with cannon trained upon the least defensible walls of Fort Mackinac. At the time Hanks believed he was even more outnumbered; three American prisoners with the British messenger told him that the invading force totaled a thousand white and Indian fighting men, that they had two pieces of artillery and carried ropes and ladders for scaling the fort walls. Commander Hanks was urged to surrender peaceably in order to prevent a slaughter of American troops and possibly of the island citizens as well. He was given thirty minutes to send his answer.

The stunned commander, who until that moment had not known that England and the United States were at war, held a consultation with his officers. There was no alternative. Under the white flag, Hanks marched with the messengers to Captain Roberts's command post on the hill.

From the "heights above Michilimackinac," where reconstructed Fort Holmes now crowns the wooded crest, Captain Roberts wrote out terms of surrender:

I. The Fort at Michilimackinac shall immediately be surrendered to the British forces.

II. The garrison shall march out with the honors of war, lay
down their arms, and become prisoners of war, and shall be
sent to the United States of America by His Britannic Majesty,
not to serve in this war until regularly exchanged; and for the
due performance of this article the officers pledge their word
and honor.

III. All the merchant vessels in the harbor, with their cargoes,
shall be in possession of their respective owners.

IV. Private property shall be held sacred as far as in my
power.

V. All citizens of the United States of America who shall
not take the oath of allegiance to His Britannic Majesty shall
depart with their property from this Island in one month from
the date hereof.

After each of these articles, Lieutenant Hanks wrote a curt
"Granted."

From this heavy errand, Hanks returned to Fort Mackinac,
but he did not see the lovely world of woods and waters under
the blue summer sky. At the fort he lined up his men, lowered
the flag and marched out the garrison. To a beat of drums, the
British regulars marched in. Three hundred savages whooped
and yelled while the British colors ran up the flagpole. Down
the hill and over the beach streamed shooting, shouting Indians;
they brandished war clubs in the air and hacked the sunlight
with their hatchets. From the hill came the boom of artillery
as British gunners emptied the American field pieces—cannon
that had been captured from the British at Yorktown in the final
battle of the Revolution.

Amid the frenzied Indians moved watchful John Askin. He
must have been bone-tired after the night voyage, the advance
through black wilderness and the restless waiting on the ridge.
Through it all he had stayed among the tribesmen, talking to
the chiefs in Chippewa and Ottawa, holding the warriors in
check. Now the lid was off, but thanks to John Askin the danger
was past. In a harmless frenzy the warriors whooped along the
beach and fired over the harbor. No life was lost in the capture

of the island. The Indians had not looted shops or houses, John Askin noted with gratitude and wonder, "nor even killed a fowl belonging to any person (a thing never known before) for they generally destroy everything they meet with."

Equally surprised and grateful was Captain Roberts. That night in his new quarters in Fort Mackinac he wrote:

> It is a circumstance without precedent and demands the greatest praise for all who conducted the Indians, that though these people's minds were much heated . . . not one drop either of man's or animal's blood was spilled, till I gave an order for a certain number of bullocks to be purchased for them.

That night the tribesmen feasted on the shore.

The British had captured an island three miles long and two miles wide and a frowning fort, with its artillery, powder and ammunition and commissary stores, including 357 gallons of wine and 253 gallons of whiskey. They also took possession of the government trading house and its stock of goods. While they were counting this plunder, two schooners came through the strait and dropped anchor in the island harbor. The *Mary* and the *Selina,* with cargoes of furs from Chicago, were promptly seized by the British. A week later, under the British flag, they sailed to Detroit with American troops and a few citizens of the island. Some of the American troops, like most of the civilian population, shifted allegiance to the victors and remained at Mackinac. Their lives were little changed by the new flag against the sky.

Much of the American loot was passed out to Captain Roberts's Indian allies. Other warriors came across the water, including a force recruited by British traders on Lake Superior; they arrived too late to join the fight but not too late to claim the plunder. With 1,500 tribesmen milling through the village and along the shore, the presents were soon exhausted, and supplies ran low. Captain Roberts tried to send an Indian army south to join the British campaign on the Maumee, but the savages—"drunk as ten thousand devils," John Askin reported—were in no hurry to leave lively Mackinac. Eventually some did set out for Detroit,

while others drifted away to their homes on Lake Michigan and
Lake Superior.

Meanwhile word of the fall of Mackinac to the British went
through all the tribal camps. Once a magic place, the island
had a mythical meaning for Indians who had never seen it. Its
possession by the English swayed minds and feelings throughout
the western country. Following his evacuation of Detroit, General Hull wrote:

> After the surrender of Michilimackinac, almost every tribe and
> nation of Indians, excepting a part of the Miamis and Delawares,
> north from beyond Lake Superior, west from beyond the Missis-
> sippi, south from the Ohio and Wabash, and east from every
> part of Upper Canada and from all the intermediate country,
> joined in open hostility, under the British standard, against the
> army I commanded . . . . The surrender of Michilimackinac
> opened the northern hive of Indians, and they were swarming
> down in every direction.

The next blow fell at the southern end of Lake Michigan,
where a growing band of Potawatomis was camped around the
fort at the Chicago river mouth. Summer was radiant over the
lake and the prairie, but gloom had come to Fort Dearborn.
At news of the fall of Mackinac Island, General Hull had sent
a messenger from Detroit ordering the Dearborn garrison to re-
tire to Fort Wayne. On the morning of August 15th, Captain
Heald dumped his spare ammunition into the Chicago River,
loaded his wagons and marched out his 64 troops, accompanied
by 27 women and children. It was a hot, clear summer day.
The fugitives started east along the lake shore—garrison troops
pacing beside the baggage wagons, then the walking women
and children, followed by a dozen civilian militia. The prairie
seemed as empty as the lake until a row of feathered heads
appeared over a ridge of sand hills. From the dunes came the
bang of rifle fire, and whooping Indians charged the caravan.
The massacre was swift and violent. In twenty minutes fifty of
Heald's company lay dead; the rest were captives. Next day the
Indians sacked and burned the fort; when the prairie sun went
down, there was only a smoking ruin beside the Chicago River.

The third blow fell at Detroit. After the fall of Mackinac, Hull feared that the British would attack down Lake Huron. While he watched and waited, they moved troops from Niagara to Fort Malden at the western end of Lake Erie. On August 15th, while the Potawatomis were slaughtering the Dearborn garrison, the British began shelling Detroit from across the river. That night several hundred Indians, led by Tecumseh in a British general's uniform, crossed the Detroit River and marched toward the American fort. Confused by this threat, still fearing another force from the north and worried over his short supplies of food and material, Hull surrendered Detroit and all of Michigan Territory. With British consent and encouragement, bands of Potawatomis, Shawnees and Ottawas made camps along the river below Detroit. From these bases, they preyed on American farms and settlements. A band of warriors was reported surrounding the post of Fort Wayne. By the end of the summer of 1812, the entire northwestern frontier seemed to be in British hands.

The long winter passed at Mackinac Island, and the spring of 1813 gave way to summer. A band of Wisconsin tribesmen came briefly and noisily to the island on their way to war in northern Ohio. At Fort Mackinac Captain Roberts, exhausted by illness, was replaced by Captain Richard Bullock, who ruled his sullen men with rigid routine. The island maple groves were turning gold when, on October 3rd, a message came from the British commander at Detroit. It was stunning news. On the cloudless morning of September 10th, an American squadron had sailed out of Put-in-Bay to engage the British fleet on Lake Erie. Commodore Oliver Hazard Perry had nine vessels mounting 55 guns; the British had six ships of superior tonnage and fire power. For two hours the cannon flashed and thundered. When the smoke blew off and the guns fell silent, the Americans were masters of the Lakes.

While the English officers at Fort Mackinac were pondering that report, another battle was taking shape. Perry's warships had landed American troops on the Detroit River, while the British and Indians retreated into Canada. The army of General

William Henry Harrison overtook them on the brushy banks of
the Thames River. In a frenzied twenty-minute battle, the Americans cut the British to pieces. Among the dead was Tecumseh,
the Falling Star of the Shawnee. Six hundred British troops were
captured. After this victory, Harrison marched his army back
to Detroit and again embarked them upon Perry's ships. He
headed north, toward Fort Mackinac, but the fleet grounded
on shallows in the St. Clair River. With winter approaching,
the northern campaign was called off.

At Mackinac the English looked at the blue water of Lake
Huron—enemy water now, by which attack would come. But
in mid-October a British ship arrived, the last English vessel
to come over Lake Huron. The schooner *Nancy* of the North
West Company had slipped through the St. Clair flats just ahead
of the pursuing Americans. When they unloaded the schooner,
the islanders knew there would be no more supplies from the
south. The waters lay blue under the arching sky, but Mackinac
Island was besieged. John Askin wrote gravely, "We will be
obliged to eat every horse that is on the island before spring
if we are not taken prisoners this autumn."

It was a hungry winter at Mackinac. When meat gave out
after Christmas, the rations were fish and cornmeal. Captain Bullock strenghtened the palisade and deepened the fort well. On
the wooded heights behind the fort, his men, augmented by
forced labor from the village, felled logs, hewed timbers and
built Fort George, a rugged blockhouse that commanded all the
island. When spring opened the waterways, the British officers
scanned the horizon of Lake Huron with hope and fear. They
hoped for reinforcements from upper Canada by way of Georgian
Bay; they feared an American expedition from Detroit.

British officials on the St. Lawrence knew what was at stake.
Possession of Mackinac meant control of the northern Indians
and of the whole northwestern fur trade. On southern Georgian
Bay at the mouth of the Nottawasaga River, boatmen were building cannon-mounted bateaux, supplies were stockpiled on the
wharf and Canadian troops were gathered. In the last days of
April this relief fleet sailed past the Georgian Bay islands,

through the dramatic spring sunsets and into the north. It reached Mackinac Island in mid-May, and the commander of the fleet, Lieutenant-Colonel Robert McDouall, took command of the fort. To McDouall's mingled gratification and worry, hundreds of Indians came to the island; they strengthened his forces, but they ate up his supplies. He urged the warriors to a pitch of anti-American fervor and waited for the Americans to come.

It was a summer of waiting. At the end of June two voyageurs arrived from the west; they reported that American troops had advanced up the Mississippi River and were building a fort at Prairie du Chien. Mackinac was outflanked, and the Indians began to waver. To meet this threat, Captain McDouall sent an expedition of Indians and volunteers, equipped with a small cannon, to the Mississippi. They set off on June 28th. Four weeks later came word that they had recaptured Prairie du Chien. Almost at the same time British lookouts sighted an invasion fleet approaching Mackinac Island.

The American fleet appeared on July 26th, and when the sun went down that evening the island village was deserted; soldiers, civilians and Indians were gathered in the fort, under protection of the British cannon. The American ships crept into the Round Island passage, just east of Mackinac Island, but artillery fire from the fort drove them back toward Bois Blanc. From their lookouts, British sentries watched a party of Americans landing on the lower shore of Round Island, where they began clearing a place to mount a cannon. When the British sent Indian warriors across the passage, the Americans withdrew, pulling back to their ships off Bois Blanc. One American did not get off in time. He was taken prisoner and brought back with whoops of triumph to Mackinac Island, where British officers rescued him from the excited savages. From him they learned that the American expedition was in command of 22-year-old Lieutenant Colonel George Croghan, a nephew of George Rogers Clark and a hero of the Ohio campaign against the British.

Next day two American warships hurled shells at the island, but their guns could not tilt upward toward the fort; the shells fell harmless in the gardens. Fort Mackinac, as its builders had intended, was impregnable from the sea. After that threat, the American ships pulled back into a cover of thickening mist.

Fog shrouded the straits for an unbroken week. When the sky cleared, the American ships moved in to an anchorage off the west side of the island, where the British had landed two years before. There, two miles behind the fort, the abrupt shore cliffs gave way to a wooded slope that offered access to the upper tableland of the island. It was the obvious beachhead.

The Americans made their landing, after blasting the shore with a heavy cannonade. Once on the island, they fought their way through dense woods full of shadowy Indians. They advanced slowly over the rise of ground to a plain of level farmland. That open place (now the tranquil fairways of the Wawashkamo Golf Course, with meadowlarks singing in the sun and a restless cloud of sea gulls over the island refuse fill) became the battlefield of August 4, 1814. The British were waiting, with artillery in the center of an arc of riflemen, when the American invaders crossed the cleared ground. In the first wave of fire, Major Andrew Hunter Holmes was killed. For a few minutes the guns volleyed and thundered, and whoops of Indians shrilled from the encircling woods. At the head of their American regiments, Captain Van Horne and Lieutenant Jackson fell mortally wounded, and Captain Desha was disabled.

Through the smoke of battle, young Colonel Croghan stared into the face of defeat. He pulled back his men, covering the retreat with rifle fire. They streamed through tangled woods, down the gashed and trampled hill and onto the landing beach. As bullets whistled around them, they climbed aboard the ships.

The next day the flagship *Lawrence* sailed into Mackinac harbor flying a white flag of truce. American officers came ashore to claim the body of Major Holmes. It was found where he had fallen; during the brief battle his Negro servant had covered it with brush and leaves. Years later people said that Holmes's body had been laid in a log dugout and towed behind a warship all the way to Detroit, where it was buried.

In a sheltered bay off Bois Blanc Island, the Americans transferred their wounded to the ships *Lawrence* and *Caledonia*, which sailed for Detroit. The rest of the expedition voyaged to Georgian Bay to cut off British supplies to Mackinac Island. At their approach, the British tried to hide their sloop *Nancy*, freshly loaded for a run to the north. The vessel was towed up the winding, hill-framed Nottawasaga River where a blockhouse could protect her. But an American landing party saw the masts of the vessel over a bare ridge, and American ships came up the river with cannon booming. Rather than surrender this prize, the British set fire to both the sloop and the blockhouse. The charred *Nancy* sank in the river, where its hull eventually formed a shoal and then an island. Now the island is parked and landscaped, and the hull of the *Nancy*, dug up in 1927, is visited each year by thousands of summer tourists.

With the *Nancy* out of commission, Colonel Croghan sailed back to Detroit in the *Niagara*, leaving two small schooners, *Scorpion* and *Tigress*, to block the supply route between Georgian Bay and Mackinac Island. When the patrol vessels sailed north to St. Joseph, for an inspection there, a young English officer named Miller Worsley slipped out of Nottawasaga Bay with twenty men in a deep-laden canoe. They reached Mackinac at the end of August. It was a hungry place, faced with starvation. In this crisis Lieutenant Worsley determined to attack the blockade vessels, which were lying off St. Joseph. With troops in four bateaux and a swarm of two hundred Indians in canoes, he traveled by night to Point Detour, where he found one of the American ships at anchor in Detour Passage. Worsley somehow kept his own mosquito fleet in hiding. The next night, September 3rd, the British craft crept up on the American vessel. In darkness, with muffled oars and paddles, they were alongside when the lookout saw them. The invaders swarmed aboard while the alarm was sounded.

The *Tigress* was now in British hands, but Worsley kept the American flag above her quarterdeck while the American crew was transferred to Worsley's bateaux and taken as prisoners to Mackinac Island. Two nights later the unsuspecting *Scorpion* appeared; it dropped anchor in Detour Passage. Next morning the *Scorpion* came alongside her sister ship. At close range, with

the two vessels within hailing distance, Worsley fired his cannon
and sent boarding parties across the intervening water. Within
a few stunning minutes, the *Scorpion* was captured.

Both vessels were sailed to Mackinac, where the *Tigress* was
gleefully renamed *Surprise,* and the *Scorpion* became *H.M.S.
Confiance.* Now Lake Huron was an English sea. The two captured vessels sailed to Georgian Bay and returned with supplies
for the island winter. Britain still held the northern straits when
the Treaty of Ghent brought an end to the war on the day before
Christmas, 1814.

The Treaty, thanks to the skill and persistence of the American
negotiators John Quincy Adams, Henry Clay and Albert Gallatin,
called for restoration of the original international boundaries.
Mackinac Island would become American, as it had been in 1812.
That word did not reach the Straits until the ice went out. On
May 15, 1815, dispatches were delivered to Fort Mackinac, and
Colonel McDouall read them with disbelief. After the British
had held it throughout the war, he was ordered to evacuate
"this most important island, this key to the whole western country." To the British captain at soon-to-be-surrendered Prairie du
Chien he wrote: "Our negotiators, as usual, have been
egregiously duped. As usual they have shown themselves pro-
foundly ignorant of the concerns of this part of the empire. I
am penetrated with grief by the restoration of this fine island—'a
fortress built by nature for herself.' "

On the 18th of July, 1815, American troops arrived under command of Colonel Anthony Butler. The British withdrew to Drummond Island, just across Detour Passage, where they hoped to
retain some control of the Indians and the fur trade. Drummon
Island was nearer to Mackinac than was their former post of
St. Joseph; in the boundary survey of 1822 it proved to be American territory, and Fort Drummond, in its turn, had to be abandoned. Meanwhile Mackinac Island had become the capital of
a famous American fur trade.

PART THREE: THE AMERICANS

The post is strong both by nature and art, and the possession of it has great influence with the Indians in favor of the United States.

U. S. ARMY INSPECTOR

FURS AND FORTUNES

In the summer of 1784, a young German immigrant in New York began working for Robert Bowne, a Quaker fur dealer. For $2 a week he pounded bugs and moths out of dusty peltry. The next year he was sent on a trading trip to the Iroquois country. When he came back down the Hudson with a boatload of skins, his pleased employer gave him a silver watch with an inscription: "Presented to John Jacob Astor by R. Bowne, 1785."

At Albany young Astor had met Alexander Henry, who had prospered in the fur trade. Soon the German youth began trading on his own. He had already tried selling flutes and peddling bakery goods, but the fur business looked brighter.

In the spring of 1788, he went by boat, horseback, canoe and wagon to Montreal, where he inquired the way to the home of Alexander Henry. The old trader told his young friend about the endless wilds of the northwest, with beaver ponds on every stream and in the great woods deer, bear, fox, wolf, martin, ermine, otter, mink and muskrat beyond counting. The upper country was still the richest fur domain in the world—and in years ahead it would make John Jacob Astor the richest man in America.

Young Astor wanted to see the British posts, to study their commerce, to watch their dealings with the Indians. The United States had annexed that country, but the trade was still in English hands. During the Revolution, the British merchants had worked together to keep control of the fur business. They formed loose partnerships, then mergers, and in 1784 they banded together in the famous North West Company. With this powerful organization, combining wealth and political influence, they held on to the trade at the strategic stations.

In 1788 an American merchant was not welcome in interior Canada, and Astor could not have made his journey without the help of Alexander Henry. The old trader, remembering his youthful venture into the northwest, saw Astor as a footloose young man who could be no threat to the entrenched and experienced British traders. He got Astor a place in a canoe bound up the Ottawa in the first brigade of the season.

It was a big canoe, forty feet long, of cedar ribbing sheathed with birchbark and calked with pine resin, and loaded with four thousand pounds of trade goods tied in hundred-pound packs for carrying over the portages—where the canoe would be borne on the shoulders of ten men. On that spring morning it was all new and exciting to the blond German youth—"yah . . . yah," he told himself—who stored every detail in his tenacious memory.

After their confession and prayer, after the last rollicking and revelry, the voyageurs took their places. At the bow a foreman watched the current and the channel; a steersman in the stern barked commands to the paddlers. Up the river they went with drunken shouts and cries. Soon they left the last outlying habitation and forgot the roistering of Montreal. With wilderness around them, they settled into the routine of paddling, portage, a pipe in slack water and then the thrust against the swift current. From dawn till dusk they toiled, hardened, half-savage men singing an old Norman ballad of a walk through the meadows on a Sunday in May:

> Behind our house there is a pond
> > Fal lal de ra
> There came three ducks to swim thereon
> All along the river clear
> Lightly, my shepherdess dear,
> > Lightly, fal de ra.

Already Astor was learning his first lesson: The whole rich fur trade was carried on the shoulders of cheerful and penniless voyageurs. Years later, when Astor persuaded the United States

Congress to outlaw foreign traders on American territory, he made sure that American merchants could employ Canadian boatmen.

Up the Ottawa, over the portages to French River, down that stream with songs and banter, they made the classic journey to Georgian Bay and through North Bay to Detour Passage. There the brigade divided, one caravan heading north to Sault Ste. Marie and to Grand Portage and Fort William on the far shore of Lake Superior, the other paddling west to Mackinac Island. If Astor went with the Mackinac brigade, he saw canoes arriving from the Illinois River, the Wisconsin and the upper Mississippi, and he watched Indians of many nations bartering furs for British merchandise. He could not have failed to see how liquor drew the Indian trade. Though Canadian law forbade that traffic, every cargo included rum and whiskey. On the American territory of Mackinac Island, the Montreal traders were beyond legal restraint.

Actually it is not known that John Jacob Astor ever set foot on Mackinac Island, though there is a story that his watch was found there long after both his life and the fur trade had ended. In the summer of 1887, a writer for *The New York Evening Post* visited Mackinac Island during a tour of the Lakes. In the John Jacob Astor House, a hotel made from the old fur-company buildings, he became acquainted with a talkative young desk clerk named John Bogan. According to his newspaper story, printed August 11, 1887, the reporter was shown a battered silver watch inscribed "Presented to John Jacob Astor by R. Bowne, 1785." It had been found three years earlier, said Bogan, by a workman who was digging near one of the fur company buildings. This story would seem proof enough that Astor had gone to Mackinac Island during that journey of 1788 and had somehow lost his watch there. Yet the watch has never appeared since the New York reporter described it, and none of Bogan's family ever knew of its existence. John Bogan had a reputation for loose talk. Perhaps the young desk clerk enjoyed baiting the New York journalist—but how could he have shown the reporter a watch with that inscription? The vanished watch is the only evidence that Astor visited Mackinac Island, though his nephew George Astor came there in 1814 to get a cargo of furs released from the restrictions of war.

Back in that season of 1788, the young German merchant did visit British fur posts. He voyaged up the St. Mary's River and over Lake Superior, and he learned some lasting lessons about the fur business. At the end of the summer, in a canoe loaded with peltry, he returned to Montreal. A month later a New York newspaper advertised that "J. Jacob Astor . . . gives cash for all kinds of Canada furs, such as beaver, beaver coating, raccoon skins, racoon blankets and spring muskrat skins; which he sells by large or small quantities." The quantities would grow larger and larger, and they would be not Canada furs but American furs when his great company spread across the continent.

In 1808 John Jacob Astor organized the American Fur Company to compete with the British merchants. In a dramatic venture, he sent two expeditions to Oregon, one by land and one by sea, and built the station of Astoria at the mouth of the Columbia River. His name had crossed the continent, but the War of 1812 halted the fur trade. When peace returned, he was ready to wrest the Great Lakes fur commerce from the British companies.

In 1816 the United States Congress passed a law providing that "licenses to trade with the Indians . . . shall not be granted to any but citizens of the United States" and making goods taken into American territory by foreign traders subject to confiscation. On this American monopoly, Astor launched his Great Lakes enterprise. With Mackinac Island as his northern capital, he sent traders to Indian tribes as far west as the upper Missouri. To his warehouses under the guns of Fort Mackinac came hundreds of clerks and voyageurs from Montreal, Albany and Niagara. Bateaux loaded with Indian goods made the journey, by way of the Niagara portage, up Lake Erie and Lake Huron to Mackinac harbor. At the Mackinac headquarters, Astor's agents hired the veteran traders and voyageurs and sent them into the wilderness; brigades of five to twenty bateaux went into the hinterlands to establish trading posts near the winter camps of the Indians. By 1820 seven-eighths of the traders in all the country from the Wabash and Illinois Rivers to the Canadian boundary had been gathered into the Astor organization. The remaining traders, trying to be independent, found the shrewd Astor men undercutting their prices and diverting their business. "It was the policy of the American Fur Company" wrote Gurdon Hubbard, "to monopolize the entire fur trade of the Northwest." After a few seasons, there were no independent traders left.

On Market Street in the Mackinac Island village stood the fur warehouse, three floors of storage space with a pulley at the peak of the roof for hauling peltry to the upper levels. Beside it stood the spacious Agency House, the home of resident managers Ramsay Crooks and Robert Stuart, with offices where the endless cargoes were recorded. A third building housed scores of clerks who exchanged weapons, blankets, clothing and frontier finery for the Indians' raw peltry. A block away in the waterfront taverns were men who knew every path and stream and portage and every Indian leader in all the country between the mouth of the Wabash and the headwaters of the Minnesota and the Mississippi.

One of Astor's wilderness traders, still remembered on Mackinac Island, was a half-breed woman, the daughter of a French fur trader and the granddaughter of the Ottawa chief Kewinaquat. For years she traveled with her trader husband, Joseph Laframboise, taking her children on long winter journeys to the Indian camps. After the War of 1812, her daughter Josette became the wife of the American commander of Fort Makinac. Though she always wore Indian costume, Mme. Laframboise spoke English, French, Chippewa and Ottawa with equal ease. She became a trader when her husband was killed by a surly Indian.

Joseph Laframboise was one of the French traders who brought fur cargoes to Mackinac Island while the flag of England, and then the flag of the United States, flew over the fort. Politics meant little to him, but religion meant much. A-

devout man he observed the Angelus on land or lake, in civilization or wilderness. At Mackinac, when church bells rang at six
in the morning, at noon and at six in the evening, he turned
from worldly tasks to prayer. In the wilds he kept the same
ritual, on the trail or in a canoe; timed by his silver watch, he
crossed himself, bowed his head and repeated the Annunciation
prayer.

At the end of the summer of 1809, Laframboise, with his wife
and children, left the gossip and bustle of Mackinac Island for
the solitude of the Michigan woods; his plan was to winter with
the Indians at the headwaters of the Grand River. With two
mackinaw boats full of trade goods and twelve boatmen, they
coasted the eastern shore of Lake Michigan. While camping at
the mouth of the Muskegon River, they had some Winnebago
visitors who asked for whiskey. Laframboise turned them away.
That night, while he knelt at prayer in his tent, the trader was
shot by a disgruntled savage.

Magdalene Laframboise voyaged on to Grand River, where
she buried her husband's body. She spent the winter trading
with the Grand River Indians and returned to Mackinac with
a cargo of prime peltry. Taking out her own license as a trader
for the American Fur Company, she returned to the Grand River
country in the fall of 1810. There the Indians brought her a
Winnebago captive, the man who had shot her husband. Mme.
Laframboise spared his life, leaving him to the Great Spirit.

Twelve winters Mme. Laframboise spent in the Indian camps,
directing her crew of voyageurs and *engagés*, and each summer
she returned to her pleasant home on Mackinac Island. There
she had the respect of the army officers and the company agents
and the trust of visiting tribesmen.

In 1816 the commander of Fort Mackinac was Captain Benjamin K. Pierce, who had left Dartmouth College during the War
of 1812 for an army career; his younger brother would become
President of the United States. At island social gatherings, he
met small, dark-eyed Josette Laframboise, who had been
educated in Montreal. A year later they were married amid the
gold braid and satins of the officers and their ladies; the bride's

mother wore a tunic of deerskin edged with colored beads and porcupine quills. That fall, when Mme. Laframboise set off on the winter's trading voyage, her daughter waved from the commandant's house on the hill.

On a cloudless June day in 1819, the bored fort sentry saw a feather of smoke on the horizon. Word went through the post—smoke on Lake Huron. Through his telescope, Captain Pierce watched the approach of the first steamship on the upper Lakes. For a year the tall-stacked *Walk-in-the-Water* had been bustling between Buffalo and Detroit; now she was making her first voyage to the north. When the bugle shrilled, the troops fell into line. They marched down the steep path, every eye on the Round Island channel. A boom came from the steamer's signal cannon and was answered by artillery on the hill. Around the point came the *Walk-in-the-Water*, sails slatting as the paddle wheels kept turning. As she crept into dock, her pennants caught the sun, and the paint work on her taffrail gleamed white, green and gold. With a rattle of drums, the troops drew up in double column while Indians lined the water.

Aboard the steamer was Major General Jacob Brown, Commander of the Northern Department, United States Army, making his first inspection tour of garrisons on the upper Lakes. Escorted by Captain Pierce and his Officers, the General marched up the hill. For a few days, life was festive at the fort. There were dress parades, dinners and toasts, a military ball with dark-eyed Josette Laframboise Pierce bowing and circling with the General. All the villagers welcomed the steamship people, and in return Captain Job Fish took them on an excursion through the straits—army officers and fur merchants, red-sashed voyageurs and feathered Indians. They were less interested in the familiar straits than in the pulsing engine, the churning paddle wheels and the double row of below-deck cabins. As she steamed through the sunset, the vessel buzzed with French and English, Chippewa and Ottawa.

After that lively week, the *Walk-in-the-Water*, freshly fueled with Bois Blanc cordwood, headed back to Detroit. Cannon boomed from the hill, and the island people watched till the last faint smoke had vanished in the sky. Then the horizon was empty, but Mackinac Island had a new link with the world.

In May of 1820 the busiest place in Detroit was the river landing in front of the old French farmhouse, scarred with bullets from Pontiac's warriors, where Governor Lewis Cass administered the affairs of Michigan Territory. Three big canoes lay there—*maître canots,* 36 feet long and 7 feet across, fitted with mast and sail. Into them went all kinds of goods and gear, Indian presents, scientific instruments and military supplies for an expedition to the Straits of Mackinac, Lake Superior and the headwaters of the Mississippi River. In 1820 Michigan Territory was a huge, wild land, and Detroit was the jumping-off place for the interior wilderness.

On May 24th the canoes were loaded. Ten Canadian boatmen and ten Indian guides and hunters (at 60 cents a day) paddled up the river. Twenty soldiers and scientists (including a young geologist named Schoolcraft) followed in carriages, accompanied by half the people of Detroit, past Windmill Point to Lake St. Clair. At the Grosse Pointe landing they embarked. To the shouts of the villagers, they pushed into Lake St. Clair—"as if a new world was about to be discovered."

After that fine send-off, a gale blew up, and the craft were forced ashore. Two days later they were under way again, through the St. Clair Flats, past Fort Gratiot and into vast Lake Huron. Paddling from dawn till starlight, they made seventy miles a day, until stormy weather halted them on the shore of Thunder Bay. On June 6th, the men beached the canoes on Mackinac Island, and the burly Governor splashed ashore. Awaiting him were Captain Pierce and an escort of troops from the garrison. For eight days the members of the Cass party were guests at Fort Mackinac.

John Jacob Astor was in Europe that summer, but the fur trade was breaking records. Mounds of peltry awaited sorting and grading in the warehouse. Indians and traders thronged the harbor taverns; in the stores men talked of La Pointe, Rainy Lake, the Butte des Morts, Bad Axe River, Mille Lacs, Prairie du Chien and Traverse des Sioux. A morning light bathed the white fort and the green island; the future was there like a presence. At no other time in its long history was Mackinac Island so full of portent. Governor Cass had a wilderness empire to explore; he would leave his name on a lake in the Minnesota wilderness near Itasca Lake, which Henry Rowe Schoolcraft would locate as the true source of the Mississippi. At Fort Mackinac as second-in-command was Lieutenant John C. Pemberton; 43 years later he would surrender Vicksburg to General U. S. Grant. In charge of the garrison hospital was young Doctor Beaumont, whose name would become known abroad when he studied the open stomach of a wounded voyageur. Mingling with the soldiers and the Indians were two young company clerks with fame and fortune ahead of them: Long-striding Gurdon Hubbard would dig the first spade of earth for the Illinois and Michigan Canal and would help to nominate Abraham Lincoln for the presidency, and John H. Kinzie would become the second Mayor of Chicago—and his wife Juliette would dedicate her classic autobiography, *Wau-Bun,* to the Hon. Lewis Cass.

Nearly a century later, when these names had become history, the Cass expedition was celebrated on Mackinac Island. On August 28, 1915, a bronze tablet was unveiled on Cass Cliff, just beyond the eastern bastion of the fort. That morning flags lined the habor street, and a procession formed at the foot of Turkey Hill. The Indians were gone, the fort was empty, the lilac trees were a hundred years older and, in place of the old garrison gardens, a green park fronted the crescent harbor. But the fort stood white against the tall blue sky, as in times past, and the parade moved up the hill as it had done when Cass and Schoolcraft arrived in 1820. With marching music came a platoon of sailors from the revenue cutter *Morrill,* followed by a company of the 9th National Guard and a line of carriages. Up Fort Street to Huron Road the procession passed to the old *portiers* of Fort Mackinac. There, with lengthy oratory, the memorial was dedicated to "Lewis Cass, Teacher, Lawyer, Explorer, Soldier, Diplomat, Statesman."

In all that eloquence, no one recalled that burley Lewis Cass was "Os-kotchee"—"Big Belly"—to the Indians; his house at

Detroit was filled with Indian portraits, snowshoes, canoe paddles, ceremonial pipes, war belts, spears, quivers of feathered
arrows. At Mackinac in 1820, Big Belly distributed tobacco,
beans, crackers and molasses. He feasted with tribesmen on the
shore and talked till the moon went down. Then he voyaged
on to plant the United States flag at Sault Ste. Marie. From
the Mackinac garrison, he took an officer and 22 troops to
strengthen his escort. Big Belly could smoke the feathered
calumet, and he could unsheathe the sword blade. He had
shrewd instincts; he seemed to know when force would be
needed.

At Sault Ste. Marie, he found the Chippewas surly and hostile.
Chief Sassaba, insolently wearing the scarlet coat that the British
had given him, kicked away the presents Cass had brought; in
front of his own wigwam, warriors raised a British flag. While
his men stood armed at the riverside, Cass strode into the Indian
camp. He pulled down the British colors, declaring that no foreign flag could fly on the soil of America. Through his interpreter,
he reminded the Chippewas that they had granted this tract
of land at the Treaty of Greene Ville. For a day and a night
there was tension beside the roaring Sault rapids. Then the Indians came over to the Governor, acknowledging the American
claim to a tract of sixteen square miles on the St. Mary's. (Two
years later Fort Brady would be planted there, and Henry Rowe
Schoolcraft would begin his term as Indian agent.) With this
agreement, the Indians opened their hands for American
presents—though Sassaba remained an America-hater until he
drowned in the rapids, after a drinking spree, in 1822. The Mackinac soldiers returned down the river, and Big Belly's expedition
went on to Lake Superior. Eventually they paddled down the
Mississippi, crossed northern Illinois on horseback and traveled
from Fort Dearborn to Detroit by the Old Sauk Trail, which
is now U.S. Highway 112. The expedition opened the way to
development of the huge and mysterious upper country.

In the summer of 1799, Father Gabriel Richard went up to
Mackinac Island from Detroit. He found the town alive with
traders, voyageurs and Indians, but the weathered St. Anne's

Church was lifeless and empty. Covering the altar with fresh
linen and filling the chalice with communion wine, he held vesper
services for French families and some curious Indians. That summer he baptized thirty Indian and half-breed children and gave
them daily instruction in the catechism. On a visit to L'Arbre
Croche he found the Ottawas "so much abandoned to drink
spirit that they do not care much about religion."

It would be more than twenty years before a resident priest
was assigned to Mackinac Island, and by that time Presbyterian-
ism would be firmly rooted there. In 1820, a few days after Governor Cass had voyaged on to Sault Ste. Marie, the steamer
Walk-in-the-Water called again at Mackinac Island. Down the
gangway strode a man in black coat and knee breeches, a white
neckcloth and a broad-brimmed black hat. This sedate figure
was the Rev. Jedediah Morse, missionary, geographer and the
father of the inventor of the telegraph. In 1820 he was Secretary
of the Society for Propagation of the Gospel among the Indians,
on a tour of inspection—"to devise the most suitable plan to
advance their civilization and happiness." He had arrived at the
right time; the island swarmed with tribesmen who had come
to receive their annuities from the United States government
and to trade. The visitor preached in the court house (later it
became the town hall) to a congregation of mixed colors and
languages. For two busy weeks he taught the children and conducted Bible study for their parents. When he returned to the
East, the United Foreign Missionary Society projected a Mackinac Island Mission and sent the Rev. William Montague Ferry
to establish it.

Young Mr. Ferry had been teaching school at Northampton,
Massachusetts, where he married Amanda White, proposing to
take her to a Presbyterian mission in Palestine. When the bride's
father objected to that, Ferry arranged to go to Mackinac Island—a place even more strenuously opposed by his father-in-
law. The couple went anyway, in the summer of 1823, by steamer
to Detroit and by a schooner loaded to the rails with barreled
cargo up Lake Huron. At Mackinac they were welcomed by
Robert Stuart, resident manager of the American Fur Company,
who made them at home in his own household.

Robert Stuart was a man of violent temper, a fiery Scot, often
brutal in dealing with his workmen. He struck first and spoke,
if at all, afterward. Once he knocked two tipsy voyageurs flat
with a piece of firewood; one of them was carried to Dr. Beaumont with a fractured skull, while Stuart strode back to the
Agency. This "severe" man underwent a change of character
soon after the missionary's arrival. He became a deacon of the
mission church, he halted Sunday work at the warehouse and
for a while he curtailed the sale of whiskey to the Indians. When
John Kinzie brought his bride to the island in 1830, they were
taken to the Stuarts', where supper was followed by Bible reading
and prayers.

The Ferrys remained house guests of Robert Stuart until late
in the summer, when they bought a home from Mme. Laframboise, on the eastern edge of the settlement. Writing to her family
in Ashfield, Massachusetts, Amanda Ferry described it as "a
little removed from the village, *toward Massachusetts,* in full
view of the lake." Nearby stood the new mission school where
Mr. Ferry had begun instruction of nine Indian boys—one of
them brought by a Chippewa woman weighed down with 130
strings of beads. In the second year, the school enrolled seventy
children, and new teachers arrived from the East. Within a few
more seasons the school was boarding two hundred pupils, giving
them instruction in classroom, chapel, shops and fields. Beside
reading and writing, the girls were taught cleanliness, sewing
and cooking; the boys learned carpentry, shoemaking,
metal-working and farming—they worked the mission farm on
the island, as well as two cleared fields on Bois Blanc across
the passage. The combination of metal, moral and manual training, wrote Juliette Kinzie, "subdued the mischievous, tricky pro-
pensities of the halfbreed and roused the stolid apathy of the
genuine Indian."

On the first day of November 1827, when the last vessel had
gone south and winter was at hand, fire broke out at the fort.
It quickly consumed the hospital and a workshop. By good fortune, there was no wind that lurid night, but sparks fell on the
roof of the commissary stable under the hill. With soldiers, fur-

company men and Indians lugging water from the harbor, the flames were confined. When fire began licking at the officers' quarters, the bucket brigade toiled up the steepening ramp and through the sally port. That winter axes and hammers thudded on the hill while the blackened buildings were repaired.

In 1829 the famous Mission Church was built beside the mission school at the end of Huron Street; still lifting its light spire and belfry against the sky, it is the oldest protestant church in the Northwest. From New York, out of his growing millions, John Jacob Astor sent a draft of $250 for the building fund. The congregation had 52 members, 25 of them Indian. On Sunday mornings, the garrison marched to worship, stacking rifles outside the church, where one man stood guard while the rest filed inside for the psalms, prayers and preaching.

The establishment of a Presbyterian church, wrote Amanda Ferry to her Massachusetts sisters, "stirred up the enmity of the Catholics," and for a few seasons religious rivalry enlivened the remote island. The half-breed woman, Mme. Laframboise, rallied the French and Indian Catholics, who had not had a resident priest for many years. At first she instructed Indian children, and, when a priest arrived, she helped him with parish duties. By the mid-1820s the old churchyard on Market Street was full of graves. The Church of Ste. Anne was then moved to a new lot, donated by Mme. Laframboise, near the eastern end of Huron Street. Re-erected there, it became a neighbor of the Mission Church. The old French church, which had been removed to the island from Fort Michilimackinac, was replaced by the present Ste. Anne's in the 1870s. During its construction, masses were said in the unused Mission Church, and so the two became good neighbors after all.

But in the 1830s, religion, as Juliette Kinzie wrote, "was every man's business," and the Presbyterians and Catholics contended for the souls of the islanders. Missionary Ferry climbed the fort hill each Sunday afternoon and held a Bible class in the soldiers' barracks. While white and Indian children were spelling out the New Testament in the mission school, other children were chorusing the catechism in Ste. Anne's. A Catholic bishop invaded the mission farm, presenting his ring to be kissed by Protestant Indian boys. At Christmas time Mrs. Ferry complained, "Whole families have gone down early to repeat their prayers and confess their sins—to a priest who does not hesitate to get intoxicated later in the day." But she gave credit to another priest who went to live in the Indian camp, sharing the savages' privation while he told them about the Blessed Virgin and the lives of the saints.

It was Fort Mackinac that brought religious peace to the island. Unwilling to join either the Presbyterians or the French Catholics, the military officers secured an Episcopalian minister as chaplain to the garrison. With a third sect there, the contest relaxed, and church bells range peacefully over the village.

Those were the palmy days of Mackinac. Wrote Juliette Kinzie in *Wau-Bun:*

> It was no unusual thing to see a hundred or more canoes of Indians at once approaching the island, laden with their articles of traffic; and if to these we add the squadrons of large Mackinaw boats constantly arriving from the outposts, with the furs, peltries and buffalo robes collected by the distant traders, some idea may be formed of the extensive operations and important position of the American Fur Company, as well as of the vast circle of human beings either immediately or remotely connected with it.

The island was full of bustle and prosperity. "The trade made all rich," a villager recalled—all except the Indians, who froze and starved as usual during the long winters in their snowbound camps. When Indian children went home from the mission school, they forgot about cleanliness and order, and they had no more taste for carpentry and farming than before their instruction. The mission was a light that failed, whereas the fur trade burned with a consuming flame. Soon it would flicker out, as the game diminished in the forest and the beaver were taken from the streams.

Meanwhile the Fort Mackinac garrison of two companies had one of the easiest assignments in the United States Army. In his report for 1828, the commander noted that the burned hospital had been rebuilt, the blockhouses were newly covered and the parade was enlarged and cleared of "certain disgusting looking root houses." New storehouses on the upper level replaced a commissary store under the hill—"a monument of false reasoning of him who erected it." The place was healthy; supplies were ample; pay, rations and clothing, Major Whistler reported, were "fully equal to the wants and expectations of the soldiers." The men had the freedom of the village very evening from after-supper retreat until the bugler sounded tattoo under the northern stars. In just one of the harbor grog shops, the troops spent $800 during the winter of 1828.

In 1834 the Rev. William M. Ferry resigned from the Mackinac Island mission; after eleven years of preaching and teaching, he was worn out. Robert Stuart sent him with his family on a rest trip in a fur-company schooner around Lake Michigan. At the mouth of the Grand River, where trader Laframboise had been killed 25 years earlier by a begging Winnebago, the Ferrys found a busy trading post and a warm welcome. This site was the headquarters of trader Rix Robinson; his agency extended from the Kalamazoo River to Little Traverse Bay. Robinson, who would become a judge and a congressman after the trading posts were closed, had left young Zenas Winsor in charge at Grand River. Winsor had the help of four veteran voyageurs; he shared his quarters with a half-breed girl, who doubled as housekeeper and interpreter. When the Ferrys arrived, this girl greeted them with a cry of delight and a stream of questions about Mackinac. She had been one of their mission students.

William Forry liked the look of that country and decided to locate there. With money borrowed from Robert Stuart, he bought a large tract of pine forest, laid out the town of Grand Haven, founded a Presbyterian church and built up a very profitable logging business. On his death in 1867, he left a part of his fortune for missionary work among the displaced Indians.

Robert Stuart left Mackinac Island and the dwindling fur trade in 1834, not even bothering to remove the accumulated records of the company. The fur warehouse was closed—it would become a "fishery" in the next generation. In 1855 Ronald McLeod bought the weathered old warehouse and so came into possession of some boxes of fur-company records. Some of the papers were used "for lighting fires and placing around cabbage plants when put in the ground, to keep them from the cut-worms"; others made linings for cake tins. One box of papers survived. It contained the outward invoices of the Mackinac Agency in 1821 and 1822, giving the names and locations of the company's traders and the goods consigned to them. Beside quantities of tobacco, whiskey, soap, cheese, biscuit, salt, gunpowder, blankets, shirts and colored ribbon, there were lists of sundries—

Trimmings for blue cloth vest
1 Jack Knife and ½ lb. Raisins
1 doz. Shirt Buttons
1 bottle Lemon Syrup
1 Curry Comb
6 lbs. small white beads

—along with the prices of furs to be given at Mackinac Island in the new season:

prime beaver	$ 4.00
black bear	4.50
silver fox	10.00
lynx	1.37½
mink	.25
buffalo robes	3.00

It was this trade that was making John Jacob Astor rich beyond the comprehension of his voyageurs, clerks and agents. When the wilderness gold was gone, he put his millions into New York real estate. After the Civil War, the old Mackinac warehouse, still redolent of fish and peltry, became a summer hotel, while in New York Astor's heirs built the Astor House, the Waldorf-Astoria and St. Regis hotels. By that time the Indians of the upper country were reduced to a few scattered bands on shrinking reservations in the land of their fathers.

. 14 .

THE SWIFT WALKER

In the summer of 1818 gangs of Irish workmen began digging the Erie Canal, the first freight wagons creaked over the National Road from Baltimore to the Ohio River and the first steamship churned the empty waters of Lake Erie. That fall Illinois became a state, and a young fur trader from Mackinac arrived at the mouth of the Chicago River.

He remembered years afterward:

> The morning was calm and bright and we, in our holiday attire, with flags flying, completed the last twelve miles of our lake voyage. Arriving at Douglas Grove, where the prairie could be seen through the oak woods, I landed, and climbing a tree, gazed in admiration on the first prairie I had ever seen. The waving grass, intermingling with a rich profusion of wild flowers, was the most beautiful sight I had ever gazed upon. In the distance the grove of Blue Island loomed up, beyond it the timber on the Des Plaines River, while to give animation to the scene a herd of wild deer appeared, and a pair of red foxes emerged from the grass within gunshot of me. Looking north I saw the whitewashed buildings of Fort Dearborn sparkling in the sunshine, our boats with flags flying, and oars keeping time to the cheering boat song. I was spellbound and amazed at the beautiful scene before me. I took the trail leading to the fort and on my arrival found our party camped on the north side of the river, near what is now State Street. A soldier ferried me across the river in a canoe, and thus I made my first entry into Chicago, October 1, 1818.

147

A descendant of a colonial governor of Connecticut, Gurdon
Saltonstall Hubbard was born in Windsor, Vermont, in 1802.
His father, after unsuccessful land speculations, settled in Montreal, where he kept a boarding house. One of his boarders was
William W. Matthews, who recruited clerks and voyageurs for
the American Fur Company. In the spring of 1818 Matthews
was looking for twelve young clerks and a hundred Canadian
voyageurs for the Mackinac organization. Gurdon Hubbard, then
a lanky fifteen-year-old, dreamed of the fur trade as a seacoast
boy would dream of the sea. Overcoming parental objections
he signed a clerk's contract—a five-year term at $120 a year—and
reported at La Chine (where La Salle had planned a voyage to
China) on the 13th of May. "To boats all!" came the command.
With yells and cheers the men took their places. A boat song
rang over the water, and the oars dipped in. Gurdon Hubbard
was on his way to the wilderness.

With heavy cargoes of trade goods the bateaux made slow
progress up the swirling St. Lawrence and into Lake Ontario.
It was mid-June when they reached "Muddy York"—the present
Toronto—and headed northward. Now that warring Iroquois no
longer blocked the approach to Lake Erie, the Astor men took
their heavy cargoes west by way of the Niagara portage and
up the lakes. On this trip, however, agent Matthews chose a
short cut. With hired ox teams he hauled boats and cargoes
straight north to Lake Simcoe, then made the Nottawasaga portage and traveled down that river to the open water of Georgian
Bay. From there it was a happy voyage, with oars flashing and
the men alternating boat songs as they coasted the northern
shores. On July 3rd from a camp on Goose Island—the outermost
of Les Chêneaux—they sighted Mackinac Island. Next day they
crossed the open water. A high wind kept them from rounding
the harbor point; they landed on the east shore at the foot of
Robinson's Folly.

On Mackinac Island the Yankee youth found a new and exciting world—Canadian voyageurs with their families of
half-breeds, the army garrison on the hill, Indians and voyageurs
streaming through the village, canoes and bateaux thronging the

harbor. It was self-contained, yet it reached out to immense distances. Young Hubbard had arrived at Mackinac in the first full vigor of the Astor company; it webbed trade routes spread over half the continent. "Here," he wrote, "during the summer months congregated the traders employed by the Fur Company, bringing their collection from their several trading posts which extended from the British dominion on the north and the Missouri River in the west, south and east to the white settlements; in fact to all the Indian hunting grounds." When he first saw Mackinac Island, the village of five hundred residents swarmed with three thousand traders. Boatmen and voyageurs, with another two or three thousand Indians, camped along the shore. Days and nights were noisy with their revelry.

In this heady setting, Gurdon Hubbard quickly took a man's place. He was quartered in the swarming clerks' barracks amid veterans of the trade; he worked in the cavernous warehouse where many-colored mounds of peltry rose to the roof. His first job was that of "second counter," tallying skins already sorted and sending them on to the pressing frame. In a reek of musk, smoke, grease and leather, he counted mink, marten, fox, lynx, badger, otter, beaver, muskrat. He worked from five in the morning, when the gulls were circling in the sunrise, until the sunset gun boomed from the fort. After dark he wandered past village houses, where music and laughter told of parties given for returning traders, and along the shore, where brigade champions fought for the black-feather trophy and Indians wrestled and gambled around their fires.

That season "the boy clerk" became a friend of John H. Kinzie, also a novice in the trade. The two youths were made welcome in the homes of Edward Biddle, Michael Dousman, Mme. Laframboise and veteran trader Deschamps, who had charge of the Illlinois "outfit." At the end of the summer, when the bateaux made gala departures for their winter stations, Hubbard was assigned to the Lake Superior brigade. At the last moment, he made a transfer to the Illinois outfit; the clerk with whom he traded places froze to death that winter on the Canadian border.

With songs and cheers, the Illinois brigade of twelve boats
left Mackinac Island on the 10th of September. Gurdon Hubbard
traveled in the lead boat with Deschamps, who sang out the
rowing songs, which his crews picked up in unison. In other
boats traveled trader Bieson, a gray-haired heavy man with
his enormous Potawatomi wife—"so fleshy she could scarcely
walk"—and several more traders with their half-breed families.
Each night they made camp on the Lake Michigan shore, the
traders pitching tents while the boatmen spread blankets under
the stars or made lean-tos of the boats' tarpaulins in bad weather.
After six weeks of travel, they reached the mouth of the Chicago
River and saw the flag of Fort Dearborn rippling against the
prairie sky. Within half a mile of the fort were a few scattered
storehouses and cottages, including the home of John H. Kinzie's
father. In that household young Gurdon Hubbard was welcomed
like a son.

After repairing the boats, the brigade rowed up the south
branch of the Chicago River. They hauled the empty craft
through the shallows of Mud Lake and portaged their cargoes
to the headwaters of the Illinois River. Then it was downstream
travel. They passed Starved Rock, where La Salle and Tonty
had built the first outpost in all that country, and came to a
southward bend of the Illinois, where the Bureau River flowed
in from the west. There, at the modern boom town of Hennepin—where a mammoth steel plant now spreads over six thousand fertile acres—stood an Astor trading post in charge of an
illiterate Frenchman named Beebeau. Young Hubbard was assigned to this place, to keep its accounts. He found Beebeau
an ill-tempered, complaining man who lived with a fat and
slovenly Kickapoo woman. The new clerk liked the Indians better, and they liked him; that winter he was adopted into the
family of Chief Waba. He learned the Potawatomi language and
became a skilled hunter and tracker. On trading trips he crossed
and recrossed the Illinois country, north to the Rock River and
west to the Wabash, his long stride covering forty to fifty miles
a day. In his mind he carried a map of the prairie creeks and

rivers, with the scattered groves rising like islands from the rolling grassland.

For a calendar the traders kept a notched stick hanging in
the store, a deep notch for each new month and a nick made
daily. In the middle of March, they loaded their winter furs
into the bateau. When the stick read March 20th, they heard
a boat song from the river. Around the bend came Deschamps
from his posts on the lower Illinois, his twelve bateaux laden
with peltry. Two days later the whole caravan rowed northward.
They reached Mackinac in mid-May among the first brigades
of the season.

That summer Hubbard worked again in the warehouse. After
beating furs to rid them of dust and vermin, he pressed them
into bales and tied the hundred-pound bundles with rawhide.
At the end of the day he worked by candlelight, writing up
records and accounts. From the bustling island he went to a
winter station on Muskegon Lake, where he had charge of the
trading post. When deep snow isolated him from his voyageurs,
he lived in a frozen solitude. "Every night," he recalled in his
autobiography, "a wolf came and devoured the remnants of the
fish I had thrown out. I could see him through the cracks of
my house, and could easily have shot him, but he was my
only companion, and I laid awake at night awaiting his
coming."

In that somber winter, the solitary boy concluded that he was
a failure. Like all the young he took his fortune seriously and
without perspective. If he survived the winter, he reflected, he
would return to Mackinac alone and empty-handed, to face the
ridicule of the company men and traders. "This," he thought,
"would be the end of all my bright anticipations."

But youthful zest followed youthful desolation. After thirty
days of solitude he found his voyageurs—laden with prime furs
of beaver, bear, marten, lynx, fox, otter and mink. Still the winter
storms howled through the woods. Before the streams broke up,
Hubbard was again lost in the snowy waste, his men went cold
and hungry and the foreman of his voyageurs died of frostbite

and starvation. There were new lines in the face of the young
trader who brought his peltry to Mackinac that spring.

Gurdon Hubbard was learning the fur trade: summer in the
warehouse, the office and the retail store, winter in the woods
and the camps of the Indians. The third winter he spent in charge
of a trading house on the Kalamazoo River with an outfit of
three voyageurs and a scarred and dented Indian who, for $100
a year, furnished the services of himself, two horses and his wife.
On a trip to a hunting camp, this Indian insisted on taking a
keg of whiskey along with two bales of merchandise. Hubbard
reluctantly agreed but insisted that the whiskey be watered
down. They had two kegs, one full and one empty, but without
a funnel how could they dilute the whiskey? They found a way:
by drawing a mouthful of whiskey from the full key and spitting
it into the other, followed by a mouthful of river water, they
ended with one full keg and one half-empty. Some hundreds
of mouthfuls of water filled the second keg, and they were ready
for trading. By the end of the season, they had a heavy load
of furs, which Hubbard valued above his own safety. To keep
the canoe upright in a swirl of rapids, he went overboard into
icy water. That spring he joined his outfit to that of trader Rix
Robinson on Grand River, the two brigades returning to Mackinac together.

In those years, there were few white men in the western country. The next winter, again assigned to the Illinois outfit, Hubbard met two landlookers scouting for likely townsites on the
windswept prairie. He gave them a turkey and raccoon dinner,
which they remembered for the rest of their lives. One of them
founded the town of Quincy on the Mississippi. His name was
John Wood, and he later became a governor of Illinois. A less
gratifying encounter that winter left Hubbard with a life-long
scar from the tomahawk of a robber Indian.

In 1824 the old trader Deschamps resigned his management
of the Illinois River posts, and Gurdon Hubbard took charge
of the entire outfit. He began with a new system—unloading
his cargoes at Chicago, mooring them in the slough where they
would not be burned by prairie fires and using pack ponies to

get trade goods and peltry to and from the Indian camps. So ended the back-breaking toil of the Illinois portages. That winter he opened "Hubbard's Trail" from Chicago to the Wabash River, with trading posts at intervals of fifty miles.

"Watseka" means "Pretty Woman" in the Potawatomi tongue, and the town of Watseka, Illinois, is named for the daughter of Chief Tamin. According to a local legend Hubbard helped his business along by marrying the chief's daughter. After two years, the story goes, he gave her to his partner, Le Vasseur, but she is remembered in Iroquois County as the wife of the "Swift Walker."

It was in this country during the winter of 1823 that Hubbard earned the Indian name that followed him all his life. As a rangy, weather-burned man in the prime of his strength, he made a cross-country race with a long-striding Indian. In one day Hubbard walked 75 miles. At sunset he swam across the flooded Illinois River at Hennepin—"reaching my house," he concluded, "about dark." The Indian was miles behind. From that day, Hubbard was known among the tribes as "Papamatabe"—"The Swift Walker."

At the end of his five-year contract, the "boy clerk" was a veteran trader, known from Mackinac to the Wabash. In 1823 he became a special partner in the American Fur Compnay, and, when John Kinzie the elder resigned his agency at Chicago, Hubbard bought from the company its entire Illinois business. After 26 trips along the shore of Lake Michigan in an open rowboat, he was ready to improve transportation; he sent cargo over Lake Michigan by schooner, and he enlarged his pack trains on the prairie trails. While conducting his fur trade, he also drove cattle and hogs from the Wabash Valley to Fort Dearborn, and so began his meat packing business, the first big industry of burgeoning Chicago. In 1833 Chicago was incorporated as a town, with Hubbard elected to its Board of Trustees. In that office, he urged the building of the Illinois and Michigan Canal. He knew the incalculable value of water transportation; ten years earlier he had made the laborious portage from the St. Joseph River to the Kankakee—tying his empty boats to horses' tails while his men staggered under endless loads of cargo. Now he headed the first Board of Canal Commissioners, and on July 4, 1836, he dug the first spade of earth for the canal that would link the Great Lakes with the Mississippi River system. With the opening of the canal, Chicago became the commerical center of the West. Meanwhile Hubbard had developed the Eagle Steamship Line, the first regular shipping service between Chicago and Buffalo. Then his vessels steamed past Mackinac Island, where the boy clerk had looked westward, wondering what land lay beyond the flashing straits.

THE FORT SURGEON

Near the western end of the parade ground, beside the three-chimneyed officers' stone quarters overlooking Marquette Park and Mackinac Island harbor stands a low pyramid—four slabs of granite topped by a smooth faced boulder. It is inscribed: "Near this spot Dr. William Beaumont, United States Army, made those experiments upon Alexis St. Martin which have brought fame to himself and honor to American medicine." The old French villagers said it more simply. To them Beaumont was "le bon docteur who mak de mer-a-cle."

In the long evening light of June 16, 1820, the historic *Walk-in-the-Water* steamed into Mackinac Island harbor. Its 29 passengers included the Rev. Jedediah Morse, missionary and geographer, and a new post surgeon, who was welcomed by Captain Benjamin K. Pierce and taken to his quarters near the one-story frame hospital at the western end of the compound. The next day Dr. Beaumont attended a dress parade and dined with Captain Pierce. Then he took up the familiar routine of military life.

After a medical apprenticeship in St. Albans, Vermont, near the Canadian border, Dr. William Beaumont had served as an army surgeon in the War of 1812. Following a few years of private practice ("Fee for each visit $0.25; doctor in night 0.38") in Plattsburg, New York, he rejoined the army and was ordered to Fort Mackinac. There he found the magic and monotony of a remote garrison perched between the northern sky and the water, with the long winter solitude followed by the excitement of the summer rendezvous of Indians, voyageurs and traders. Dr. Beaumont served the village, as well as the fort, but in that vigorous and salutary place there was little illness. On September 10, 1820, the surgeon's diary noted: "Visited my patients in village and discharged garrison duty before 9 A.M. Settled my hospital account with commandant and perused scripture and Pope's *Essay on Man* till eve."

William Beaumont was a descendant of a Huguenot family that had settled in Saybrook, Connecticut, in 1640. Though professing no religion, he had the best qualities of the Puritan tradition: conscience, honesty, modesty, patience, perseverance. During that first season at Fort Mackinac, he was a bachelor, attending to his duties, observing men and nature, reading Shakespeare, Ben Franklin, the Bible and the English poets. At the age of 35 he had a youthful idealism and aspiration—"September 9. Commenced a diary of conduct on Dr. Franklin's plan for attaining moral perfection." Amid roistering voyageurs, drunken Indians and the callous men of the garrison, William Beaumont kept an account of his progress in virtue. His devotion to a young woman in Plattsburg must have heightened his idealism. "Your dear image," he wrote at his desk in the fort hospital, "do I cherish with increasing fervency and love."

In August, 1821, after fourteen months of duty, the surgeon was granted a furlough to be married. A few weeks later he returned with his bride, blooming white-bonneted Deborah Green Beaumont, whose Quaker "thees" and "thous" charmed the entire garrison. On the 8th of June, 1822, she bore her first child, Sarah, and on that day Dr. Beaumont divided his time between two patients. From his wife's bedside, he hurried to the hospital, where a young voyageur lay with his stomach blown open by a shotgun wound.

The sound of gunfire was commonplace on Mackinac Island, where the garrison held target practice and Indians and voyageurs fired salutes to themselves and greetings across the water. If Dr. Beaumont heard the shotgun blast on the morning of June 6, 1821, he thought nothing of it. But it changed the course of his future and opened a dramatic chapter in the history of medicine.

On that bright summer morning, the retail store of the American Fur Company, at the foot of the steep road to the fort, swarmed with Indians, traders and voyageurs. John Kinzie had charge of the store, and young Gurdon Hubbard was helping him in this busy season. Through the buzz of voices in English, French and Algonquian came the roar of a shotgun. A customer, examining the gun, had accidentally fired it, and onto the floor fell a young voyageur, Alexis St. Martin. "The muzzle was not over three feet from him—I think not over two," wrote Hubbard in his autobiography. "The wadding entered [his stomach], as well as a piece of his clothing; his shirt took fire; he fell, as we supposed, dead." Someone raced up to the fort to call the surgeon; another ran to the Agency. Dr. Beaumont and Robert Stuart arrived in a few minutes, while Kinzie and Hubbard were laying the stricken man on a cot at the back of the store.

From the gaping wound, Dr. Beaumont removed balls of shot and bits of clothing. As he reported in a book that became famous: "The whole mass of materials forced from the musket, together with fragments of clothing and pieces of fractured ribs, were driven into the muscles and cavity of the chest." He found a part of the lung, burned and lacerated, protruding through the wound and below it another mangled tissue that proved to be a part of the stomach "pouring out the food he had taken for his breakfast." There seemed little to do for a man in this dire state. Dr. Beaumont applied a dressing. "The man can't live thirty-six hours," he said. "I will come to see him by and by." When he returned a few hours later, he was surprised to find the voyageur recovering from shock. The next day, after trimming and cleaning the wound, the surgeon told Robert Stuart that he thought the lad might live.

St. Martin was carried up to the fort hospital, where Dr. Beaumont tended him between preparations for his wife's childbirth. The next day the child was born, and the voyageur was alert and hungry. Observing that food passed out through the wound, Dr. Beaumont applied firm dressings, walling in the stomach, so that the contents were retained.

"After the fourth week," wrote Beaumont "the appetite became good, digestion regular." (Fourteen years later the English author

Harriet Martineau observed that Mackinac Island was so healthful that people had to go away to die.) The inner abrasions were then healing, but the flesh at the surface showed no sign of closing. Wrote the surgeon: "After trying every means within my power to close the puncture of the stomach by exciting adhesions between the lips of the wound of its own proper coats, without the least appearance of success, I gave over trying."

When Dr. Beaumont began the medical record of this case, he knew almost nothing of his patient. Having heard his name spoken, he wrote phonetically—"Alex Samata"—identifying him as "a Canadian lad of about 19 years old, hardy, robust and healthy." The name was changed later to "San Maten" and finally to "Alexis St. Martin." He learned little from the patient; St. Martin could not speak English, and Beaumont had trouble understanding the French Canadian patois. At first the stolid voyageur remained silent during medical treatments, but as time went on each learned the other's language.

Ten months after the accident, St. Martin was hobbling about with a compress holding in the contents of his stomach. He had no funds or friends, and there was no welfare agency on Mackinac Island. The villagers wanted to send him back to Montreal in an open bateau, and again it was the surgeon who saved him.

> Knowing that his life must inevitably be sacrificed in such an attempt, I resolved to rescue him from the pending misery and death. I took him into my own family [Beaumont's pay was $40 a month] . . . . In this condition he remained with me, gradually improving, for a year or two, when he became able to walk about and help himself a little, but unable to provide for his own necessities. During this time I nursed him, fed him, clothed him, lodged him and furnished him with every comfort, and dressed his wounds daily and for the most part twice a day.

The wound did not close, but a fold of flesh grew, like a flap, to cover the stomach opening. Raising the flap, the surgeon could watch the stomach at work. With a new note of curiosity and discovery, he wrote in his record:

I can look directly into the cavity of the stomach, observe its motion, and almost see the process of digestion. I can pour in water with a funnel and put in food with a spoon, and draw them out again with a siphon . . . . It would give no pain or cause the least uneasiness to extract a gill of fluid every two or three days, for it frequently flows out spontaneously in considerable quantities; and I might introduce various digestible substances into the stomach and easily examine them during the whole process of digestion.

Three years after St. Martin's accident, Dr. Beaumont realized that he had a unique and living laboratory for medical experimentation. During the next few years, he made 238 detailed observations of the digestive process under various conditions. When he was a medical apprentice in Vermont, Beaumont had copied a maxim that honored honest labor and faithful pursuit of real and useful knowledge. Now he put that maxim into practice. "At twelve o'clock noon I introduced through the perforation into the stomach the following articles of diet, suspended by a silk string and fastened at proper distance so as to pass without pain: a piece of highly seasoned à la mode beef, a piece of raw salted lean beef, a piece of boiled salted beef, a piece of stale bread, and a bunch of raw sliced cabbage." Every hour he pulled up the string and examined the process of digestion on each item. He inserted a thermometer and kept a record of the stomach's temperature. He siphoned out gastric juice, suspended bits of food into it and studied their changes. With these observations, Beaumont was discovering the chemical action that makes up the process of digestion.

In the summer of 1825, Beaumont was ordered to Fort Niagara. Taking his family—there were two children by then—and his patient with him, the surgeon continued his experiments. But St. Martin was growing restless. That winter, without as much as a farewell to his benefactor, he ran off to Canada. (Wrote Washington Irving: "The Canadian voyageur was as full of tricks and vice as a horse.") It was four years before Beaumont saw him again.

While serving at Green Bay in 1827, Dr. Beaumont had word from William W. Matthews, the Fur Company's recruiting agent in Canada: St. Martin was married, impoverished and living in a village 57 miles from Montreal. Beaumont began a correspondence with him, a communication made doubly slow by distance and by St. Martin's indifference. Meanwhile Beaumont was transferred to Fort Crawford near Prairie du Chien; at that post on the upper Mississippi, he sat in the officers' mess with Stephen Watts Kearny, commander of the fort, and the junior officers Zachary Taylor and Jefferson Davis. At last, in the summer of 1829, a fur brigade brought to Fort Crawford Alexis St. Martin, his wife and two children. Beaumont agreed to board and lodge the family and to pay St. Martin $300 a year, in return for which the voyageur would submit to medical experiments and his wife would help in the Beaumont household.

For a year and a half the studies went on—the timing of digestion; the effects of various kinds of drink; the stomach's reception of warm and cold food, of animal and cereal products, of chewed and unchewed substances. Then Mme. St. Martin got homesick for Canada, and Beaumont's laboratory left him again. In an open canoe the man with the flap on his stomach took his family down the Mississippi and up the Ohio River. They portaged from the headwaters of the Ohio to Lake Ontario and voyaged on to Montreal.

The Black Hawk War occupied the men at Fort Crawford in 1832. When the campaign had ended, Beaumont was given a six-month furlough to complete his medical experiments. Alexis St. Martin was placed on the United States Army roll as a sergeant on special duty. Both he and Dr. Beaumont signed a contract that bound St. Martin for one year to

> serve, abide and continue with the said William Beaumont . . . that he, the said Alexis will at all times faithfully during said term when thereto directed or required by said William, submit to, assist and promote by all means within his power such philosophical or medical experiments as the said William shall direct or cause to be made on or in the stomach of him, the said Alexis, either through and by means of the aperture or opening in the side of him, the said Alexis, or otherwise, and will obey, suffer and comply with all reasonable and

proper orders of or experiments of the said William in relation
to the exhibiting and showing of his said stomach and the powers
and properties, and situation and state of the contents thereof.

For this "service" St. Martin was to be paid his board and lodging
and $150 for the year.

"The man with the lid on his stomach" had been derided by
his comrades of the fur brigades. A long-remembered Mackinac
story tells how his brother Etienne had stabbed Charlie Charette
for ridiculing Alexis. "If they do not let my brother's stomach
alone," he threatened, "I will kill the whole brigade." For St. Martin the contract was a kind of surrender. Though he did not
grasp his role in history, he realized that his exposed stomach
was his best means of support.

Beaumont made plans for extended experiments and consulta-
tions. He hoped to engage St. Martin for five or six years, and
he wrote to the United States Minister to France, suggesting a
trip to Paris, where French scientists could look into the open
stomach. At the same time, the Medical Society of London raised
a travel fund to bring Beaumont and his man to London. Nothing
came of these designs, but St. Martin traveled to New York, Philadelphia and Washington to be observed by physicians and medical students. Then the death of one of his numerous children
took St. Martin to Canada, and his wife kept him there. After
1834 Beaumont never saw him again.

But in 1833 Beaumont's little book had appeared, and with
it medical service took a giant step. *Experiments and Observations
on the Gastric Juice and the Physiology of Digestion* contained
seven sections: "Of Aliment"; "Of Hunger and Thirst"; "Of Satisfaction and Satiety"; "Of Mastication, Insalivation and Degluta-
tion"; "Of Digestion by the Gastric Juice"; "Of the appearance
of the Villous Coat, and of the Motions of the Stomach"; "Of
Chylification and Uses of the Bile and Pancreatic Juice." The
principles were all substantiated by 238 detailed observations
begun at Mackinac Island eight years before.

In 1835 Beaumont was transferred to the St. Louis Arsenal. Four
years later he resigned from the army and took up private practice in St. Louis. He prospered there, but his mind kept returning

to St. Martin's stomach and to new experiments that could enlarge medical knowledge. In 1846 he sent his son Israel to Canada in an attempt to persuade the old voyageur to come to St. Louis. Alexis would not budge. A final letter in 1852 expressed Beaumont's "most fervent desire" to have St. Martin with him again. By that time Alexis was the hard-drinking head of a large family on a small farm near Montreal. He did not reply to Beaumont's offer. On a winter night in 1853, Dr. Beaumont slipped on an icy step, which struck his head. He died a few weeks later. The voyageur lived to ripe old age. When he died in 1880, at St. Thomas de Joliette near Montreal, his family refused urgent requests for an autopsy. To deter grave-robbers, the body was buried eight feet deep.

William Beaumont is buried in one of the famous cemeteries of America, the wooded spacious Bellefontaine Cemetery above the Mississippi at St. Louis; he lies among illustrious dead—Governor William Clark, Senator Thomas Hart Benton, General Stephen Watts Kearny, Captain Henry Miller Shreve. But he is best remembered on Mackinac Island, where the American Fur Company store had been restored and furnished as a Beaumont memorial. The old stone building, containing lifelike scenes of the wounded voyageur and the attending doctor, was dedicated by the Michigan Medical Society on a summer day in 1954. It stands now as it was on that June morning in 1822 when a shotgun banged in the crowded store and a man raced up to the fort surgeon on the hill.

. 16 .

INDIAN SUMMER

Henry Rowe Schoolcraft first met "Michilimackinac" in his
spelling book in a village school near Albany, New York. He first
saw Mackinac Island in 1820, when he traveled with the Cass
expedition as a young geologist on the government payroll at
$1.50 a day. "Nothing can exceed the beauty of this island," he
wrote in his journal, which lingers over the grandeur of the cliffs,
the picturesque village around the harbor and above it the fort
like an alhambra with white walls gleaming in the sun. Like
countless people since, he walked around the island—easier now
than then, before the brush and rock had been cleared for a
smooth roadway. On the northern shores where the cliffs fell sheer
to the water, he waded at the base of the precipitous rock. In
the nine-mile circuit, he picked up pieces of quartz, striped horn-
stone and iron oxide. His specimen bag grew heavier as the expedition journeyed on to Sault Ste. Marie and the wild shores
of Lake Superior.

Two years later, in 1822, he was appointed Indian agent on
the northwestern frontier. For eleven years he resided at Sault
Ste. Marie; there he married Miss Jane Johnston, daughter of an
Irish trader and granddaughter of an Ojibwa chief. In 1833 he
transferred the Agency headquarters to Mackinac Island, where
he lived until 1841. During his twenty years as Indian agent,
he traveled to scores of Indian towns and villages and negotiated
treaties with many tribes. His official letter book, in Washington,
fills 1,822 pages and ranges over men and matters from Detroit
to the Canadian border and the Dakota prairies.

Schoolcraft knew both the poetry and the squalor of savage life. He saw the Indian with reality and compassion—"A man spending his time painfully to catch a beaver, or entrap an enemy, without stores of thought, without leisure, with nothing often to eat and nothing to put on but tatters and rags, and withal, with the whole Anglo-Saxon race treading on his toes and burning out his vitals with ardent spirits."

During the long northern winters, he studied Indian languages and legends. With his wife's help, he compiled the native mythology, which other writers used in romantic portrayals of the noble savage. In a Cambridge, Massachusetts, study, far from the snowy forests and smoky lodges of the Ojibwas, Longfellow read and reread Schoolcraft's *Algic Researches* before shaping its tribal lore into the epic *Song of Hiawatha*.

> Should you ask me, whence these stories,
> Whence these legends and traditions,
> With the odors of the forest,
> With the dew and damp of meadows,
> With the curling smoke of wigwams,
> With the rushing of great rivers,
> With their frequent repetitions,
> And their wild reverberations,
> As of thunder in the mountains?
>   I should answer, I should tell you,
> "From the forests and the prairies,
> From the great lakes of the Northland,
> From the land of the Ojibways,
> From the land of the Dacotahs,
> From the mountains, moors and fen-lands
> Where the heron, the Shu-shu-gah,
> Feeds among the reeds and rushes
> I repeat them as I heard them
> From the lips of Nawadaha
> The musician, the sweet singer.

Elsewhere he answered more literally, "I pored over Mr. Schoolcraft's writings nearly three years."

In June of 1833 Henry Rowe Schoolcraft put his family, his Indian servants, his books and papers and his household goods aboard the schooner *Mariner* at Sault Ste. Marie for removal to Mackinac Island. That summer he settled into the Agency House, in the east garden of the fort, beyond the army stables, wagon sheds and blacksmith shop. A rambling house with many gables, it stood amid orchard trees and arbor vines under the steep green hillside. Briar roses climbed its lichen-stained walls and rough stone chimneys. Its windows had weathered shutters held back by "S"-shaped iron flanges. In a back wing of the house there was a carved door, said to have been brought from France for Father Marquette's first chapel at St. Ignace across the strait. The front door held a brass knocker and a metal plate inscribed "United States Agency." For eight years this house was Schoolcraft's home and office.

After the remoteness of Sault Ste. Marie, Mackinac Island seemed a crossroads.

He wrote in his journal:

> Here the great whirl of lake commerce from Buffalo to Chicago continually passed. The picturesque canoe of the Indian was constantly gliding, and the footsteps of visitors were frequently seen to tread the sacred island, rendering it a point of contact with the busy world. Emigrants of every class, agog for new El Dorados in the West, eager merchants prudently looking to their interests in the great area of migration, domestic and foreign visitors, with notebook in hand, and some valetudinarians, hoping in the benefits of pure air and whitefish— these constantly filled the harbor and constituted the ever moving panorama of our enlarged landscape.

Schoolcraft's mind had many horizons. He pondered biblical revelation and the evidence of geology, the shimmer of northern lights and the flitting of the sandpiper, Egyptian antiquities and the lives of the English poets. But he was most ardently interested in the island life and lore. From visiting Indians he pieced together the myths of Michilimackinac, the record of the military removal to Mackinac Island, the long struggle for possession of

the straits. In his home he entertained the officers of the fort—
Major Whistler, Captain Barnum, Lieutenants Kingsbury and Pen-
rose and their wives; he was a familiar guest in the officers' quarters on the hill.

After the siege of winter, he turned from books and papers
to his garden, pruning the orchard trees and bushes and planting
flower beds along the gravel paths. On spring days he would
order his carriage and took his family driving to Arch Rock, Sugar
Loaf, Skull Cave, Lover's Leap and the Devil's Kitchen; while he
reflected on the geology of the formations, his wife and children
would gather wildflowers. When business took him to Detroit,
Sault Ste. Marie or elsewhere, he would return gratefully to his
island home.

From a trip to Green Bay he brought back a fawn named
"Nimmi," which became a family pet. Browsing in the Schoolcraft
garden the animal grew to full size but remained as tame as
ever. When the door was open, it foraged in the kitchen and
took bread from the dining table. It had the freedom of the
Agency grounds and of the adjoining property as well; it leapt
lightly over the six-foot picket fence and browsed on the crops
in the garrison gardens. Finally, because of overfondness for
young plum leaves, Nimmi was turned out to roam the island.
After three years he was shot by a vexed villager.

Though he knew the savage character of the Indians, Schoolcraft hoped to domesticate their lives. On the Agency grounds
he had a carpenter shop and a forge, where visiting tribesmen
could learn to work with wood and metal. In his mind, while
he tended his own garden and replaced the old cedar posts
around the Agency, he made some calculations. Estimating that
every hunter required 50,000 acres to supply his family's needs,
he concluded that Indian education should stress agriculture. He
provided spades, hoes, seeds and plantings and encouraged Indian gardening and farming. It greatly pleased him when Chabo-
wawa, a Chippewa chief, took slips from his currant bush to
the mainland village—where they promptly died. At the Old
French Mission on Grand Traverse Bay, he stationed a blacksmith,
a carpenter and an Indian farmer for the instruction of the tribes-

men. On a trip to Lake Superior in 1838, he asked the Indians about their fields and gardens. They showed him nineteen apple trees in the forest and a few ragged potato patches.

After the Rev. William Ferry left Mackinac Island, Schoolcraft occasionally conducted services in the Mission Church. For a time, in the mid-1830s, a sergeant from Fort Mackinac led the choir, which included two privates. In the congregation were army officers and their wives, Indians in buckskin and blankets and a few Protestant villagers. For a season or two a company of soldiers marched down the hill and along the harbor to the Mission Church. Rules at the fort had been tightened since the 1820s, and church attendance was a diversion from post routine. In 1833 Captain Cobbs, after deploring drunkenness among the troops, issued an order to the village tavern-keepers: "You are hereby forbid to sell or give any spirituous liquors at any time to any soldier in service within two miles of the military ground or military reservation on the Island of Mackinac under penalties of the Act of the Legislative Council of the Territory of Michigan, approved March 1st, 1831." He even declared the village out of bounds: "Passes may be granted in fatigue dress for the purpose of gunning or other recreation on the back part of the island until retreat beating . . . but it is strictly forbidden for men obtaining such passes to visit the village unless on duty or by order of an officer." But a man could march to church without a pass or a question.

To join the Indians and whites in worship, Schoolcraft had prepared a hymnbook with English and Chippewa on opposite pages—if they sang together it could hardly have been in unison. The missionaries had prepared a Chippewa New Testament, which reached beyond that people, as Chippewa was the lingua franca of the tribes, their common language of trade and commerce. In the Indian Gospel, "It came to pass, when Jesus had finished all these sayings" was filled with the hard "g"s and "k"s of the Chippewa tongue: *Gipugumiaiamugut su api au Jesus gauaiekua-sitot kukinu ono ikitouinun.*

To the island came tribesmen from St. Ignace, L'Arbre Croche and the Chêneaux and Beaver Islands, asking for alms and presents. Beaching their canoes, they splashed ashore, ragged and hungry with their bony dogs behind them, and made straight for the Agency. Their standard greeting was *Kitte-mau-giz-ze Sho-wain-e-min*—"I am poor; show me pity and charity." Mrs. Schoolcraft always let them into the kitchen and gave them something from her pantry. Schoolcraft issued kettles, blankets, pieces of cloth, a gun, a hoe and requisitions for supplies from the Agency storehouse. When a tattered Chippewa announced that he had become chief of his village, Schoolcraft gave him a flag, along with a double ration of bread and tobacco.

After nearly twenty years of the great Astor fur harvest, the tribes were indeed destitute. Furs and game were depleted throughout the lower peninsula of Michigan. In midwinter of 1834, Schoolcraft received a delegation from the village of L'Arbre Croche stating the wish of the Chippewas and Ottawas to see the President in Washington about the sale of their lands. These tribes were in debt to the traders, their lodges were empty and their only livelihood was the supplying of cordwood to the steamboats—some of which, they said, was never paid for. Settlement was encroaching on their lands, for which they had received no compensation. It was time for a treaty council.

In the fall of 1835, Schoolcraft went to Washington to prepare for a tribal conference. Back to Michigan he sent for chiefs from all parts of the territory, so that a major cession could be negotiated. In the spring of 1836, the tribal leaders—some in boiled shirts and stovepipe hats, others in Indian blouses and headdresses—were assembled in the old Masonic Hall in Washington. After days of discussion with government officials, they agreed to cede all the land in the lower peninsula north of Grand River and west of Thunder Bay and in the upper peninsula from Point Detour through the Straits of St. Mary, west to the Chocolate River on Lake Superior and south to Green Bay. The principal Indian towns were reserved for the tribes, who could use any of the ceded lands until they were required for actual settlement. An incidental clause in this treaty of March 28, 1836, called for construction of an Indian dormitory on Mackinac Island, where chiefs could be housed on official visits. An abrupt, steep-roofed, three-story building, it rose starkly beside the rambling Agency. With an Indian boardinghouse established where warriors had once danced in the firelight, the old wild ways were past.

This treaty was quickly followed by agreements with a delegation of Saginaws and a Chippewa band for Wisconsin. The final cessions were signed in May 1836. For about $2 million the Indians had surrendered claim to nearly twenty million acres. The tribesmen could now pay their debts to the traders. They would collect perpetual annuities from the government, which would also support schools, shops and model farms in their villages.

Meanwhile on Mackinac Island there was a rumor of Indian revolt—as though the tribesmen sensed the threat of dispossession. On May 27th at Fort Mackinac, Captain John Clitz alerted the garrison. It was followed by specific plans and orders:

> Two guns in quick succession from the battery or either of the blockhouses will be the signal for alarm. On the alarm being given the officers and men selected as above will immediately repair to their posts and prepare for action. The remainder of the companies will be posted where their services will be most required and where they can annoy the enemy and do the most execution. Each man will be supplied with twenty-six rounds of ammunition and two spare flints. Should it be necessary [if besieged] barrels will be furnished by the Quarter Master for all the blockhouses and store buildings and kept constantly full of water.

It proved to be a false alarm. During the radiant summer only the sunrise gun boomed over the quiet island.

In Washington the chiefs were gratified by the treaty terms, and so was Schoolcraft, who felt that the tribes had been treated fairly, whereas the new State of Michigan had gained title to nearly all the lower peninsula and huge territory beyond the Straits. He traveled back to Mackinac Island in the steamer *Columbia,* arriving on June 15th. He found his family well, except for the Chippewa girl whom the Schoolcrafts had adopted when her father was killed in a quarrel at Sault Ste. Marie. A happy and dutiful child—"of pleasing piety and gentle manners"—she had

died of tuberculosis during the winter past. If her fate suggested
to him the fate of the domesticated Indians, Schoolcraft did not
say so.

Late that summer of 1836, four thousand tribesmen gathered
on the beaches and coves of Mackinac Island for their first annuity
payment. They feasted on rations handed out by Schoolcraft's
busy storekeepers, while the fort garrison was kept on alert and
a company of troops from Detroit patrolled the village streets.
"So large an assemblage of red and white men probably never
assembled here before," Schoolcraft noted, "and a greater degree
of joy and satisfaction was never evinced by the same number."
The Indians said it more simply—it was a time of fine weather
and plenty to eat. On the island were 143 chiefs with their bands
of men, women, children and dogs in clustered camps all the
way from the sea cliff of Robinson's Folly to the steep west bluffs.
At sunset, which was ration time, a gun boomed from the fort,
and the noisy camps welcomed the commissary wagons. In the
dusk campfires twinkled for miles along the shore, and the wind
was spiced with wood smoke, pork and bacon. During the last
days of September, as the hillsides were turning gold and scarlet,
wagonloads of flour, pork, rice, corn and tobacco were piled on
the trampled beach, and the paymaster distributed $150,000
worth of traps, kettles, knives, axes, hoes, shovels, blankets, coats
and stockings. In Indian-summer weather, the canoes pushed off,
laden with this bounty.

When the tumult had died and the last canoes had vanished
over the radiant water, Schoolcraft indulged in a backward look
and quiet self-congratulations. He wrote in his slanting, open
hand:

> Fourteen years before, I had taken the management of these
> tribes in hand, to conduct their intercourse and to mold and
> guide their feelings, on the part of the government. They were
> then poor, in a region denuded of game, and without one dollar
> in annuities. They were yet smarting under the war of 1812,
> and all but one man, the noble Wing, or Ningwegon, hostile
> to the American name. They [are] now at the acme of Indian
> hunter prosperity, with every want supplied, and a futurity of

pleasing anticipation. They [are] friends of the American government . . . . I [am] gratified with a result so auspicious to
every humane and exalted wish.

Than he summarized his satisfaction in a heroic couplet:

> War, ye wild tribes, hath no rewards like this;
> 'Tis peaceful labors that result in bliss.

A few days later, the guard troops under Major Hoffman were
embarked on a steamer for Detroit. An east wind washed the
shore clean of blackened campfires, and Schoolcraft's journal
listed 23 species of birds observed on the island.

A year later, in 1837, the chiefs asked for part of their payment
in cash. Government paymasters counted out 42,000 silver half
dollars, throwing the coins—two hundred, three hundred, four
hundred—into the Indians' greasy blankets, and the braves
whooped off with their jingling burden. Island merchants would
lessen that load, and other traders would be waiting with whiskey and trinkets when the tribes came home.

With the white man's money, the Indians learned of various
evils. To Schoolcraft an Ottawa brought a half-dollar, which he
had been told was counterfeit. Not attempting to explain a poor
joke, the Agent gave him another coin in its place. Eighteen
months after the gratifying Treaty of 1836, Schoolcraft observed
sadly:

> This tribe [the Chippewas], like all the other leading tribes
> of the race, is destined to fritter away their large domain for
> temporary and local ends, without making any general and per-
> manent provision for their prosperity. The system of temporary
> annuities will, at last, leave them without a home. When the
> buffalo, and the deer, and the beaver are extinct, the Indian
> must work or die. In a higher view there is no blessing which
> is not pronounced in connection with labor and faith. These
> the nation falter at.

For years the annual disbursement would continue at Mackinac
Island, with dwindling bands camped on Mission Point, or Biddle's
Point (the present Windermere Park) and along the southwest

shore. At payment time the village streets swarmed with government officials, army men, traders and visitors. Men from the fort
patroled the Agency, more to please the tourists than to protect
the property. The chiefs, in white man's clothing, collected their
dole in silence and went back to their dwindling towns.

In 1841 Henry Rowe Schoolcraft ended his stay at Mackinac
Island. In the interest of his literary pursuits, his wife's health
and his children's education, he had decided to move to New
York. On his first arrival at the island, he had come in a birchbark
canoe; he left in a commodious steamer. He had outlived the
frontier period of the upper country. In his first season at the
island Agency, on the night of November 13, 1833, he had mar-
veled at a display of northern lights—the astonishing *Jebiug
nemeiddewaud* of the Ojibwas—ghostly banners shimmering
across the midnight sky. It was a sight of mysterious grandeur,
touching the ancient wonder and dread of the Indians. Now the
wonder had gone, and the once magic island was becoming real
estate. "An opinion arose," Schoolcraft wrote in his journal, "that
Michilimackinac must become a favorite watering place, or refuge
for the opulent and invalids during the summer; and lots were
eagerly bought up from Detroit and Chicago."

As Indian agent, Schoolcraft was succeeded by Robert Stuart,
who served until 1845, when the Agency was removed to the
Apostle Islands in Lake Superior. Still the Agency House stood,
haunted with memories, an island landmark until it burned on
a snowy New Year's midnight in 1873.

Constance Fenimore Woolson, a niece of James Fenimore
Cooper, used the rambling house as the setting of her romantic
novel *Anne*. She was in Italy when the house burned, and word of
its disappearance led her to write her nostalgic tale of "The Old
Agency." She pictured it "stretching back from the white limestone road that bordered the little port, its overgrown garden
surrounded by an ancient stockade ten feet in height, with a
massive, slow-swinging gate in front, defended by loopholes."
The house stood empty and forgotten, "under a cloud of confusion as regarded taxes, titles and boundaries . . . belonging
legally to no one." But one winter night the fort commander

saw a flickering light in a back window, and morning showed a curl of smoke from the kitchen chimney. A homeless old Frenchman on his way to Canada had crept into the lifeless house, like a fox finding an empty den. He lived there for a few seasons, according to the story, and on a clear autumn day after a stormy night he died, sitting in sunshine under the cherry trees in the garden.

The Indian dormitory, next door to the vanished Agency, had become a public school, which served the island children until the mid-twentieth century. In 1965 it was restored to its original construction, the belfry was removed and the stone fireplaces and the kitchen oven were rebuilt. As an Indian museum, it now stands as it was in Schoolcraft's time under the gun platforms of Fort Mackinac on the hill.

. 17 .

MACKINAC AND THE MORMONS

In the summer of 1835, Schoolcraft watched a tide of migration flowing through the Mackinac Straits. "The great lakes," he wrote, "can no longer be regarded as solitary seas, where the Indian war whoop has alone for so many uncounted centuries startled its echoes. The Eastern world seems to be alive and roused up to the value of the West. Every vessel, every steamboat, brings up persons of all classes, whose countenances the desire of acquisition, or some other motive, has rendered sharp, or imparted a fresh glow of hope to their eyes . . . . Sitting on my piazza in front of which the great stream of ships and commerce passes, it is a spectacle at once novel and calculated to inspire high anticipations of the future glory of the Mississippi Valley."

At mid-century this tide of migration carried hundreds of Mormon converts to the religious settlement on Beaver Island, and the Mackinac gentiles watched it with hostility. For a few turbulent years the Mormons contested with Mackinac Island for commercial and political dominance in the upper country.

To Burlington, Wisconsin, in 1843 had come a restless and accomplished man—teacher, editor, lawyer, farmer—from western New York. His name was James Jesse Strang; he would become "St. James" to his submissive people. In 1844 on a visit to the Mormon capital of Nauvoo, Illinois, he was converted to the Mormon faith—just four months before Joseph Smith was killed by a gentile mob. Strang was a short man with a tall ambition. He had a high forehead, a bushy red beard, burning eyes and a voice that could both coax and command. Seeking the leadership of the Mormons, he attracted a motley group to his "holy city"

174

of Voree, Wisconsin, where he ruled with rigid authority and
aroused the rancor of neighboring communities. In 1846 he told
his followers of a "revelation" that directed them to "a land amid
wide waters," where they would find prosperity and peace. The
next year he led an exploring party to Big Beaver Island, forty
miles west of the Straits of Mackinac. They found a few traders
and some Indian and Irish fishermen living on a commodious
harbor amid waters teeming with trout and whitefish, and they
learned that the entire island was about to be opened to legal
settlement. There, Strang believed, the Mormons could establish
their theocracy without interference. The traders and fishermen
were clustered on Whiskey Point at the entrance to the harbor,
which Strang called "Paradise Bay." On his map of the wilderness
island he lettered some Biblical names—"Lake Genesareth,"
"River Jordan," "Mount Pisgah." Like Moses, he was leading his
people to a promised land.

Already Beaver Island had a history of religious persecution.
In 1833 Bishop Frederick Baraga had landed on Big Beaver, where
there were a few Christian Indians, along with pagan tribesmen
who sacrificed dogs to grotesque wooden idols. He found a half-
built chapel in the woods—

> and they told me that the pagans on this island are so hostile
> to the religion that every time the Christians began to erect
> their chapel they pulled out the poles from the ground and
> overthrew them. Finally they succeeded once in building half
> the chapel. However the pagans threatened them with burning
> it down as soon as it will be finished. This is why they have
> no desire to finish it, but are rather resolved to move to Arbre
> Croche [on the mainland] in order to avoid the persecutions
> of these stubborn pagans.

On his next visit, Baraga brought gifts—"small scissors, sewing
needles, pins, thread and the like, and very much smoking tobacco which the Indians passionately love"—promising the pagan
tribesmen that he would bring more presents if they would tol-
erate the Christians. Only in this way, he concluded, could Chris-
tianity be sustained on the island.

By 1849 some fifty Mormon families were clearing woods and building their town of St. James on the inmost shore of the roomy harbor. Most of Beaver Island was wilderness, but at Whiskey Point there stood a cluster of shacks, a couple of trading houses and a post office. Mormons who called there for mail were given rough treatment. When government land went on sale, the Mormons and the fishermen contested claims to certain waterfront lots, and the Mormons lost. The disputed ownership of a cow ended in a general clash with clubs and cudgels. Repeatedly the Irish islanders broke up Mormon meetings and chased off Mormon wood-cutters, who were hewing timber for their tabernacle. So history was repeated—gentiles harrying the Latter-Day Saints—on the wave-washed island.

In the fall of 1849 Strang went east to recruit converts in Boston, New York, Philadelphia and Baltimore. Steamboats from Buffalo brought new settlers to Big Beaver. But there was anti-Mormon talk in the upper lake ports, and steamboat captains were reluctant to call at St. James. On the *Empire State* fifty New York emigrants who had bought passage to Beaver Island were carried on, protesting, to Wisconsin. Still the settlement grew.

By the summer of 1850 Mormons outnumbered the island fishermen, who called for help from their gentile neighbors. To Mackinac Island and Pine River (the present Charlevoix) went word of a Fourth of July celebration at Whiskey Point, a celebration that was to culminate in driving the Mormons off the island. Over the water came canoes, skiffs and slant-sailed mackinaw boats. On Whiskey Point they unloaded food, drink, guns and ammunition. At St. James, Strang countered by calling a "conference" of his followers and marching his men in drill squads. On the night of July 3rd, Mormon spies visited the carousing gentiles on Whiskey Point and threw some kegs of gunpowder into the lake.

Next morning the Mormons pointed artillery across the harbor and saluted the Fourth with cannon balls that whistled toward Whiskey Point. Mormon squads patrolled the half-built tabernacle, and one of Strang's men told a gentile trader that his house would be smashed by cannon fire if the fishermen attacked St.

James. The day wore on with no foray from Whiskey Point; the fishermen had lost their zest for battle. They ate their beans and bacon, drank up their liquor and boarded the boats. Sunset found them heading home to Mackinac and the mainland.

Twenty years later Constance Fenimore Woolson described the Battle of Beaver Island in a nostalgic article in *Putnam's Magazine.* Having heard it from the Mackinac people, she described the Mormons as profligates, pirates and robbers. With false lights they lured ships to destruction on the shores of Beaver Island, where they plundered "the numerous wrecks on the beach." These acts, she wrote, inflamed the Mackinac men, but they took no action until a young French girl was enticed to the wicked island. Then an avenging fleet put out from Mackinac, manned by Frenchmen and half-breeds armed with shotguns and rifles, with "a sprinkling of uniforms from the fort on the heights giving Uncle Sam's sanction to the enterprise." When they entered Paradise Bay and opened fire on St. James, the Saints fled to the woods. Soon afterward, her story concluded, the Mormons forsook Big Beaver, which was restored to the occupancy of loons and sea gulls.

Actually the Fort Mackinac troops were never involved in the Mormon hostility, though it must have enlivened their talk in the taverns and their routine on the hill.

Four days after the Fourth of July "battle" the Mormons held a ceremony that angered and astonished the gentiles. On July 8th beside the blue waters of Paradise Bay, Strang was crowned "King" of Beaver Island. In fulfillment of one of his "revelations," the Saints were assembled in the unroofed tabernacle. Clad in a crimson robe, the ruler marched to the platform with his twelve apostles. There he was crowned with a tinsel circlet encrusted with stars (a property provided by a former actor, who had left the stage to become a Latter-Day Saint), and he read a decree imparted to him by revelation. It ordained "the Islands of the Great Lakes" as the "Kingdom of the Saints" and delegated the "King" to apportion the lands among his people. After this bizarre ritual, sacrifices of cattle and poultry were prepared for a public feast.

One of Strang's first royal pronouncements sanctioned polygamy among his people: He imparted a new revelation stating that God required the Saints to practice plural marriage. The "King" set an example by taking four wives into his household. Not many of his followers had prospered enough so to enlarge their families, and, besides, there were few unmarried women in the colony. Of the five hundred heads of Mormon families, perhaps twenty took additional wives. But the doctrine of polygamy quickly added to the notoriety of the Mormons and to the outrage of their gentile neighbors.

During the early 1850s the Mormon numbers grew, with colonies spreading to Pine River, Grand Traverse Bay and Drummond Island in Lake Huron. On Beaver Island, Strang's rule was undisputed. The Saints had driven out the earlier settlers, who fled to neighboring islands with only what possessions they could carry. To Mackinac, smoldering with resentment and hatred, went the Cables, Coopers, Wrights, McKinleys and Bennets. On Mackinac Island "Mormon" was an ugly word.

Beyond this personal animus, a commercial conflict was at work. With a fine harbor, rich fishing waters and limitless wood for supplying fuel to steamers, Beaver Island threatened to dominate the economy of the Straits; and, when in 1852 Strang was elected to the Michigan legislature, the Mormons had a threatening political power. In his first term of office, Strang accomplished the creation of Emmet County, comprising the Beaver Islands and a tract of neighboring mainland; thus he separated his "kingdom" from the authority of Mackinac County. In Emmet County there were some five hundred Indian fishermen, who turned over their catch to traders in return for quantities of whiskey and flimsy trade goods. When Strang clamped down on the liquor trade, the teetotaling Mormons were charged with counterfeiting, stealing government timber and robbing the mails. A warfare of words began.

In his *Northern Islander* newspaper, Strang accused the Mackinac people of avarice, corruption and hypocrisy, charges elaborated in his rambling *Ancient and Modern Michilimackinac, Including an Account of the Controversy between Mackinac and the Mormons.* This little book, half local history and half dynamite, sketches the French, English and American occupations of

the Straits and arrives at the present with the heading, "Decay
of Mackinac." Finding little to commend in the island's physical
resources, Strang quickly turned to an appraisal of its people.
He wrote:

> The poorer classes, are excessively dissipated. Their only change
> is from dissipation to want, and from want to dissipation. Ten
> times more liquor is drunk in Mackinac than any other town
> of the same population. Among the halfbreeds, who formerly
> made most of the population, the deaths are as two to one
> birth, and the class are rapidly disappearing. The Irish, who
> are supplying their places, are running the same race.

He dismissed Fort Mackinac in a sentence—"The fortress is
reduced from an important military position to a mere hospital
to recruit the health of soldiers long employed in sickly
climates"—but he gave a paragraph to Indian whiskey.

> The most profitable and at the same time the most ruinous trade
> Mackinac ever had is that in Whisky. Indian whisky is made
> by putting two gallons of common whisky, or unrectified spirits,
> to thirty gallons of water, and adding red pepper enough to make
> it fiery and tobacco enough to make it intoxicating. Its cost
> is not above five cents per gallon. Thousands of barrels have
> been sold every year, the prices generally being fifty cents a
> gallon by the cask, twenty-five cents a quart by the bottle, and
> six cents a drink.

After discussing political controversies, his voice rose in a shrill
and sweeping diatribe.

> In Mackinac, where at the Indian payments the most respectable
> men have heretofore considered stealing from the Indian annui-
> ties honorable; where hundreds of inexperienced whites, and
> thousands of Indians, have been victimized and their lives de-
> stroyed for the sole purpose of obtaining their property; where
> gambling, drunkenness and debauchery swallow up all things,
> and during one third of the year are the sole employment of
> the population; where twenty cold-blooded murders have been
> committed within the memory of man, and not one punished;
> where, till recently, poor men were imprisoned and sold without

law and without process; where law is scarcely resorted to, except to gull or destroy someone by the perversion of it; and where the public officers, the sworn conservators of the peace, openly and shamelessly appeal to the mob power to override the authority of the law, and publish their perjured infamy with their names signed to it; there, in such a place, the men are found to complain of the Legislature for giving a legal organization to Emmet County, the [Mormon] inhabitants of which have never been guilty of an offence against the peace and good order of society.

To Strang the lawless men of Mackinac seemed the enemy, yet it was his own disaffected followers who brought down his "kingdom." The leader of the revolt was Dr. Hezekiah D. McCullough, an ex-surgeon of the United States Army, who had become one of Strang's high councilors and an official of Emmet County. Though St. James was a bone-dry community, McCullough sometimes went aboard ships in the harbor for a drink of whiskey. Rebuked by Strang and deprived of church and civil office, McCullough began plotting against the "kingdom." On a trip to Detroit he repeated the gentile charges against the Mormons—counterfeiting, robbing United States mails, cutting government timber—and somehow he got the United States gunboat *Michigan* sent north to arrest Strang and his leaders. McCullough himself returned to Beaver Island on the gunboat.

At noon on July 16, 1856, the *Michigan* steamed into St. James harbor and was moored to the dock. It loomed large—pointed bowsprit, three masts with tilted spars and a tall stack smoking above the iron-sheathed paddle boxes. All afternoon the ship lay there with cannon pointed at the roofless tabernacle, while the Mormons wondered and waited. That evening, while the sun sank over the woods, the gunboat's pilot went ashore to summon Strang to the captain's quarters. Strang came willingly, striding along the dock with pilot St. Bernard. As he reached the gangplank, two men sprang up from behind a wall of fuel wood. At point-blank range they emptied pistols into Strang's back and head. As he fell, the two assassins ran aboard the gunboat for protection.

Faithful Mormons carried Strang to the nearest house, where
the gunboat's surgeon came to dress his wounds. Next morning
the *Michigan* steamed through the sunrise toward the Straits.
At Mackinac Island the assassins—apostate Mormons named
Wentworth and Bedford—were turned over to Sheriff Granger,
who took them to the island jail. After five minutes behind bars
they were released, to the cheers of an excited gathering.

Ten days later, with McCullough and his confederates still
aboard, the *U.S.S. Michigan* returned to Beaver Island. Learning
that Strang was still alive, though barely, Captain McBlair
demanded surrender of the "King" and his leaders. Getting no
response he sailed the gunboat back to Mackinac.

Two days later the steamer *Louisville* called at Beaver Island,
and the sorrowing Saints carried Strang aboard. He was taken
to his original Mormon colony at Voree, Wisconsin, thirty miles
below Milwaukee. There he died on the 9th of July with two
of his wives, Betsy and Phoebe, at his bedside.

Meanwhile the faithful, fearful Mormons clung to their belief
in the goodness of God and the sainthood of their fallen leader.
Looking out of her door at sunset, a St. James woman saw a
golden cloud, which, dissolving, formed the letters "Z-I-O-N" and
then reformed in the letters "J-S" for the dying king. These signs
were seen by other Mormons, who talked of them with wonder
and hope.

Early in July a vessel from Mackinac brought Sheriff Granger
to arrest the Mormon leaders. He found no leaders there, only
a bewildered people who were warned to leave the island before
they saw their cattle slaughtered and their houses burned.
Prodded by jeering fishermen from St. Helena and Mackinac islands, 2,600 Mormons, men, women and children, crowded into
vessels in the harbor. Behind them a yelling mob set fire to the
tabernacle and plundered the town. It was the harvest of a
decade of hate, and it left a sorry page on Lake Michigan's history.

No Mormons remained on Beaver Island, though their plain
and solid farmhouses still stand, mostly empty, in the ragged
grass, with the old orchards around them. A few hundred Indians
and Irish fishermen and farmers live today in the village of St.

James, and on summer mornings the black-robed Christian Brothers walk down the King's Highway from their retreat in the woods. Every day the ferry *Emerald Isle* brings visitors from Charlevoix. They look at the King Strang Hotel and the Mormon Print Shop and stop in at the newer Shamrock Bar, which offers *Caed Mille Failte*—"a hundred thousand welcomes." In October sportsmen come by air and water to hunt Beaver Island deer, coyotes, grouse, duck, geese and squirrel.

Back in 1856 the Mormons were dispersed near and far. Hundreds of them, dazed and destitute, were unloaded on the docks of Detroit and Chicago in the searing July sun. Others went to Green Bay, Milwaukee and Racine. Some found a nearer refuge on the Emmet County mainland, where they were slowly accepted by their gentile neighbors.

One of these displaced families was recalled by U. P. Hedrick, when he wrote the story of his youth in *The Land of the Crooked Tree*. Hedrick's father had arranged to buy a cow from a Mormon who lived twelve miles back in the woods from Little Traverse Bay. Early in the morning, the day before Thanksgiving, young Ulysses Hedrick started off, carrying a lead rope and a lunch bag, his pockets sagging with sixty silver dollars. Soon it began to snow. He ate his lunch in a spruce thicket and trudged on over a blank, white road. In late afternoon he came to a two-story cabin in a stump-dotted clearing.

A family of eight lived there—a weathered man, a wan woman, six children with a dog and a cat, in two rooms, which the red-hot cookstove filled with heat and suffocation. The walls were covered with wrinkled sheets of Strang's newspaper, the *Northern Islander*. After the children were put to bed, the old Mormon took off shoes and stockings and propped his rheumatic feet on a slab of wood in the oven. While baking himself, he told the visiting boy the story of his life.

He had grown up and married in the old cathedral town of Canterbury, learning to be a printer; his father had turned to the printing trade after spending half his life as Charles Darwin's gardener. From a Mormon missionary the young man and his wife heard of Joseph Smith's revelation in America and of the

Mormon promised land in Utah. Converted to the faith, the two left Canterbury for the long journey to the Great Salt Lake. But at Buffalo, New York, while waiting for a lake steamer, they met "King" Strang, who persuaded them to join the Beaver Island colony. There the Englishman became a printer for Strang's "Royal Press." When the Mormons were driven off the island, this family came to the mainland and made a clearing in the woods of Emmet County.

When the tale was told, young Hedrick climbed upstairs and crawled into a feather bed with a couple of Mormon boys. In the morning he found the bed dusted with snow and a swirling white curtain outside the frosted window. It was Thanksgiving Day. At noon there was a meal of salt pork and boiled potatoes beside the suffocating cookstove. All day, while snow deepened in the woods, he read the mysteries of Mormonism in a box of books in the drafty upstairs room. Just before dusk the sky cleared, and the boy was overwhelmed with homesickness. Supper was laid out—bread, pork and potatoes—but the visitor insisted on starting home. He counted out the sixty dollars and claimed a balky cow. With the boy pulling the lead rope and the farmer prodding from behind, they went two miles down the snowy road. By then the cow was tamed, and the Mormon turned back. Through silent snow-hung woods, under the cold and distant stars, the boy plodded homeward.

It was past midnight when he saw through the winter darkness the lamplight in the window—his mother had left it burning. At his call the family wakened. They put the cow in the barn, poked up the kitchen stove and brought out roast turkey, ham, spiced peaches, mincemeat and pumpkin pie. Over this Thanksgiving feast, the boy told about the Mormon household, the patience and poverty and the strange saga of wandering and revelation. It seemed he had returned from a far journey.

. 18 .

THE CRUMBLING FORT

Solemn sentinels pace the ancient walls, and rusty cannon frown sullenly from the battlements, but in spite of mounted guard and severe military etiquette we fear it must be acknowledged that one gunboat could easily level Fort Mackinac to its limestone foundations.

—CONSTANCE FENIMORE WOOLSON, 1870

On the Morning of March 11, 1873, the Hon. Thomas W. Ferry took the floor of the United States Senate to propose a resolution:

> That so much of the island of Mackinac, lying in the Straits of Mackinac within the county of Mackinac, in the State of Michigan, as is now held by the United States under military reservation or otherwise (except Fort Mackinac and so much of the present reservation thereof as bounds it to the south of the village of Mackinac, and to the west, north, and east respectively by lines drawn north and south, and east and west, at a distance from the present fort flag-staff of four hundred yards) hereby is reserved and withdrawn from settlement, occupancy or sale under the laws of the United States, and dedicated and set apart as a national public park, or grounds, for health, comfort and pleasure, for the benefit and enjoyment of the people.

At the Treaty of Greene Ville in 1795 (Article 3, Section 13), the Indian tribes had ceded to the United States "the post and island of Michilimackinac, and portions of the mainland adjacent

184

thereto, also a piece on the mainland to the north to measure six miles on Lake Huron or the Strait; also the Isle de Bois Blanc, the latter being an extra and voluntary gift of the Chippeway nation." After that cession, resident householders had legal title to their own property, though land was not offered for public sale. Most of the strategic island had remained in government possession.

In 1827 Thomas White Ferry was born in the Mission House at the eastern end of Mackinac village. When Tom Ferry was a boy, learning his lessons in his father's mission school, romping on the beach with Indian and half-breed children, steering a canoe with a torn-blanket sail, Fort Mackinac dominated the island and the straits. Every morning its sunrise gun reverberated over woods and water; through all seasons its flag commanded the northern sky. But when he spoke in the Senate chamber Senator Ferry acknowledged that the island was no longer a military stronghold. The fort was not needed for protection, but protection was needed for the crumbling fort that had long guarded the vital straits.

Since Tom Ferry's boyhood the fur trade had vanished, the Indian traffic had dwindled, fish and tourists had become the island's business and Fort Mackinac, seemingly as permanent as the limestone cliffs, had slowly lost its sway. In the 1850s the rotting old stockade—made of cedar logs tipped with iron spikes—came down. For a season daily details of soldiers labored to remove the pickets that British troops had planted seventy years before. That left the stone and earthworks exposed to view; Fort Mackinac was more picturesque without its bristling palisade. In 1861 the two-story soldiers' barracks were occupied by two artillery companies, each with its own mess; at inspection the two outfits faced each other across the green parade ground. But Mackinac Island was a thousand miles away from the Confederate battle line. The fort was left empty when its two companies sailed out of Mackinac Harbor to join the Union armies.

On a breezy May day in 1862, the steamer *Illinois* whistled at the harbor entrance. When she was moored at the wharf, a company of Michigan Volunteers marched off, escorting three

prisoners of war from Tennessee. They were high-ranking men—
General William G. Harding, General Washington Barrows and
Judge Joseph C. Guild. While quarters at the fort were being prepared for them, they were lodged in the Mission House, with
sentries patrolling the street outside. After a week there they
were marched up the fort road to three suites of rooms in the
wooden building between the stone quarters and the guardhouse.
There they spent a tranquil summer (visitors file past their life-
sized wax figures in the fort museum today) while the island
steamers brought news of the battles of Bull Run and Cedar Mountain. In September, like other summer residents, the prisoners
packed their trunks and departed. They were taken to the growing prison for Confederate officers on Johnson's Island in Sandusky
Bay at the western end of Lake Erie.

For the rest of the war Fort Mackinac stood empty while the
men of its former garrison fought and died in distant battles.
One roll call lists "the gallant General Williams who was killed
at Baton Rouge; the tall young Virginian, Captain Terrell, who
was shot while leading a charge in one of the early battles of
West Virginia; the brilliant engineer, General Sill, and two lieutenants, Bailey and Benson, whom we remember as light-hearted
boys."

A cadence of booted feet was heard on the hill in 1867, when
Company B of the 43rd Infantry arrived. For the men the leaking
and drafty barracks were repaired. Curious summer visitors admired their dress parade, and dignitaries were entertained in
the officers' mess. But the gun platforms were a tourists' lookout,
commanding a far view of forest shores and wind-stirred water.
Across the channel Round Island and Bois Blanc were still wilderness, with legends haunting their old Indian burial grounds. A
carriage road took visitors past the old stone quarry and the
ruined lime kiln, built by the British in 1780. Tourists passed
through the north sally port, where on a July morning in 1812
two lines of redcoats had presented arms while the American
garrison marched out in surrender.

The frowning blockhouses had outlived the primitive warfare
of whooping Indians. In the northwest blockhouse, the highest

point of the fort, a wooden water tank was installed in the summer of 1881. Then the soldiers had a pumping detail in a pump
house down on Spring Street; each morning they pumped water
from a bubbling pool (later named "La Salle Spring") at the foot
of the bluff. From the blockhouse tank, water was piped to the
fort buildings. Gone was the water wagon that had creaked up
Turkey Hill when the fort cisterns failed in dry weather. In 1885
a bathhouse was built at the east end of the parade, on the
site of the old sutler's store.

The fort that had overlooked the traffic of Indians, voyageurs
and traders now watched the arrival of excursion boats, and the
village overflowed with vacationists and health-seekers. The old
buildings of the Fur Company were converted into the Astor
House, with rocking chairs on the verandah and a billiard table
in the public rooms. The St. Cloud Hotel, just east of the fort
gardens, "furnished in Queen Anne style," advertised a corps of
colored servants, operatic singers and a "Famous String Band."
The Mission House, once filled with Indian and half-breed children, had "good accommodations for 200 guests." Other choices
were offered by the Northerner Hotel, the Mackinac Hotel, the
Island House and the Commercial House. The Miners' Arms was
patronized by copper and iron men who waited at Mackinac for
boats to Lake Superior.

One of these early hotels became known to the world when
a Boston clergyman wrote a short story for a Boston magazine.
On the first page of the *Atlantic Monthly* for December 1863, readers found a traveler "stranded at the old Mission House in Mackinac, waiting for a Lake Superior steamer which did not choose
to come." In an old newspaper the restive traveler chanced upon
the name of Philip Nolan, Lieutenant in the United States Army—
and so began the tale of "The Man Without a Country." Island
readers took the story literally, and even today a visitor may
be shown Room 16 overlooking Mission Point, "where Edward
Everett Hale wrote his immortal story." Though the Mission House
had some famous guests—Generals Sherman, Sheridan and Han-
cock were regulars there—Edward Everett Hale never saw the
hotel or the island.

After an 1880 survey of the national park, certain lands went on sale for summer residents. From a Chicago office Gurdon Hubbard, once the "boy clerk" of the Astor agency, advertised eighty acres of building lots on the west bluffs, near the cliff known as Lover's Leap and above the caves of the Devil's Kitchen. In 1885, when the first towered and balconied "cottages" were built on the bluffs, workmen began felling timber from the slope beyond the government pasture, which lay west of the village and the fort. There two years later the Grand Hotel opened its doors to the public. Built by a combination of the Grand Rapids and Indiana Railroad, the Michigan Central Railroad and the Detroit and Cleveland Navigation Company, this famous hostelry attracted guests from near and far.

To five busy wharves came daily steamers from Traverse City and Petoskey and liners on regular schedule from Chicago and Detroit. At the Hoban Brothers Livery Stable, across from the present Chippewa Hotel, visitors could step into carriages for the drive to Arch Rock, Fort Holmes and Robinson's Folly. Next door in Fenton's Indian Bazaar they could find all kinds of native souvenirs—feather fans, moccasins, miniature canoes and mococks of maple sugar and baskets woven of sweet grass and decorated with porcupine quills. A surprising number bought Lieutenant Kelton's pocket-sized *Annals of Fort Mackinac* (between 1882 and 1895 it went through twelve editions), and most of them accepted its friendly offer: "Now follow us, and we will show you through the fort." The old stronghold had become a tourist attraction.

Even on Sunday mornings island visitors climbed the hill to attend church services in the fort chapel, an upper room overlooking the parade ground. They fell in behind the lined-up garrison and marched to worship to drum and bugle. The officers attended in full uniform, sitting rigid on the narrow front benches. Precisely an hour later the bugle sounded to marshal the congregation out. "If the sermon was not finished," wrote one of the visitors, "so much the worse for the sermon, but it made no difference to the bugler—out marched the soldiers,

drowning the poor chaplain's hurrying voice with their tramp
down the stairs."

In the Episcopal service the Old Testament readings appointed
for August Sundays were from the Book of Numbers, the chapters
about Balaam and Balak. "As it was in August that summer visitors
came to Mackinac," Constance Fenimore Woolson recalled, "the
little fort chapel is in many minds associated with the patient
Balak, his seven altars and his seven rams."

In 1873 Senator Ferry's resolution was lost in the press of other
business. But it was presented again years later, with approval
of the Secretary of War and of both military committees of Congress. It was adopted on March 3, 1875, and Mackinac Island
became a national park. In 1884 the government offered for sale
military lands on Bois Blanc Island, where for nearly a century
firewood had been cut for the stoves and hearths of the fort.
The income was used to improve carriage roads and bridal paths
on Mackinac Island.

In those years the policy of the United States Army was to
consolidate troops at large permanent posts and to abandon
smaller outposts. At the end of 1884, Robert Todd Lincoln, Secretary of War, stated, "The Army has enjoyed almost complete rest
from field operations." The frontier was quiet, and there had been
no disturbance that year to cause the firing of a single musket.
In 1891 the Secretary of War reported evacuation of a quarter
of the army posts that had been occupied in 1889, with others
marked for closing within the next few years. In 1892 there were
96 active army posts in the United States. By 1895 the number
was reduced to eighty.

In 1894 a company of men marched down the hill from Fort
Mackinac. From Bennett's Wharf they boarded a steamer for transfer to Fort Brady at Sault Ste. Marie. With them, to a scuffle of
hooves and a creaking of caissons, went five brass field guns and
a ten-inch iron mortar. Other Mackinac cannon were shipped
down the lakes as scrap iron; some were set into the wharves
of Buffalo for mooring posts. Left at Fort Mackinac were Lieuten-

ant Woodbridge Geary and a single squad of the 19th Infantry. That winter ten men mustered for reveille and retreat on the snowy parade ground. Their footsteps must have made a hollow sound in the empty barracks.

On March 3, 1895, just twenty years after its designation as a national park, Mackinac Island was transferred to the State of Michigan. Fort Mackinac was included in the then established Mackinac Island State Park, with provision that the flag of the United States should be kept floating over the parade ground as in the century past. On September 16, 1895, the few remaining troops fell into line with knapsacks and rifles on their shoulders. From his quarters in the morgue a civilian caretaker watched them march down the hill in the autumn sunlight. Behind them stood the empty fort, with its flag against the sky.

. 19 .

BRIDGING THE STRAITS

Now follow us, and we will show you through the Fort.

—DWIGHT H. KELTON

On November 1, 1957, the first wheeled traffic crossed the Straits of Mackinac. The great bridge hanging from its twin steel towers is a product of twentieth-century engineering and technology, but its approaches, from Old Mackinaw and St. Ignace, are rooted in the past. When the lofty span began to carry a new commerce over the wide blue water, the State of Michigan began a reconstruction of the forts of Mackinac. Neither the bridge nor the historical restoration was a new idea. Both had waited for their time to come.

The dream of a bridge across the four-mile narrows is older than the search for a Northwest Passage. In their winter lodges before white men came into the country, the Chippewas told of a great chief who gathered stones on the Lake Huron shore and made a path across the northern narrows. Their legend described an autumn storm that broke the bridge and carried the stones away—except those that remained as Bois Blanc, Round and Mackinac Islands.

In 1853 "King" Strang of the Mormons, with less fervor than accompanied his other revelations, foresaw a bridge over the narrows:

The early construction [of a railroad to Lake Superior] is now probable; the plan being to ferry across the Straits, which at

191

that point are only three and a half or four miles wide. The
plan of a ferry, however, will not succeed; because the ice forms
in such quantities as to entirely prevent the passage of boats
long before sleighs can cross it. If the road is located across
the Straits it will necessarily cross on a bridge, in order to secure
the winter business.

Thirty-one years later a Traverse City editor proposed a bridge
or a tunnel to provide "a sure and permanent crossing of the
Straits." In the early twentieth century there were proposals for
a floating tunnel and for a series of causeways and bridges making
a hop, skip and jump, from Cheboygan by way of Bois Blanc,
Round Island and the tip of Mackinac Island to St. Ignace.

In 1923 the state ferry service was established. It was efficient
and dependable, the big steamers breaking a passage through
the pack ice of midwinter and paving a white wake across the
summer straits. But its capacity of 416 cars an hour was inade-
quate in rush seasons; at times automobile traffic backed up for
twenty miles from the ferry docks, and drivers waited all day
and all night for a crossing. Work began on the massive bridge
piers in the summer of 1954. On November 1, 1957, after 34 years
of service, the ferries made their last trip, and the first cars drove
across the soaring bridge.

A dramatic past is one of the magnets of the north country,
and awareness of its history was quickened by the new flow of
traffic across the Straits. In 1958, when the bridge was formally
dedicated, the State of Michigan began a historical-development
program. Spanning two centuries of tradition at the Straits, it
would link the present to the storied past.

When Fort Mackinac was abandoned as a military post in 1895,
the Mackinac Island State Park Commission opened its gates to
the public. After admiring the view from the lofty fort, visitors
could only guess what memories it held of peace and war. In
1900 a simple monument to Dr. Beaumont recalled that a fort
surgeon had made medical history with his studies of a voyageur's open stomach. Half a century later the old Fur Company
store, where the young French Canadian had been injured in
a shotgun accident, was rebuilt and furnished as a Beaumont

memorial museum. By that time much of the island's history had
been reclaimed from the deepening past.

The first reclamation of military property took place, not at
Fort Mackinac, but at the outpost of Fort Holmes (which the English, who first built it, called "Fort George") on the highest point
of the island. The primitive redoubt consisted of a blockhouse
with an underground magazine, surrounded by a cedar stockade
and an earth embankment. Sometimes after 1815, American gunners at Fort Mackinac shattered the blockhouse for target practice.
Its timbers were used to build a stable in the fort gardens near
the harbor. In 1836 the English traveler Harriet Martineau came
to Mackinac with an ear trumpet, a lively curiosity and an ob-
servant eye. She exclaimed about the view from the island's
crest—"No words can give an idea of the charms"—but said
nothing about a fortification. A visiting missionary climbed to the
height in 1843 and found some grassy ditches yawning around
"two posts and a beam of the gateway, on which many have as-
pired to immortality by carving their names." Sometime after the
island became a national park, an observation tower said to be
seventy feet high was constructed to mark the Fort Holmes site.
When a tourist fell from the stairway, the tower was taken down.

In 1904 the Commission began to plan a park between the
island harbor and Fort Mackinac. At that time the stable built
of the old Fort Holmes timbers was removed; the timbers went
back to their original airy site and became again a blockhouse
with two doors, two narrow windows and a four-sided roof. It
stood until 1933, when a brush fire blackened the height. The
fort was rebuilt in 1936—an authentic reproduction this time,
with moat, timbered earthworks and a two-story blockhouse—
under the direction of army engineers. Since then it has guarded
the island crest, with visitors again carving their names on the
weathered doors.

In the woods below Fort Holmes lay the neglected Post Cemetery, with brush, ferns and wildflowers hiding the graves of the
garrison dead. From 1901 to 1911 the president of the Park Commission was the Hon. Peter White of Marquette, a pioneer in iron
mining and shipping on the lakes. In Washington he lobbied for

an appropriation to improve and maintain the post burial ground. By Memorial Day in 1907, the work was complete. Visitors found sunlight and shadow falling across the 142 weathered stones enclosed in a white picket fence. A flag flew over the entrance, and individual flags decorated each grave. On a stone platform in the center stood a cannon from Fort Sumter. Its bronze tablet was engraved:

> On fame's eternal camping ground
>   Their silent tents are spread,
> And glory guards with solemn round
>   The bivouac of the dead.

Among them are six British soldiers who died in the War of 1812.

Under Peter White's direction the park planned by the commissioners took shape at the foot of the fort hill. In 1909 it received its name and its central feature—a bronze statue of Father Marquette who had come to Mackinac Island with a band of homeless Huron and Ottawa Indians in 1671. Later the Park Commission added a bark chapel with a cedar cross beside it—the simple structure that the Jesuits erected as the house of God in the wilderness.

In 1915 Mackinac Island had its most fervent revival of history. With due ceremony, the Nicolet tablet and the Cass memorial were unveiled on the wooded cliffs. At the Cass Day exercises Colonel William P. Preston, then mayor of the village and a veteran of the Fort Mackinac garrison, reminded a crowd of notables that they were gathered on one of the most historic places of America. A review of that history was at hand in the list of more than two hundred names recently given to island landmarks. In an excess of spirit an excess of names had been assigned to features large and small. Pontiac's Lookout and the Duluth Lookout shared the western bluffs with Agatha Lookout, named for a nun who had once looked after Mackinac orphans. On the eastern shore Langlade's Craig jutted over Hennepin Point near Tonty Spring. The Allouez Cascade dripped down the limestone cliff, and Parkman Prospect overhung Echo Grotto, which re-echoed the whistle of passing steamboats. The old public pasture, surrounding Hanks

Pond, became Richard Park, for Father Gabriel Richard, who had lived on the island during the summer of 1799. Hanks Pond—now a water hazard of the Grand Hotel Golf Course—recalled the gallant Lieutenant Porter Hanks of 1812; it was fed by La Salle Spring and Wawatam Brook. All the history of the upper country was echoed in these names, though no islander could use or remember a fraction of them.

In the same year, 1915, the first Fort Mackinac museum was created. For two decades visitors had climbed the hill, peered at the blockhouses, strolled over the parade grounds and sat on the airy gun platforms. Now in the old officers' quarters they could linger over a collection of Indian and pioneer implements— stone-tipped spears, axes, arrowheads, snowshoes, traps, guns, kettles, gourd rattles, feathered pipes and necklaces of bears' claws. These things gave visitors a glimpse of early life in the region, but they told nothing of the old post that had dominated the straits for a hundred years.

Another year of commemoration came in 1934, the three hundredth anniversary of Nicolet's journey through the straits. The celebration began on July 1st, with the raising of colors by the United States 2nd Infantry, a regiment once quartered at the post, at the south sally port of Fort Mackinac. Exhibition drills on the parade ground, band concerts in Marquette Park and parades down Huron Street enlivened a festive week. Army aircraft dedicated the new airstrip on the Early Farm, where British and American troops had clashed in 1814. In two of the fort buildings, historical displays featured an Indian lacrosse stick used in the game that preceded the Michilimackinac massacre, a copy of the deed given by Indian chiefs in transfer of Mackinac Island to George III of England, the petrified skull of a prehistoric animal found on Round Island and the original pilot's license for navigation of the Mississippi River issued at St. Louis in 1859 to Samuel L. Clemens (Mark Twain). The formal celebration ended with a Nicolet memorial program on the parade ground at Fort Mackinac and the Nicolet pageant, enacted by four hundred costumed characters in the tea gardens of the Grand Hotel. All that summer the historical fair drew visitors to the fort, but what they saw was more like an old curiosity shop than a reconstruction of times past.

In 1958 a historical interpretation was begun at Fort Mackinac, a picturing of men and events from the storied past. This museum program had so much public appeal that the Park Commission began a reconstruction of the British fort at Old Mackinaw Point on the southern mainland.

It was nearly two centuries since the British had moved to Mackinac Island, leaving a lifeless station behind them. The winds blew, the restless lake lapped at the shore and slowly the sand buried old Fort Michilimackinac. When Schoolcraft first visited the Point in 1820, he found some tilted timbers studding the windswept shore. In 1845 Parkman spent a day pacing the outlines marked by the stumps of rotting pickets; he made a rough drawing of the vanished palisade. The modern Mackinaw City slowly grew up on the highway, a mile to the east, and only some curiosity seekers disturbed the historic site. In 1934 a rude stockade and some small cabins were built on the point, where the great bridge began to rise two decades later. This stockade, plus some historical records in London and Ottawa and some maps, letters and diaries in Detroit, Ann Arbor and Lansing, was what museum men had to begin with. The work was started in 1958 while the first summer traffic streamed across the bridge.

At first the digging looked like any excavation. But it was not done from blueprints; it was a search for blueprints buried in the earth. Slowly the buildings' guidelines were uncovered—patterns of sand, stone, soil and charcoal, remnants of charred logs, stone floors and cedar puncheons. The archaeologists traced five expanding stages of Fort Michilimackinac, from the first rude stockade built by the French in 1715 to the fortified town abandoned by the British in 1780. They identified building materials and methods of construction. Sifting and resifting the sand, they collected beads, bullets, buttons, pipe shards, fish hooks, flint locks and crucifixes. Hundreds of these metal, glass and clay artifacts enriched their knowledge of the commercial, military and religious life of the old fort.

Now, after a remarkable collaboration of archaeological and historical research and restoration, Fort Michilimackinac stands, with walls, blockhouses and a score of buildings, as it did when the Indians massacred the British garrison. The work, which still goes on, is wholly supported by admission fees.

After their painstaking reconstruction, the fort buildings were furnished to portray their eighteenth-century life. Onto plank shelves in the King's Storehouse went blankets, guns, tobacco, bar lead, bagged and baled goods, jugs of wine and barrels of rum—with life-sized figures taking inventory. In the soldiers' barracks a sequence of thirty displays tells the story of the fort and its leading characters through the French and British periods. In the restored Chapel of Ste. Anne, a famous marriage of 1754 is re-enacted, several times a day, with music, candlelight and French and English voices.

At Fort Mackinac on the island the fort buildings have been made into a historical museum portraying the life of the post in its active years. Up the long ramp from Marquette Park visitors enter through the south sally port; others come through the main entrance on the upper side, passing through an avenue of flags of the three nations that have occupied the Straits. Inside the walls they find themselves in another century.

In the north blockhouse, a period reproduction on the second floor shows the scene at daybreak on July 17, 1812—with American soldiers sounding alarm at sight of British troops on the island heights. A representation on the ground floor shows the surrender of the fort to the British on that same day. The west blockhouse contains the figures of British troops hoisting cannon and supplies onto the upper level to resist the American attack of 1814. The ground floor of the east blockhouse shows British troops making bullets; on the upper floor British soldiers are hurriedly cleaning muskets and cannon.

In the officers' stone quarters, which like the blockhouses date from the 1780s, period reproductions portray the fort at peace, with white-wigged officers engaged at the cribbage board and the tea table. From these scenes, visitors can step onto the long piazza outside. There the fort tea room offers a luncheon menu

with the same harbor view that pleased the captains and their
ladies long ago.

The adjoining officers' wooden quarters now contain a life-sized
portrayal of the three high-ranking Confederate prisoners who
were confined there in 1862. There also is a display of three
famous local products—the mackinaw coat, the mackinaw boat
and the mackinaw blanket—with an account of their origins. Next
door the old guardhouse grimly recalls the confinement of soldiers
who had broken regulations.

Across the shaded green parade ground stand the soldiers' barracks, where the men of the 10th and 22nd Infantry once answered morning call and mess call; there visitors see historical
displays, mural paintings and dioramas that review the long history of the Straits region.

Every half-hour brings the ferry boats from St. Ignace and Mackinaw City, and visitors stream ashore. They take the carriage drive
to Arch Rock, Sugar Loaf, the Post Cemetery and Fort Holmes on
the heights. Up the long ramp they climb to Fort Mackinac; a
quarter of a million people pass through its gates during the
short summer season. Their admission fees support the entire
historical development program at the Straits.

In the long shadows of afternoon, the boats fill again, and visitors return to the mainland. By evening the village is quiet. Over
Biddle's Point, where the Indians and voyageurs once tended supper fires, gulls circle in the sunset. From the far side of the harbor
the Straits Transit ferry sounds its deep steam whistle for the
last trip to Mackinaw City. With dusk the flashing brightens from
the light tower in the Round Island channel. Gulls settle on the
breakwater; the night wind freshens, and the lake is loud along
the shore. Above the twinkling harbor lights the fort stands dark
against the stars. Then from the storied hilltop come the serene
clear bugle notes of taps, ending another day at old Fort
Mackinac.

BIBLIOGRAPHY

BIBLIOGRAPHY

The first references to the strategic Straits of Mackinac appear in the *Jesuit Relations;* the literature of the region begins with this great work, whose seventy-one volumes are a mine of material about French exploration, evangelism and trade in the Great Lakes area. I have drawn on many of the volumes in matters large and small. The forty volumes of *Historical Collections* published by the Michigan Pioneer and Historical Society and the 31 volumes of *Wisconsin Historical Collections* published by the Wisconsin State Historical Society contain a vast variety of information about men and movements in the upper country. The Straits region and Mackinac Island especially have been the subjects of much writing—some historical, some literary, some descriptive. A general survey and sampling of this literature appears in the two thick volumes of *Historic Mackinac* by Edwin O. Wood, published in 1918. In a current publishing program, the Mackinac Island State Park Commission is issuing a series of booklets and leaflets on various phases of its research and restoration. I am indebted to all of these writings.

Other works are listed with reference to specific chapters.

Chapter 1 THE GALLANT NORMAN

Bayliss, Joseph E., and Estelle Bayliss, in collaboration with Milo M. Quaife. *River of Destiny; The St. Mary's.* Detroit: Wayne University Press, 1955.

Biggar, H. P., ed. *The Works of Samuel de Champlain.* 6 vols. Toronto: The Champlain Society, 1922–1936.

Bishop, Morris. *Champlain, Life of Fortitude.* New York: Alfred A. Knopf, Inc., 1948.

Butterfield, C. W. *History of the Discovery of the Northwest by Jean Nicolet in 1634.* Cincinnati: R. Clarke & Co. 1881.

Eccles, W. J. *Frontenac, The Courtier Governor*. Toronto: McClelland & Stewart, 1959.

Garneau, F. H., and J. B. Ferland. "Jean Nicolet," *Wisconsin Historical Collections*, 10: 41–6.

Jouan, Henri. "Jean Nicolet, Interpreter and Voyageur in Canada, 1618–1642," *Wisconsin Historical Collections*, 11: 1–25.

Poetker, Albert H. "Jean Nicolet," *Michigan History Magazine*, 18: 305–15.

Shea, John Gilmary. *Discovery and Exploration of the Mississippi Valley*. New York: Redfield, 1852.

Sulté, Benjamin. "Notes on Jean Nicolet," *Wisconsin Historical Collections*, 8: 188–94.

Chapter 2 THE CROSS ON THE SHORE

Abbott, John S. C. *The Adventures of the Chevalier de La Salle and His Companions*. New York: Dodd & Mead, 1875.

Brebner, J. B. *The Explorers of North America, 1492–1806*. Garden City, N.Y.: Doubleday & Company, 1955.

Goodrich, Calvin. *The First Michigan Frontier*. Ann Arbor: The University of Michigan Press, 1940.

Hunt, G. T. *The Wars of the Iroquois: A Study in Intertribal Trade Relations*. Madison: University of Wisconsin Press, 1960.

Parkman, Francis. *The Jesuits in North America*. Boston: Little, Brown and Company, 1895.

———. *La Salle and the Discovery of the Great West*. Boston: Little, Brown and Company, 1907.

Repplier, Agnes. *Père Marquette*. Garden City, N.Y.: Doubleday, Doran and Company, 1929.

Shea, John Gilmary. *Discovery and Exploration of the Mississippi Valley*. New York: Redfield, 1852.

Thwaites, Reuben Gold. *Father Marquette*. New York: D. Appleton & Co., 1902.

———. "The Story of Mackinac," *Wisconsin Historical Collections*, 14: 1–16.

Chapter 3 TO THE GREAT RIVER

Delanglez, Jean. *Life and Voyages of Louis Jolliet, 1645–1700*. Chicago: Institute of Jesuit History, 1948.

———. *Some La Salle Journeys*. Chicago: Institute of Jesuit History, 1938.

Parkman, Francis. *The Jesuits in North America*. Boston: Little, Brown and Company, 1895.

Shea, John Gilmary. *Discovery and Exploration of the Mississippi Valley*. New York: Redfield, 1852.

Thwaites, Reuben Gold. *Father Marquette*. New York: D. Appleton & Co., 1902.

Winsor, Justin, ed. *Narrative and Critical History of America*. Boston: Houghton, Mifflin and Company, 1884–1889.

Chapter 4   THE END OF THE JOURNEY

Abbott, John S. C. *The Adventures of the Chevalier de La Salle and His Companions*. New York: Dodd & Mead, 1875.

Charlevoix, Pierre F. X. de. *History of New France*. New York: John G. Shea, 1868.

"The Discovery of Father Marquette's Grave at St. Ignace in 1877, as Related by Father Edward Jacker," edited by George S. May, *Michigan History Magazine*, 42: 267–87.

Duffield, George. "On the Recent Discovery of the Long Lost Grave of Père Marquette," *Michigan Pioneer and Historical Collections*, 2: 134–45.

Kellogg, Louise Phelps. *The French Regime of Wisconsin and the Northwest*. Madison: State Historical Society of Wisconsin, 1925.

Repplier, Agnes. *Père Marquette*. Garden City, N.Y.: Doubleday, Doran and Company, 1929.

Stebbins, Catherine L. "Marquette's Death-Site," *Michigan History Magazine*, 48: 333–68.

Chapter 5   THE LOST GRIFFIN

Baker, Wallace J., Sr. "On Manitoulin Island," *Inland Seas*, 3: 211–17.

Delanglez, Jean. "A Calendar of La Salle's Travels," *Mid-America*, 22: 278–305.

Fleming, Roy F. "The Search for La Salle's Brigantine *Le Griffon*," *Inland Seas*, 8: 223–8; 9: 19–26.

Jacks, Leo Vincent. *La Salle*. New York: Charles Scribner's Sons, 1931.

Kellogg, Louise Phelps, ed. *Early Narratives of the Northwest*. New York: Charles Scribner's Sons, 1917.

Parkman, Francis. *La Salle and the Discovery of the Great West*. Boston: Little, Brown and Company, 1907.

Chapter 6   THE LAWLESS POST

Charlevoix, Pierre F. X. de. *Journal of a Voyage to North-America*. London, R. and J. Dodsley, 1761.

Goodrich, Calvin. *The First Michigan Frontier*. Ann Arbor: The University of Michigan Press, 1940.

Innis, H. A. *The Fur Trade in Canada*. Rev. ed. Toronto: University of Toronto Press, 1956.

Lahontan, Louis Armand, Baron de. *New Voyages to North America*. Edited by R. G. Thwaites. Chicago A. C. McClurg and Co., 1905.

Phillips, Paul Chrisler. *The Fur Trade*. 2 vols. Norman: University of Oklahoma Press, 1961.

Quaife, Milo M., ed. *The Western Country in the Seventeenth Century. The Memoirs of La Mothe Cadillac and Pierre Liette*. Chicago: The Lakeside Press, 1947.

Sandoz, Mari. *The Beaver Men*. New York: Hastings House, 1964.

Skinner, Constance Lindsay. *Beaver, Kings and Cabins*. New York: The Macmillan Company, 1933.

Chapter 7   A MAN FROM OLD MACKINAW

J. C. B. *Travels in New France*. Edited by Sylvester K. Stevens, Donald H. Kent and Emma Edith Woods. Harrisburg: The Pennsylvania Historical Commission, 1941.

"The British Regime in Wisconsin, 1760–1800," *Wisconsin Historical Collections*, vol. 18.

"The French Regime in Wisconsin, 1634–1727," *Wisconsin Historical Collections*, vol. 16.

"The French Regime in Wisconsin, 1727–1760," *Wisconsin Historical Collections*, vols. 17 and 18.

Grignon, Augustin. "Seventy-two Years' Recollections," *Wisconsin Historical Collections*, 3: 197–295.

Kelton, Dwight H. *Annals of Fort Mackinac*. Chicago: Fergus Printing Company, 1882.

"Langlade Papers," *Wisconsin Historical Collections*, 8: 209–23.

Tasse, Joseph. "Memoir of Charles de Langlade," *Wisconsin Historical Collections*, 7: 123–87.

Chapter 8   TALE OF AN OLD TRADER

Alexander Henry's Travels and Adventures. Edited by Milo M. Quaife. Chicago: The Lakeside Press, 1921.

Parkman, Francis. *The Conspiracy of Pontiac*. Boston: Little, Brown and Company, 1895.

Porlier, Louis B. "Capture of Mackinaw, 1763—A Menomonee Tradition," *Wisconsin Historical Collections*, 8: 227–31.

Russell, Nelson Vance. *The British Regime in Michigan and the Old Northwest*. Northfield, Minn.: Carlton College, 1939.

Schoolcraft, Henry Rowe. *Personal Memoirs of a Residence of Thirty Years with the Indian Tribes on the American Frontiers*. Philadelphia: Lippincott, Grambo and Co., 1851.

Chapter 9 ROGERS AT MICHILIMACKINAC

Carver, Jonathan. *Three Years' Travel Throughout the Interior Parts of North America*. Walpole, N. H.: Isaiah Thomas & Co., 1813.

Clements, William L. "Rogers' Michilimackinac Journal," *Proceedings of the American Antiquarian Society*, vol. 28.

Cuneo, John R. *Robert Rogers of the Rangers*. New York: Oxford University Press, 1959.

May, George S., ed. *The Doctor's Secret Journal*, by Daniel Morison, Surgeon's Mate. Mackinac Island: The Fort Mackinac Division Press, 1960.

Peckham, H. H. *Old Fort Michilimackinac at Mackinaw City*. Ann Arbor: The University of Michigan Press, 1938.

Riddell, William Renwick. "A Petty Quarrel Over Rum at Old Michilimackinac," *Michigan History Magazine*, 13: 278–300.

Rogers, Robert. *Concise Account of North America*. London: J. Millan, 1765.

———. *Journals*. London: J. Millan, 1765.

Chapter 10 THE ISLAND FORT

Goodrich, Calvin. *The First Michigan Frontier*. Ann Arbor: The University of Michigan Press, 1940.

Jenks, William L. "Patrick Sinclair, Builder of Fort Mackinac," *Michigan Pioneer and Historical Collections*, 39: 61–85.

The John Askin Papers. 2 vols. Edited by Milo M. Quaife. Detroit Library Commission, 1928.

Russell, Nelson Vance. *The British Regime in Michigan and the Old Northwest*. Northfield, Minn.: Carlton College, 1939.

Schoolcraft, Henry Rowe. *Personal Memoirs of a Residence of Thirty Years with the Indian Tribes on the American Frontiers*. Philadelphia: Lippincott, Grambo and Co., 1851.

Williams, Meade C. *Early Mackinac.* St. Louis: Buschart Bros., 1898.

Chapter 11 TWO FLAGS IN THE WIND

Bayliss, Joseph, and Estelle Bayliss. *Historic St. Joseph Island.* Cedar Rapids: The Torch Press, 1938.

Bolz, J. Arnold. *Portage Into the Past.* Minneapolis: University of Minnesota Press, 1960.

The John Askin Papers. 2 vols. Edited by Milo M. Quaife. Detroit Library Commission, 1928.

Kellogg, Louise Phelps. *The British Regime in Wisconsin and the Northwest.* Madison: State Historical Society of Wisconsin, 1935.

Ogg, Frederick Austin. *The Old Northwest.* New Haven: Yale University Press, 1919.

Wilson, Frazer Ells. *Around the Council Fire.* Greenville, O.: 1945.

Chapter 12 GUNS ON THE GREAT TURTLE

Baird, Elizabeth Thérèse. "Reminiscences of Early Days on Mackinac Island," *Wisconsin Historical Collections,* 14: 17–64.

Bayliss, Joseph E., and Estelle Bayliss, in collaboration with Milo M. Quaife. *River of Destiny: The St. Mary's.* Detroit: Wayne University Press, 1955.

Kelton, Dwight H. *Annals of Fort Mackinac.* Chicago: Fergus Printing Company, 1882.

Lucas, C. P. *A History of Canada 1763–1812.* Oxford: The Clarendon Press, 1909.

May, George S. *War 1812.* Mackinac Island State Park Commission, 1962.

"Papers Pertaining to the Relations of the British Government With the United States During the Period of the War of 1812," *Michigan Pioneer and Historical Collections,* vol. 15.

"Personal Narrative of Captain Thomas G. Anderson," *Wisconsin Historical Collections,* 9: 137–206.

Chapter 13 FURS AND FORTUNES

Baird, Elizabeth Thérèse. "Reminiscences of Early Days on Mackinac Island," *Wisconsin Historical Collections,* 14: 17–64.

Chittenden, Hiram Martin. *The American Fur Trade of the Far West.* 2 vols. Stanford: Academic Reprints, 1954.

Irving, Washington. *Astoria.* New York: G. P. Putnam and Son, 1868.

Kinzie, Juliette. *Wau-Bun.* Preface by Milo M. Quaife. Chicago: The Lakeside Press, 1933.

"Letters of William Montague and Amanda White Ferry," *Journal of the Presbyterian Historical Society,* 25: 197–223; 26: 101–29, 182–93.

Phillips, Paul Chrisler. *The Fur Trade.* 2 vols. Norman: Oklahoma University Press, 1961.

Terrell, John Upton. *Furs By Astor.* New York: William Morrow and Company, 1963.

Woodford, Frank B., and Albert Hyma. *Gabriel Richard.* Detroit: Wayne State University Press, 1958.

Chapter 14 THE SWIFT WALKER

Andreas, A. T. *History of Chicago, History of Cook County, Illinois.* Chicago: A. T. Andreas, 1884–1886.

The Autobiography of Gurdon Saltonstall Hubbard. Chicago: The Lakeside Press, 1911.

Currey, Josiah Seymour. *Chicago: Its History and Its Builders.* Springfield, Ill.: S. J. Clarke Publishing Co., 1912.

Masters, Edgar Lee. *The Tale of Chicago.* New York: G. P. Putnam's Sons, 1933.

Quaife, Milo Milton. *Chicago and the Old Northwest.* Chicago: University of Chicago Press, 1913.

———. *Pictures of Chicago 100 Years Ago.* Chicago: The Lakeside Press, 1918.

Schoolcraft, Henry Rowe. *Travels in the Central Portions of the Mississippi Valley.* New York: Collus & Hannay, 1825.

Chapter 15 THE FORT SURGEON

Beaumont, William. *Experiments and Observations on the Gastric Juice and the Physiology of Digestion.* Plattsburg, N.Y.: 1833.

Flexner, James Thomas. *Doctors on Horseback.* New York: The Viking Press, 1937.

Meyer, Jesse S. *Life and Letters of Dr. William Beaumont.* St. Louis: C. V. Mosby Co., 1912.

Osler, William. *An Alabama Student and Other Biographical Essays.* London: Oxford University Press, 1908.

White, George H. "Alexis St. Martin of Mackinac," *Michigan Pioneer and Historical Collections,* 26: 646–50.

Chapter 16 INDIAN SUMMER

Davis, Marion M. "Three Islands," *Michigan Pioneer and Historical Collections,* 12: 513–53.

Jameson, Anna B. *Winter Studies and Summer Rambles.* New York: Wiley and Putnam, 1839.

Mason, Philip P., ed. *The Literary Voyager.* Michigan State University Press, 1962.

Osborn, Chase, and Stellanova Osborn. *Schoolcraft-Longfellow-Hiawatha.* Lancaster, Pa.: The Jacques Cattell Press, 1942.

Schoolcraft, Henry Rowe. *Algic Researches, Comprising Inquiries Respecting the Mental Characteristics of the North American Indians. First Series: Indian Tales and Legends.* New York: Harper & Bros., 1839.

———. *Oneota, or the Red Race of America.* New York: Burgess, Stringer & Co., 1844.

———. *Personal Memoirs of a Residence of Thirty Years with the Indian Tribes on the American Frontiers.* Philadelphia: Lippincott, Grambo and Co., 1851.

Woolson, C. F. *Castle Nowhere.* New York: Harper & Bros., 1875.

Chapter 17 MACKINAC AND THE MORMONS

Backus, C. K. "An American King," *Harper's New Monthly Magazine,* 64: 553–9.

Cronyn, Margaret, and John Kenny. *The Saga of Beaver Island.* Ann Arbor: Braun and Brumfield, 1958.

Hedrick, U. P. *The Land of the Crooked Tree.* New York: Oxford University Press, 1948.

Legler, Henry E. "A Moses of the Mormons," *Parkman Club Publications,* Nos. 15, 16, 1897.

"Letters of Rev. Frederic Baraga, L'Arbre Croche, to Leopoldine Foundation, Vienna." Typescript. Bishop Baraga Historical Commission. Marquette, Michigan.

Quaife, Milo Milton. *The Kingdom of St. James.* New Haven: Yale University Press, 1930.

Strang, J. J. *Ancient and Modern Michilimackinac.* Edited by George S. May. Mackinac Island: W. S. Woodfill, 1959.

Watrous, E. F. "King James of Beaver Island," *Century Magazine,* 63: 685–9.

Woolson, C. F. "Fairy Island," *Putnam's Magazine,* 6: 62–69.

Chapter 18 THE CRUMBLING FORT

Andrews, Roger. *Old Fort Mackinac on the Hill of History*. Menominee, Mich.: Herald-Leader Press, 1938.
Bailey, John Read. "The Province of Michilimackinac," *Michigan Pioneer and Historical Collections*, 32: 395–404.
Disturnell, J. *The Great Lakes or Inland Seas of America*. Philadelphia: W. B. Zieber, 1871.
Kelton, Dwight H. *Annals of Fort Mackinac*. Chicago: Fergus Printing Company, 1882.
Prucha, Francis Paul. *A Guide to the Military Posts of the United States, 1789–1895*. Madison: State Historical Society of Wisconsin, 1964.
Spooner, Harry L. "At Fort Mackinac a Century Ago," *Michigan Pioneer and Historical Collections*, 12: 505–12.

Chapter 19 BRIDGING THE STRAITS

Clark, E. M. "Restoration of Old Fort Holmes on Mackinac Island," *Michigan History Magazine*, 20: 295–300.
Perry, Henry A. "Mackinac Island's Historical Fair and Ter-Centennial," *Michigan History Magazine*, 18: 291–304.
Petersen, Eugene T. *Michilimackinac: Its History and Restoration*. Mackinac Island, 1962.
Pitezel, John H. *Lights and Shades of Missionary Life*. Cincinnati: Methodist Book Concern, 1857.
Ratigan, William. *Straits of Mackinac*. Grand Rapids: William B. Eerdmans Publishing Company, 1957.
White, Peter. "Old Fort Holmes and Fort Michilimackinac," *Michigan Pioneer and Historical Collections*, 38: 85–92.

INDEX

INDEX

ABOUT THE AUTHOR

Walter Havighurst was born in Appleton, Wisconsin, in a house overlooking the Fox River where the French priests, explorers and traders passed on their way from Lake Michigan to the Mississippi River. He now lives in Oxford, Ohio, where he is a Research Professor of English at Miami University.

Mr. Havighurst had his first view of Mackinac Island from the pilot house of a Great Lakes freighter in 1920. His college course, at Ohio Wesleyan University and the University of Denver, was interrupted by service in the U.S. Merchant Marine, in both the Pacific and the Atlantic trade. After a year's study at King's College of the University of London he took an M.A. degree at Columbia University in 1928. Since then he has been a college teacher and a writer of fiction, biography and regional history. With his wife, Marion Boyd Havighurst, he has collaborated on several junior historical novels.

He has received awards from the Friends of American Writers, the Rockefeller Foundation, and the Association for State and Local History.

His first book, *Pier 17*, a novel of a waterfront strike on the Pacific coast, was followed by *The Upper Mississippi* in the Rivers of America series. His subsequent books include: *The Winds of Spring, The Long Ships Passing, Signature of Time, Wilderness for Sale, The Heartland, Voices on the River,* and *The Great Lakes Reader.*

Typography and Binding Design

by

CARL A. KOENIG

977.48   S
H
        Havighurst, Walter
          Three flags at the
        Straits.

    18 JAN 69   W P 3967
                       W P 32332

Forts Michilim